Mexico, Interrupted

CRITICAL MEXICAN STUDIES

CRITICAL MEXICAN STUDIES
Series editor: Ignacio M. Sánchez Prado

Critical Mexican Studies is the first English-language, humanities-based, theoretically focused academic series devoted to the study of Mexico. The series is a space for innovative works in the humanities that focus on theoretical analysis, transdisciplinary interventions, and original conceptual framing.

Other titles in the series:

The Restless Dead: Necrowriting and Disappropriation, by Cristina Rivera Garza

History and Modern Media: A Personal Journey, by John Mraz

Toxic Loves, Impossible Futures: Feminist Living as Resistance, by Irmgard Emmelhainz

Unlawful Violence: Mexican Law and Cultural Production, by Rebecca Janzen

Drug Cartels Do Not Exist: Narcotrafficking in US and Mexican Culture, by Oswaldo Zavala

Monstrous Politics: Geography, Rights, and the Urban Revolution in Mexico City, by Ben Gerlofs

Robo Sacer: Necroliberalism and Cyborg Resistance in Mexican and Chicanx Dystopias, by David Dalton

The Mexican Transpacific: Nikkei Writing, Visual Arts, and Performance, by Ignacio López-Calvo

Mexico, Interrupted

Labor, Idleness, and the Economic Imaginary of Independence

Sergio Gutiérrez Negrón

Vanderbilt University Press
Nashville, Tennessee

First printing 2023

Library of Congress Cataloging-in-Publication Data
Names: Gutiérrez Negrón, Sergio, author.
Title: Mexico, interrupted : labor, idleness, and the economic imaginary of independence, 1821–1867 / Sergio Gutiérrez Negrón.
Description: Nashville, Tennessee : Vanderbilt University Press, [2023] | Series: Critical Mexican studies ; 9 | Includes bibliographical references and index.
Identifiers: LCCN 2022034837 | ISBN 9780826505538 (paperback) | ISBN 9780826505545 (hardback) | ISBN 9780826505552 (epub) | ISBN 9780826505569 (pdf)
Subjects: LCSH: Mexico—Economic conditions—19th century. | Mexico—Economic policy—19th century. | Mexico—History—1821–1861.
Classification: LCC HC135 .G85 2023 | DDC 338.972—dc23/eng/20220808
LC record available at https://lccn.loc.gov/2022034837

Para Ana María y Tomás

Contents

Acknowledgments

This book could have been many other, lesser books were it not for the direct or indirect influence of a lot of good people. It has already had multiple lives. It began as an introduction to a dissertation that was meant to be something else, led by Ricardo Gutiérrez Mouat, may he rest in peace. It then served as research for what ended up being a novel on contemporary labor, *Los días hábiles*, which is this book's shadow. Upon meeting Zachary Gresham, Vanderbilt University Press's acquisitions editor, it took its current and best form, in many ways because of his encouragement. I am indebted to him, and also to Ignacio Sánchez Prado for offering a model of a rigorous and curious scholarly life, and for curating the Critical Mexican Studies series, of which I am happy to be part. I am also beholden to my colleagues in the Department of Hispanic Studies at Oberlin College, Ana Cara, Sebastiaan Faber, Kim Faber, Claire Solomon, Patrick O'Connor, Patty Tovar, Yorki Encalada, and Blanche Villar, for their overall generosity.

Many of the ideas that underlie this project were explored while in conversation with the *Conservative Sensibilities* research group, led by Kari Soriano Salkjelsvik and Andrea Castro, and I feel lucky to collaborate with all its wonderful members. During Summer of 2018, two Oberlin College-funded research assistants, Zoe Kaplan and Sonia Bloom, helped me go through decades-worth of nineteenth-century newspapers, and their laborious notes and smart insights proved to be tremendously helpful as I found myself writing in the middle of a pandemic in 2020 and 2021. During the day-to-day wordsmithing and paragraph-crafting, I was virtually accompanied by my *comadre* Naomi Campa and Curtis Dozier, the two coolest classicists with whom to share a writing accountability group. Thank you, friends.

I am, of course, lucky to have had Ana María Díaz Burgos, my colleague and wife, at my side from the very beginning, and I am forever grateful for her love and support. Ana kept me on track whenever a new idea or unrelated primary sources promised the excitement of the new. Tomás, born during the writing of this book, also taught me to focus and be more intentional, and made my language and life all the richer, and I am thankful for him, too. This book is for them.

Introduction

Mexican independence was an economic event. From the earliest days of the insurgency, images of Spanish economic and fiscal exploitation were used to legitimize the uprising and its demands. The first insurgent periodical, *El Despertador Americano* (The American Awakener, 1810–11), consistently accused the Spanish of having "plundered, devastated and annihilated America" and of keeping the territory "always exhausted, always weak, in the most deplorable scarcity, the most absolute misery."[1] For its editor, priest Francisco Severo Maldonado, the Spanish had not only taken control of the richest mines and the most productive soils, they had also, among other things, imposed monopolies that made it impossible for the honest individual to work so as to "provide himself at least an average subsistence."[2] To add insult to injury, imperial functionaries had heavily taxed the population for decades, to the point that the poorest of the poor "finds himself forced to invoke death, as the only available end of his misery."[3] In the face of such dire exploitation—the "yoke of this hardest and most horrible condition of all"— true liberty could only be, as Severo Maldonado had written in an earlier issue, "the freedom to break all obstacles to industry, to give occupation to our own so that they do not fester as they now fester in a forced idleness, so that we supply ourselves with all we need and free them from the obligation of buying everything from a seventh or eighth hand."[4]

The army general who would be Emperor, Agustín de Iturbide, insisted on this, too. More than ten years after *El Despertador Americano*, on October 13, 1821, the *Gaceta Imperial*, the recently rebranded official mouthpiece of Iturbide's Army of the Three Guarantees, published and publicized two broadsheets that promised such release. These had originally been issued strategically and arbitrarily by Iturbide during his campaign months earlier, on June 30 of that year. One of the broadsheets argued that the previous "fatal administration" had, for the last decade, exacted disastrous duties on the populace just to enrich foreign coffers, in turn driving the locals to misery. "It is high time," it read, "for [the newly independent nation's] meritorious inhabitants to begin to experiment the difference that exists between the state of a people that enjoys its political liberty, and that of one that is subject to a foreign yoke."[5] As a testament to the new regime's commitment to fiscal liberation, the document went on to call for, and soon after to implement, the radical reduction and elimination of the fiscal and commercial burdens that had driven "all classes of men" to penury. The industry of a free population, the providential wealth of the land, and the workings of the free market would take care to yield the aggrandizement that was inevitable.

After a decade-long war, the economic promises of independence built a common ground between different sectors of the population.[6] Most, if not all, imagined separation from Spain, before and during its first decades, as a feat that nationalized, or that could have nationalized, a rich and productive economic apparatus.[7] A new, independent era of territorial sovereignty and autonomy was supposed to guarantee that the providential wealth of the land, its plentiful resources, and the labor of its peoples sustain the existence, survival and improvement of a just state and polity.[8] Freed from restraints, it was only a matter of time until the new Mexican nation would "shine its bright beacon of liberty" over Europe, the United States, and all other nations of the globe.[9]

These expectations did not materialize, of course. The next half century would be marked by economic crises, political instability, foreign interventions, and a bloody civil war. *Mexico, Interrupted: Labor, Idleness, and the Economic Imaginary* investigates the fate of these economic hopes during the difficult decades between the year of the country's definite separation from Spain and the aftermath of the US-Mexico War. Drawing on pamphlets, legislation, congressional debates, reports, and newspapers of the period, this book studies the Mexican intelligentsia's obsessive engagement with the labor and idleness of the citizenry in their attempts to create a wealthy, independent nation. By focusing on three key and interrelated figures of work and their opposites in the period, *Mexico, Interrupted* attempts to piece together elements of the period's economic imaginaries, the repertoire of political and cultural discourses, images, and stories that structured the understandings, beliefs, and fantasies about the relationships between the economic futures of the nation and the life of an independent polity.

In its first months of existence, the new Mexican state fulfilled some of the promises it had made. It dissolved many of the viceregal fiscal instruments that survived the war, cut taxes and duties, paid the armies, and nationalized all of the standing debts the Viceroyalty owed to the remaining monied interests, whether local or international. The unspoken expectation behind such moves was that, soon enough, silver would fill and overflow the national coffers. The opposite happened. During the decade of insurgency that went from 1810 to 1821, the territory's renowned mines had been destroyed or otherwise stopped, and commercial agricultural output had fizzled out. International markets, as a result, had starved, and internal markets had struggled to re-articulate their shattered local networks in the face of the expansion of subsistence farming, demonetized commerce, a jeopardized transportation infrastructure, and the pull of regional autarkies. The capital that had sustained mining, imports, and commercial cultivation, along with much of the available specie, vanished in the pockets of fleeing financiers, merchants, and peninsular elites. Local capital became scarce, exhausted in the conflict, hidden away, or drained earlier in the century by Spain's own debts. Thus, from having been one of the engines of silver commercial capitalism, its treasury rich enough to sustain its own dynamic society, support Spain's Caribbean possessions and the Philippines, all the while transferring its surpluses to the metropolis, the territory suddenly discovered itself incapable of paying its armed forces, meeting its fiscal obligations, or fulfilling its end in multiple national and foreign (British) loans.[10] In other words, after independence, the Mexican economy spiraled downward, and its ruling elites spent much of the following decades trying to regain the economic prosperity that had characterized the eighteenth-century—a prosperity that had nursed early Creole patriotism.

This economic maelstrom was not entirely the result of the insurgencies sparked in the heartlands in 1810. The preceding thirty years had seen wars and revolutions interrupt and remake an Atlantic economy that once linked New Spain's and Peru's silver mines, indigenous exploitation, African enslavement, and Caribbean plantations to European imperial competition and to each other. The intranational and international conflicts of the "age of revolutions" cemented the shift away from "polycentric commercial competition" and paved the way for the commercial integration to Anglocentric industrial capitalism."[11] England, and the United States to a lesser degree, crept into the openings created by the sudden eruption of free and freed ports, establishing or formalizing links between regions of commodity production and industrial centers, and inaugurating the hegemony of Anglocentric industrial capital.

The disarticulation of the viceregal economy and the transformation of the international panorama put the lettered elites of the new Mexican nation in a material and intellectual bind. The territory's wealth and the myth of Mexico's proverbial riches, as scholars have called it, had been constitutive elements in the making of the Creole subjectivities that underpinned elite visions of independence. While the myth had been present as a rhetorical trope since Hernán Cortes's early chronicles, it had not been until the latter half of the eighteenth century when, as Pedro Salmerón Sanginés put it, it expanded "to the rhythm of the spectacular boom of the silver and gold mines" that fueled the rise of global capitalism.[12] Where Francisco Javier Clavijero's and other enlightened Creoles' discursive defense and apology of the territory and its history served as the ideological foundation for Creole political imaginaries, the mining boom that centered the global silver economy in the Mexican heartland and launched subsequent speculation about as-of-yet untapped resources served as the material foundation for the Creole economic imaginaries that, after 1821, became the economic imaginaries of independence.

ECONOMIC IMAGINARIES OF INDEPENDENCE

An imaginary is an "ideal architecture" or interpretative grid through which subjects order material reality. Like their political and social counterparts, economic imaginaries correspond, to a greater or lesser extent, to real material circumstances, to the infinite agglomeration of economic activities that conform an economic life. Thus, talk of economic imaginaries entails the recognition that there is no such thing as the economy, singular. What there is, instead, as Jessop and Oosterlynck write, is an infinite and chaotic stream of economic acts and actions concerned with the provisioning of life and/or with the creation of profit through the mediation of intersubjective practices.[13] What there is, moreover, is the simplification of this infinite set which involves, again with Jessop and Oosterlynck, "discursively-selective 'imaginaries' and structurally-selective institutions."[14] Any reference to "the economy" in the abstract only gestures toward the images, figures, discourses, and genres furnished by imaginaries that organize and narrate economic activity around particular conceptions of the economic and the economy. Like all others, these imaginaries are always grounded spatio-temporally and refer, as Érika Pani has written, to the shared, collective, and complicated "framework of worldviews; of symbols and representations, of principles, aspirations and prejudices; of experiences and influences; of philias and phobias—those that are repressed and those that are not—that make up the intellectual and cultural horizon shared by a group of men."[15]

Economic imaginaries encapsulate contrasting idealizations, discourses, ideologies, and theories. They are productive matrices charged with constitutive force. Once institutionalized and operational, imaginaries normativize "a substratum of substantive economic relations and instrumentalities," and transform (or create and constitute) them into "objects of observation, calculation, and governance."[16] That is, subjects interpret economic activities through imaginaries, but also act in accordance. Likewise, subjects in power, like the ones I study in this book, forge legislation and policy that affect the life of the population according to their understanding of the working of "the economy." By economic imaginaries of independence, then, this book refers to the shared and impersonal interpretative framework, between 1821 and 1852, through which Mexican Creole elites understood and engaged with the economic life of the new nation. These imaginaries entailed the dreams, ideologies, and expectations vis-à-vis Mexico and the world economy held by elites. These imaginaries were impressively consistent, as we will see, and remained active throughout the many disturbances the country would face in the first half of the nineteenth-century.

Mexico, Interrupted specifically studies the anthropological figurations of labor within these imaginaries, as I will explain later in this introduction. Yet, despite the importance and centrality of the figures I study, it is fundamental to note that they were ultimately secondary to a constitutive pair of images that structured them: the myth of Mexico's proverbial riches and the certainty of the territory's underpopulation. The independence-era myth of Mexico's proverbial natural wealth was buttressed by the eighteenth-century silver mining boom. Yet it was Alexander von Humboldt's *Political Essay on the Kingdom of New Spain* (1811) which allowed for the myth's transference to, and operativity within, these imaginaries.[17] The *Political Essay* did more than simply confirm the patriotic beliefs of an earlier generation of Creole lettered men. It *proved* them scientifically by mobilizing the power of statistics for their cause.[18] Unlike the other statistical accounts that abounded in the period, which studied the formation of states and their growth in terms of population, production, and territorial expansion, Humboldt's disciplinary approach, a field called political arithmetic, figured as a science geared toward the future, interested in the current performance of a state for what it could reveal about the potential of a polity's political existence.[19] To the glee of Mexican pro-independence elites, the Prussian's procedure spoke of a prosperous future. Mexico's imminent place as an economic giant was guaranteed by its territorial extension, the diversity of climates, the fecundity of its soil, its mineral riches, and its commercial location between two oceans.[20] This potential, for Humboldt, was being restrained only by the unenlightened administration of the viceroyalty and its deleterious effects on the territory's social and political life.[21] The *Political Essay* gave confidence to independence-era elites, confirmed the territory's promise, and determined the economic imaginaries of independence well into the second half of the nineteenth-century.[22] As the 1824 Minister of State and Interior Relations Lucas Alamán put it in a letter in which he invited the Prussian naturalist to visit Mexico, the *Political Essay* had made it possible "to form a complete concept of what Mexico could be under a good and liberal

Constitution, insofar as it has all the elements of prosperity within it, and [the] reading [of the *Political Essay*] has contributed significantly to enliven the spirit of Independence that was already germinating in many of its inhabitants, and to awaken others from the lethargy in which a strange domination had them."[23]

The Creole ruling elite also took another element of the *Political Essay* to heart. For Humboldt, Mexico's proverbial wealth could easily sustain a population that was ten times its size. Such demographic capacity was deeply connected to its potential, insofar as, put to work, it would generate economic demand, production, and lead to the general well-being of the nation.[24] The interrelationship between population and economic development predated the *Political Essay*, and had been an essential element of the mercantilist programmes of the eighteenth century. Yet, again, Humboldt's scientific approach and sheer enthusiasm provided a different emphasis, one which strengthened the claims and structured the expectations (and policy) of the post-independence political class. For these men, reading Humboldt or reading those who had read Humboldt, if one bracketed the political and institutional restraints the Prussian scientist critiqued—restraints which independence was thought to have largely undone—what remained was the image of a natural plenitude presently undercut by demographic scarcity.

This idea of a demographically scarce or underpopulated Mexico echoed throughout the nineteenth-century and well into the twentieth. Humboldt had offered some respite to the problem, holding that the Mexican population naturally doubled every twenty-two years. The lettered elites either ignored this detail or found it unsatisfactory in the face of the imperious necessity of the present. Interestingly, even if Humboldt's population-growth estimate had been exaggerated, it held some truth. Demographic historian Robert McCaa has shown that, "[f]rom a nineteenth-century perspective, Mexico's population growth was surpassed by few countries, mainly those attracting large contingents of immigrants, such as Argentina, Brazil, and Mexico's covetous neighbor, the United States of America."[25] Unlike these, "the peopling of Mexico," as McCaa calls it, "grew solely by means of native stocks."[26] That said, despite this, it is also true that, as many observers and historians of the time noted, the decade-long "independence wars, with [their] accompanying epidemics and scarcities, wiped out the demographic growth of an entire decade and spilled over into a second."[27] Likewise, the existing population was not uniformly spread through the territory, and remained scarce in the the northern regions, which had barely been settled by Spain and depended on its weak missions-system and an isolated archipelago of settlements—a territory that included parts of what historian Pekka Hämäläinen calls the "Comanche Empire."[28] Thus, the inaugural demographic shock that was the biological cost of the war of independence, the realization of Imperial Spain's territorial overreach, and the subsequent political instability, cast a shadow on any optimistic account of natural demographic growth, and cemented the certainty of an underpopulated Mexico, launching the fevered quest, among elites, for economic measures and policies to expedite the necessary peopling of a territory on which the new state's providential futures depended.

Almost a hundred years after independence, in the first half of the twentieth century, post-revolutionary economist and intellectual Daniel Cosío Villegas argued that the myth of Mexico's proverbial wealth was and had always been, ultimately, misanthropic subterfuge. He believed that the position—first professed by foreigners, but as Pedro Salmerón Sanginés has annotated, also comfortably wielded by elites and the general public—had been historically deployed as a way to delegitimize Mexico's population. He writes:

> Nature—it is argued—has been prodigal on the Mexican: it has given him all climates, the tropics and perpetual snows; agriculture and minerals; extensive territory; long shores; rivers; a blue sky, always clean. But the Mexican is ignorant, lazy, undisciplined, lavish, unpredictable, susceptible, rebellious. What can be done under these circumstances? [In light of this,] [t]here is nothing strange in the backwardness of the country, in the fact that is poverty and even misery, despite and in the midst of so much wealth?[29]

If the myth continued to be operative throughout the nineteenth and twentieth century, Cosío Villegas held, it was because it allowed for the rhetorical and discursive disqualification of whatever demographic element (the indigenous, the mestizo, the Spanish, the soldier, the army, the priests, the politicians, etc.) a speaker believed perverted, limited, or misdirected the Mexican population. Cosío Villegas's position was, at the end of the day, a philosophical argument that attempted to break with the dual pressures of geographic determinism and possibilism, both of which had characterized Mexican political and cultural thought since independence.[30] These dual pressures haunted the post-independence Creole elite, an elite intentionally or unintentionally caught in the misanthropic collateral of the myth of Mexican proverbial wealth.

The *colono* or settler, the artisan, and the vagrant are three significant points of entry into economic imaginaries that were ultimately misanthropic, caught as they were between the certainty of a providential future and a disappointing present. Throughout the first half of the nineteenth century, these three figures played a central role in the fevered quest to expand, improve, and modernize that Mexican population which limited or undermined Mexico's providential wealth. Whereas the colono encapsulated the hopes of the political class for an influx of productive and modern citizens, the artisan embodied the technical and cultural limits of the actually existing Mexican laboring population, and the vagrant haunted all figuration of labor. These figures functioned as what Fredric Jameson has called ideologemes. An ideologeme, for Jameson, is "an amphibious formation, whose essential structural characteristic may be described as its possibility to manifest itself either as a pseudoidea—a conceptual or belief system, an abstract value, an opinion or prejudice—or as a protonarrative."[31] Its vagueness or incompleteness allows it to take the "finished appearance of a philosophical system on the one hand, or that of a cultural text on the other."[32] The three figures made possible discursive and narrative answers to the increasingly frustrating and anxiety-ridden question of how to yield the prosperity promised by a territory that made the nation potentially prosperous, but which, on one hand, was limited by demographic scarcity and, on the other, had never been completely or satisfyingly subsumed into the productivist control of a central government. Indeed, these figures offered powerful narratives, capable of surviving through internal revolts, foreign interventions, civil wars, and multiple constitutional arrangements. Each of these figures were "a form of social praxis, that is, a symbolic resolution to a concrete historical situation."[33]

The economic imaginaries of independence were emphatically elite, Creole imaginaries. This is no surprise if we consider that post-independence public life was dominated by the approximately two thousand or so men whom Eric Van Young calls "the political nation."[34] These men belonged to a Creole lettered class invested in the founding of independent, decolonized American nation-states that, despite their autonomous existence, retained European values and cemented Creole supremacy.[35] Like other hemispheric Creole elites of the period, they "aimed, from the outset, to preserve the privileges that, as the descendants of Europeans, they enjoyed at the expense of Indigenous and [black communities]," as Joshua Simon has written.[36] Thus, "[t]hey designed constitutions with an eye to containing the conflicts that they knew their still-stratified colonial societies might produce.[37] As a result, the working and popular masses were largely shut out of the (Creole) political, and their economic or social prospects were as limited as they had been before independence.

The Creole political nation represented a minority not only in the urban spaces it largely occupied and from where it wielded its power, but also in the national territory as a whole. Out of approximately 6.1 million inhabitants at the close of the eighteenth-century, some sixty percent or 3.7 million were indigenous. According to Yasnayá Elena Gil, this means that only about 2.4 million or forty percent of the Mexican population were Spanish-speaking or, at the very least, bilingual.[38] "With a population composed primarily of indigenous people," writes historian José Ángel Hernández "the demographic reality on the ground necessarily provided the reference point for most legislation [and discourse, I might add] dealing with the makeup of the population following the wars for Independence."[39] In other words, for Hernández, most if not all post-independence legislation entailed, in one way or another, "the acceptance of Mexican hegemony or the targeted extermination of indigenes."[40] In the immediacy of independence, this very same Creole political class began "the ideological, legal, and physical assault on communal village lands and other indigenous community institutions such as hospitals, public political offices, schools, and the management of community chests," as a "state tactic for incorporating those who had resisted the imposition of alternative modes of citizenship, like Indios Bárbaros and Independent Indians."[41] The economic imaginaries of independence likewise emerged from this minoritarian elite minority—an elite which, after the war, found itself consistently threatened and under siege. In this sense, elite anxiety over the performance of the economy was inevitably tied to the fact that the economic performance of the (Creole) nation-state was intrinsically limited by the very minority status of the culturally Creole population. For this reason, the economic horizon of post-independence policies, politics, and discourse always entailed the subsumption not only of the territory, but of the existing population and the transformation and modernization (understood as creolization) of its customs.[42] In truth, as Allan Knight has written about another context, the problem faced by these elites was not necessarily the lack or quality of working bodies, but that the bodies that populated the now-Mexican territory were "recalcitrant."[43] That is, still paraphrasing Knight, Indians with subsistence holdings did not readily abandon their land to take up wage labor and central Mexicans, "though dispossessed and proletarianized," were embedded in their landscape and not rootless enough to follow the demand and the imperatives of labor that were to drive elite's dreams of a wealthy nation-state. Surely, shortages in labor were oftentimes related with demographic density, but they had also to do with the fact that the total population had not been transformed in that detached reservoir of labor that grounds "free labor."[44]

In other words, what was often at stake in the economic imaginaries was not simply the question of the economic well-being and aggrandizement of the nation, but of national and capitalist accumulation of the territory and its population. Karl Marx called this process "primitive accumulation." By this, Marx referred to "an accumulation which is not the result of the capitalist mode of production but its point of departure."[45] Political Economy had erased this prior accumulation and had replaced it with "magical elements." He continues, "In the tender annals of Political Economy, the idyllic reigns from time immemorial. Right and 'labour' were from the beginning the sole means of enrichment, 'this year' of course always excepted."[46] This prior accumulation functioned like the original sin in Judeo-Christian theology, offering a vague historical narrative that explained the present through fictional justification, jettisoning the complexities of politics and economic struggle. Against this "insipid childishness," he insisted that "[i]n actual history it is a notorious fact that conquest, enslavement, robbery, murder, in short, force, play the greatest part . . . As a matter of fact, the methods of primitive accumulation are anything but idyllic."[47] In Mexico, the myth of the proverbial wealth of the land and the certainty of demographic scarcity played a similarly "magical" role for the Creole elite in that it flattened the territory and its history, erasing the genealogies of indigenous settlements and forms of life, as well as the regional, national, and international commercial networks and markets which had activated past economic gains, and the forms of labor and modes of production that had in the past and present exploited these riches. The economic imaginaries of independence, then, generated a multiplicity of elite, economic narratives that attempted to articulate the harmonious story of the economic future of the nation; a story whose plot belonged to the genre of capitalist accumulation. Put differently, the economic imaginaries of independence were imaginaries of (capitalist) accumulation.[48] What was at stake in the narratives and conceptual apparatuses they engendered was not simply the nation's production, but also the production of Mexico as a collective entity, as a national market, and of "the Mexican" as a particular (Creole) form of subjectivity. That is, the economic imaginaries of independence articulated the narratives and images of the modernization of the nation's modes of production and of the subsequent production of subjectivity.

COLONO, ARTISAN, VAGRANT

This book is divided into three chapters to explore three quintessential figures: the colono, the artisan, and the vagrant, respectively. Each of these figures captures a conceptual and symbolic quandary vis-à-vis labor in the economic imaginaries. By tracing the unfolding and development of these figures through the contexts studied, I emphasize the ways in which they offered symbolic resolutions to the political-economic situation stemming from the disjuncture for the political nation that existed between a prodigal nature and a population believed by the elites to be insufficient, both in terms of quantity and quality. These figures—doggedly gendered as male throughout the period—converge, then, not only in the sense that they belong to the same imaginative horizon and establish overlapping points of resonance, but also insofar as they are structurally isomorphic, and reproduce the same symbolic gestures and ideological effects in differing contexts. As will become evident, the lettered elite that participated in the political nation rarely spoke of labor beyond abstract reflections on the moral value of work, its relationship to freedom and the nation, and its public benefits. However, each of the figures in question prompted specific reflections that made explicit the constellation of ideologies, narratives, images, and concepts through which labor and its opposites were conceived beyond the platitudes of a vague liberal grammar and the ascendant languages of political economy. Therefore, when speaking of the colono, for example, the figures studied spoke of the relationship between freedom and work, between landlord and peasant; about the prefatory need for slavery or unfree forms of labor that would prepare the ground for a truly free worker-laborer. An engagement with the artisan as a key figure brought about reflections on labor and technology, on capitalist production and the limits of nature, and the relationship between morality, production, and the creation of a new modern form of life.[49] Finally, when speaking of the vagrant, liberal clichés about the modern freedom to work broke down, and the interrelation between police and production emerged as a matter of contention, along with questioning of the limits of freedom when it had to do with labor, and long disquisitions about the relationship between a people's customs and the capacity to work. Each chapter works individually, but read together they offer an impressionistic portrait of the economic imaginaries of independence. The three chapters explore the same period and, in parallel and through the shifting emphases, allow for a more comprehensive appreciation of the economic imaginaries and their conceptual limits. In a more programmatic manner, Chapter 1 centers on the colono as the protagonist of a nineteenth-century hemispheric narrative which coupled labor, population and the territory. Even if did not belong strictly to the domain of economics, *colonización* as settlement, occupation, and exploitation of the land drew the economic imaginaries of independence well into its orbit.

The chapter argues that, in the economic imaginaries of the period between 1821 and 1852, the subject of Mexican aggrandizement was not the concrete and actually existing Mexican laborer—not the urban artisan, domestic weaver, peasant, fisherman, muleteer, carpenter, blacksmith, government employee, obraje worker, Totomac vanilla gatherer, coffee harvester, shepherd, wage laborer, henequen grower, miner, tlachiquero, etcetera—but the ever-industrious colono in all his abstract glory; the colono as a figuration of the state's will, as the active agent in the accumulation and exploitation of the national territory. Surely, if the centrality of the figure held steady through the decades, its conceptualization did not and the chapter surveys the limits of its diverse iterations—the imperial colono imagined by Juan Franciszco de Azcárate y Lezama in the immediate aftermath of independence; Tadeo Ortiz de Ayala's liberal colono entrepreneur, the slave-owning American colono; and the soldier-colono, to name a few. The chapter is divided in two parts. The first focuses on the period from 1821 and 1836, a "generative" period in which individuals such as Ortiz de Ayala were consistently and intentionally trying to conceptualize a working blueprint for the actual colonization of the Mexican territory. During this period, important debates took place, in pamphlets and in Congress, vis-à-vis the relationship between the state and the colono as an autonomous, productive individual; and the question of unfree labor, whether it be slavery or other forms of exploitation. Texas secession and the avalanche of conflicts that lead to the US-Mexico War, conflicts in which actually existing colonos starred, put an end to this first period. The second part of the chapter, which covers from 1846 to 1852, focuses on the colono's fate after Texas. Many attempted to dismiss the figure in light of the circumstances, yet it continued to exert gravitational force and was quickly rehabilitated and reconceptualized—and transformed into polemical object by a better-funded press—not as an autonomous individual, but as a direct agent of the state under the strict guidance of a new institution, the Dirección de Colonización (the Directorate or Bureau of Colonization). Despite its return, though, the period saw a consistent critique of the figure from the perspective of landowners, industrialists, and a new conservative, elite position. This consistent critique would shed light on the aporias that haunted the figure, even if they would ultimately fail to undo the colono's powerful hold on the economic imaginaries of independence and beyond.

Chapter 2 and 3 move to the figures through which the economic imaginaries of independence interpreted the real Mexican citizen. If the figure of the colono embodied the fantasy of free labor for elites, the artisan and the vagrant, as its opposites, indexed the social, political, and economic fears of national modernity. Chapter 2 looks at the figure of the artisan as it was imagined by the Creole elites of the period, intent on the industrial transformation of Mexico. The artisan was the most readily available urban figuration of labor. Yet, after the 1830s, he—and he was conceived of in the masculine—was consistently found to be lacking, insufficiently industrious. He was neither free nor faithful to productivity for productivity's sake, and perpetually constricted by what remained of the customs of the by-then-abolished guild structure. In the immediate aftermath of independence, the figure had enjoyed a period of honorability and republican righteousness, deployed as a representation of the popular working class. Yet, by the 1830s, in the midst of an economic crisis and an attempt at the industrialization of the cotton textile industry, the artisan was demoted and seen more often than not as an obstacle to the modernization not only of the nation's production but also the polity's customs. The first part of the chapter focuses on Lucas Alamán, one of the most important Mexican statesmen of the first half of the century, and on Estevan de Antuñano, the self-avowed father of Mexican industry. Both men, Alamán and Antuñano, played leading roles in Mexico's first industrialization and worked toward the articulation of the economic imaginaries of independence with a new language of capitalist modernization and technology absent before their interventions, and which entailed the replacement or displacement of the artisan. Both men were also seen, for more than a decade, as the main enemies of the Mexican working classes.

Alamán inaugurated the argument that Mexican autonomy depended not simply on the recognition of foreign governments, but on the economic independence of the territory; an independence he believed could only be achieved through industrialization. In these arguments, Alamán insisted that the economic agent of Mexico's transformation had to be the state, and not the artisan or individual worker. Only the state could direct modern industry's "perpetual duration," and channel it to improve the well-being of the population. For this to be possible, a strict police force and a vertical politics were necessary. As we will see, Alamán's logic was more than simply discursive, and launched a series of policies and institutions, which would flourish and survive him. The chapter studies Alamán's reports as either Ministro de Relaciones (Minister of Interior and Exterior Relations) or Director General de Industria (Director General of Industry) Industry, between 1830 and 1845, as well as his creation of Mexico's first developmental bank, the Banco de Avío.

Estevan Antuñano was a close associate of Alamán, and soon became the main publicist and beneficiary of Alamán's projects. In the years before and after the founding of his Constancia Mexicana, Mexico's first industrial factory, Antuñano was a steady presence in the press, evangelizing on the benefits of the industrialization of textile production, what he called the "industrial regeneration of Mexico." Put simply, he would consistently hold that the economic aggrandizement of Mexico required the technological replacement of artisan labor. Were the traditional artisan workshop replaced with modern factories, Mexico could quickly catch up with its providential future. For him, as for Alamán, technologization had the potential to transform artisan labor and also democratize employment and alter the customs of the population. For him, his factory, like all modern factories, was an engine of production, both of profit and customs.

The second part of the Chapter focuses on the Junta de Fomento de Artesanos (Artisan Development Junta, 1843–1846), an official institution dedicated to artisan protection. Through its activity in the press of the period and the founding of a mutual fund, the Junta would offer a counter-narrative to Alamán and Antuñano, one which preached the inherent morality of artisan labor. That said, insofar as the Junta de Fomento de Artesanos was led by wealthy master-artisans, it could only imagine futures that, similarly to those crafted by Alamán and Antuñano's institutions, hinged on the control and suppression of the worker, on the emptying of his interiority and on his transformation into mere procedure, mere instrument.

Chapter 3 focuses on the vagrant as the figure which allowed for the development of new mechanisms to discipline and force the transformation of the idle and unproductive population. In the years after independence, Bourbon-era and viceregal anti-vagrancy discourse and policy, understood as the persecution and expulsion of idle and unmoored populations, became essential elements to the economic imaginaries. Anti-vagrancy offered the new ruling classes a policy through which to identify, police, persecute, and prosecute those citizens whose lack of employment or general idleness threatened the productivist morality they believed proper to a modern nation-state. Independence-era politicians tried, at first, to adapt anti-vagrancy to a new republican circumstance, seeking a balance between the state's police—that is, its right over the administration of subsistence and markets so as to guarantee the economic well-being of the nation and, consequently, the liberty of its polity—with the citizen's newfound rights. As I show in the chapter, throughout the 1820s, they attempted to fashion an anti-vagrancy policy that could rid the state of the idle population and rehabilitate it, without transforming the State into a despotic apparatus. Yet, as the congressional proceedings studied show, government agents consistently ran into anti-vagrancy's despotic disposition; the fact that, if the state was to require all citizens to work, forceful intervention inadequate to a liberal republic was required. These republican qualms would be dismissed by the end of Mexico's first decade, when a Thermidorian reaction began to limit the democratic gains of the first years.[50] This period of conservative retrenchment, which extended from the 1830s to 1848 and was also a period of deep economic crisis, recuperated a series of Bourbon legal instruments that dismissed the "modern" separation of public and private and intervened directly in the personal life of the citizen. The intensifying ideological polarization of the period did not hamper the fact that the widespread adoption of anti-vagrancy as a tool to make the population productive offered a common ground between members of the political class. Such police intervention was sheltered under the argument, made by politicians but also by the press of the period, that idleness, the intentional rejection of the duty to be productive, constituted a crime against the republic. This united front against idleness began to show cracks after the US-Mexico War, when the understanding of vagrancy started to shift from the foundation of moralistic voluntarism on which it had rested until then, and move to a sociological understanding, that acknowledged the effects of social and economic circumstance on the life of working people.

Chapter 3 tells this story through an analysis of a series of laws, provisions, legislative debates, and journalistic coverage between 1826 and 1852. Through these instances, we see the political classes both tackle the question of vagrancy and engage in a process through which they hoped to better define the category, so as to establish a definite and clear border between the realms of labor and its opposites. In the process, it explores, from a different perspective, the place occupied by the relationship between freedom and labor (as it applied to the urban poor) and the role of police in the economic imaginaries of independence. Ultimately, it shows how the figure of the vagrant, and anti-vagrancy as the instrument to suppress it, functioned as symbolic resolutions to what the elite saw as the problem of development in a post-war economy plagued by the interspersed threats of demographic scarcity and pre-capitalistic habits. Whereas colonization sought to subsume and transform the national territory into a productive engine of industriousness, one which launched it to the forefront of commercial export capitalism, all the while growing a deficient population with laboring and exemplary elements from abroad; anti-vagrancy sought to capture and discipline the elements of the population that escaped work imperatives and which, its proponents believed, damaged the proper functioning of the social and economic spheres through their activity and example, so as to integrate them to the great chain of national production.

All in all, each instance studied throughout these chapters captures the attempt, by Mexico's lettered elite between 1821 and 1853, to materialize these imaginary figures; the adventure of their unfolding and their eventual failure. As I summarize in the book's brief conclusion, these figures fail not because it was a time of failure, but because every attempt to shape reality according to abstract, economic ideas that ignored the material obstinacy of the territory was bound to fail. Ultimately, this book engages with the cultural repertoire of the economic imaginaries of independence to delineate, sound, and explore the symbolic and economic horizons of the Creole elite of the first half of the nineteenth century. In this sense, it seeks to contribute to the deployment of the critical and theoretical approaches that the last decades of cultural and literary analyses have brought to bear on contemporary processes, but that have largely and until recently remained foreign to the scholarly study of nineteenth-century Latin American cultural production in US academia, where the emphasis on the period's literary production continues to hold a central place.[51] A critical approach to the economic imaginaries, as this book shows, overrides traditional grand narratives—such as the distinction between liberal and conservative thought in Mexico— as well as the quintessential debates about political form like the clash between monarchy, centralism, and federalism, and emphasizes the surprising stability and continuity that characterized narratives of economic growth and development. This book reveals that, when all was said and done, beyond the colono, there was no operative positive figuration of labor during the period. That is, in short, the nineteenth-century Mexican economic imagination was constructed on a vertical and misanthropic worldview. Most, if not all, of the members of the Creole and elite political nation were incapable of seeing Mexico for what it was: a society composed, in its majority, of indigenous communities, rural and urban Indian, mestizo and white peasants and artisans, and legions of unpaid soldiers, all of whom labored without respite with the hope not of leading the nation into a providential future of economic aggrandizement, but of simply making do.

CHAPTER 1

The Colono

The Territory, the Future of Labor, and the Subject of Production

And they knew that sooner or later their sanctuary's land was going to be claimed by that insatiable Republic that, who knows when, decided that it had to rule every square millimeter of the immense territory in which it sat, as if it had a use for the impenetrable heights of the Sierra Madre—it didn't: they're still empty.

Álvaro Enrigue, *Ahora me rindo y eso es todo*

The colono is very much the protagonist of a nineteenth-century hemispheric narrative that coupled labor, population, and the territory. Male and, ideally but not necessarily, a foreigner, the colono was a citizen only of the republic of labor. Recruited by a government for the settlement and exploitation of idle lands, he would, in time, fuel the wealth of the nation. His appeal predated independence. In both Spain and New Spain, he had starred the pipedreams of Enlightened proyectistas such as José de Escandón (1700–70), José de Gálvez (1720–92), Pablo de Olavides (1725–1803), Pedro Rodríguez de Campomanes (1723–1802) and Gaspar Melchor de Jovellanos (1744–1811). But it was only after the creation of the Mexican nation that colonización became an all-consuming narrative whose force warped the economic imaginaries of the period. As Moisés González Navarro put it, colonización became "the grand illusion of an independent Mexico."[1]

While not belonging strictly to the domain of economics, colonización drew most nineteenth-century economic discourse into its orbit. The newborn republics of the Americas looked at the United States' successful projects of population-increase, settlement, and the subsequent effects on its industry and wealth as a model and a path forward. Argentinean intellectual and politician Juan Bautista Alberdi best summarized the aspirations of

Latin American Creole elites in 1852 when he held that "to multiply a small population in just a few days–that is the heroism of the modern statesman."[2] The idea's gravitational pull, with its emphasis on land, labor, and agriculture, so enamored politicians that a frustrated early industrialist like Estevan Antuñano, who we study in Chapter 2 and who aspired to another form of economic development, termed colonización in 1844 the *noli me tangere* of economic matters.[3] That is, for Antuñano, colonización, like Christ's body in the immediacy of his resurrection, was the desired object of the age and yet, despite being in sight, it was one which could not be accessed, touched.[4] Unfortunately for the Creole lettered men I study in this chapter, Antuñano was right.

The word colonización or colonization refers, most directly, to the act of settlement, the creation of settler-colonies. This was the definition given by the daily *El Monitor Constitucional* in 1845 when, because of the term's preponderance over the past two decades of independent life, it felt the need to define it. This word, they wrote, "comes from the noun colonia, which means a certain portion of peoples that are sent, under the orders of a prince or a republic, to establish in another country recently conquered or discovered."[5] Their definition echoed the 1729 *Diccionario de Autoridades*, which put it so: "A population or allotment of land that has been populated by foreign people, brought from the Capital City or from elsewhere."[6] Yet, was colonization simply a question of population and settlement? In 1824, during a discussion of one of the earlier colonization projects, a congressman had asserted that it indeed was, observing "that the word [colonización] is not proper to the project, and that it would be convenient to replace it with population, which is truly the object of the measure."[7] Yet, this suggestion fell by the wayside and would continue to do so through the decades whenever similar acts of clarification were staged. The truth of the matter was that colonización, as it was most often used throughout the century, did not simply refer to the creation of colonies or the increase of population. In fact, the *Monitor*'s own 1845 definition went on, in a second paragraph, to note: "When all the points of the globe of which we have news became better known through the descriptions of travelers, many families abandoned their homelands to procure for themselves a soil that was richer and a comfortable and [thus] secure subsistence."[8] Colonización, for the authors, then, spoke of populations, surely, but more importantly of rational individuals who, moved by interest and necessity, seek lands which through labor can improve their lot. That is, at the stem of the word beat not the settler, but the etymological colono, from the Latin *colonus*, the "tiller of the soil, farmer." Made legible through the lens of a somewhat physiocratic liberal political economy, the colono as a figure melded territory, population, and industry and, as such, personified the economic aspirations of Creole elites.

As this chapter will show and as was said in the introduction, colonización was a sign, an ideologeme much more than a concept or ideology; serving both as a pseudoidea and a narrative. As a pseudoidea, colonización offered a conceptual resolution to the problem of postcolonial economic development in a postwar territory that had suffered massive demographic loss, but enjoyed the certainty of an abundance of natural resources. As a narrative, it imbued that problem with a historicity, a teleology, and a geography. This flexibility allowed it to serve as an anchoring point for productive and productivist liberal ideologies which, as scholar Evelyne Sánchez has said, narrowed down Mexico's difficulties to two elements: the lack of hands and the system of property, both of which could be solved through colonización.[9] Sánchez writes that "in the immediate aftermath of independence, policies of internal colonización served as one of the immediate resources to concretize the desired nation."[10] This was consistent with the liberal disposition of Mexican economic imaginaries, considering that, as critic Joshua Lund, who has studied the question of colonization in the last decades of the nineteenth century, has written, "if liberalism . . . relates to space, it does so through its tenacious drive to make space productive, in the capitalist sense, enlisting the state (the government and its armed forces) in this task."[11] In the aftermath of independence, the newborn Mexican nation's economic imaginaries tied the territory's future and inevitable economic aggrandizement, first, to liberty, and then to the power of industry and labor—its citizens', surely, but more importantly, the colono's.

In a nutshell, that is the argument espoused in these pages. What follows subscribes, then, to historian José Ángel Hernández's claim that, despite the significant amount of scholarly attention that the question of colonización has received, it remains largely unexplored. The existing historiography does "little to explain these policies on their own merits and in accordance with a sensitivity to their historical temporality."[12] One of the main reasons for this, Hernández points out, is that the trope of failure has pervaded accounts produced since the end of the nineteenth century. These narratives of colonización's failure find their epitome in post-revolutionary historian González Navarro's influential works on the matter.[13] In his three books on the subject, Mexico appeared "emplotted within a narrative of a young nation growing up" and, in the process, "tripping up at the same time," failing "to whiten its indigenous population" through multiple colonization policies.[14] Thus, González Navarro's account of colonización remained caught in the horizon of post-revolutionary historiography, dictated as it was by a liberal constitutionalism which took Benito Juárez' Restored

Republic (1867) as the starting point of Méxican modernity. It was also ideologically committed to what Lund calls the mestizo state, understood as "a historical-political process of state formation and capitalist penetration that explains itself to itself, indeed sustains itself, by drawing on a discourse of race."[15] That is, moving beyond Hernández's criticism of these accounts' emphasis on failure, one could say that what held back this historiographical tradition, with regards to a critical engagement of colonization, was not simply the trope of failure, but its very inscription in the racial logics of the mestizo state, which led it to proleptically racialize, simplify, and sterilize the polysemic nature of the colono. In the period studied, that of the earliest iterations of national colonization policies, the racial imperative was not as central as it would become in the second part of the century when "colonos blancos" (white settlers) became a working category. Between 1821 and 1852, as we will see, whether because the authors were offering lip-service to the newfound republican ideal of equality, or because they were desperate for population, they considered different European nationalities, different indigenous groups, and the Chinese as potential migrants. Surely, these policies were undoubtably and explicitly anti-black and participated in Creole racial logics, and yet, by transplanting one of the many discursive strands of colonization—race, which became paradigmatic only after 1862 and not before—the historiography has flattened and disregarded the depth and influence of the colono as a quintessential figure in the economic imaginaries of nineteenth-century Mexico.

In the subsections that follow, I focus on determining instances in the imaginary life of the colono, placing particular (but not exclusive) emphasis on its articulation of labor and territory. While not exhaustive, the moments I have chosen shed light on how the lettered men of the period turned to the figure to suture a series of historical crises and conceptual impasses. The sections are organized chronologically and, individually, should give insight into particular conjunctures. Cumulatively and in conversation with the other chapters of this book, these instances offer an expansive account of the economic imaginaries of the period between independence and the War of Reform.

THE STATE, COLONIZATION, AND THE FUTURE OF LABOR, 1821–1835

On October 6, 1821, the *Gaceta Imperial de México*, the recently rebranded official mouthpiece of Agustín de Iturbide's Army of the Three Guarantees, which gave Mexico its independence less than a month before, published an untitled editorial under the heading "Mexico" that set the ground for an image that would take hold in certain lettered quarters and become recurrent during those first years of effervescent patriotism. It was also an image that set the ground for the independent-era's colonization discourse and the deployment of the figure of the colono. According to it, Mexico figured as the end of history, as the westernmost point of a European teleology of liberty and, consequently, as the future of labor. The article in question, much like the other pieces published in the previous three issues of the *Gaceta*, sang praises to the newly formed governing body, the Junta Provisional Gubernativa (Provisional Governing Junta, September 1821–February 1822), charged with summoning a Constituent Congress and with the regency of the newborn Mexican Empire. The Empire, the authors caroled, held proudly to its place in history surrounded not only by the happiness which announced its road to aggrandizement and the current and future wisdom of its legislators, but also because of the "abundance that tears its breast to communicate its bountiful treasures" and the "industry that will activate a multitude of arms that for three hundred years have remained inert and without action."[16] These elements, glimpsed by the Empire only from the "plenitude of liberty" (plenitud de la libertad), affirmed what seemed as an all-but-certain truth: "This blessed country will be the hope of the discrete and industrious European."[17]

Because of its location, riches, and "feracidad" (fertility, fecundity of land), "América Septentrional" (North America), they noted, could be understood to have been groomed (criada) to "give the law to the entire world" (dar la ley al mundo entero).[18] The feat of Independence had been so brilliant, so characterized by "extraordinary events of human virtue" (aquellos extraordinarios acontecimientos de las virtudes humanas), that it not only placed Mexico among the "great nations" (naciones grandes), but also guaranteed its future place as the "center of liberty" (centro de la libertad).[19] This prediction was not only articulated from the buoyancy of a recent victory. The authors arrived at it after considering recent world-historical events. As they explained, it must have been Divine Providence, that force which "rules the events of the world according to its inscrutable dispositions," that animated Agustín de Iturbide to conceive and consummate "the sublime undertaking of the independence of the kingdom" in only seven months. This was at the same time in which, in Europe, the Congress of Troppau signed its onerous Troppau Protocol, confirmed further in the Congress of Laibach, which made the Holy Alliance the effective instrument of the ancien regime's repression of revolutionary change.[20] For the authors, the providentiality of Mexican independence was evident in the fact that just as Iturbide effectuated Mexico's most complete liberty, Europe's old sovereigns rallied and conspired to sustain and conserve an age of despotism which had begun, they believed, three hundred years earlier with the extinguishing of the prosperous empire of the Aztecs.[21] The coincidence of these two events further cemented the certainty of the economic futures of this new Septentrional Empire insofar as its independence was made all the more significant in the face of European liberty's dire outlook. At that moment, more than ever before, the authors insisted, the prospects of uninfringeable rights and the possibility of free industry resided nowhere else than in American soil.[22]

Framed in this manner, as a new, providential Empire built on solid economic grounds and modern sensibilities at the same moment in which the old empires asserted their political backwardness, the expression to "give the law to the entire world" (dar la ley al mundo entero) becomes noteworthy. As Sophus Reinert has written, the idiom of "giving" laws played a key role in the early modern development of political economy. The expression was a variation on the equation, in classical antiquity, of power with the ability to "give laws;" "a condition derived from the idea that liberty demanded subjection only to one's own legislation."[23] "To give law" or "dar la ley" was used to refer both to concrete as well as to de facto conquests. Yet, in the context of the eighteenth century, the idiom was universally employed in early modern political economy to refer to conquest through commerce, through "purely economic means."[24] This usage was not simply analogical. That is, the presentation of economic power in the language of war was not merely a question of simile, but of a material and symbolic synergy between the two forms of conquest.[25] Says Reinert, "[c]onquest was not always a corruption of trade's intrinsic telos; it could be its most natural consequence."[26] Against the trope of "doux commerce," which saw trade as a moderate, civilizing force that checked humankind's destructive drives, this idea of commerce as the necessary expression of economic power appeared as much in the writings of "economic imperialists" who saw it as a means of indirectly achieving *imperium*, as well as in texts concerned with guaranteeing the national independence of small states such as the Kingdom of Naples.[27] In this panorama, early modern political economy was not simply the science of enlightened reform and the increase of wealth, but the necessary science to both render nation-states viable as political entities in a contentious international landscape, as well as to educate people to the "congruence" between conquest and commerce.[28] "[S]uccess in trade, the ability to give laws, and commercial jealousy were impossible to extricate as the modern world economy took shape, and would resonate as such into the nineteenth century. Where a state was located in the architecture of the global economy—what it produced and how—remained of literally existential importance," writes Reinert.[29]

The commercial sense of the idiom "to give laws" was latent within the *Gaceta Imperial*'s usage. In those first months, the incipient state was indeed concerned with both its aggrandizement and with securing the economic grounds of its independence. Yet it was also concerned, insofar as it envisioned itself as an empire, with amassing "that conflux of conquest and commerce known, and feared, as *imperium*."[30] Under the spell of patriotic effervescence, it was manifest that this latter goal would easily be carried out once a "moderate" government was consolidated and commerce liberalized. It would simply be a matter of instrumentalizing the territory's natural resources. After all, unlike Europe's outlook, and thanks to the unexploited riches of the land, Mexico's future economy was to be an economy of abundance.

For the *Gaceta*, under the new enlightened government, the providential copiousness of the land would consequently activate the idle arms of a once-subjugated populace, while also serving as a hopeful horizon for the "discrete and industrious European."[31] Thus, the *Gaceta* anchored its discourse of economic aggrandizement on a particular anthropology of labor, pregnant with significance. On the one hand, it promised to imbue with activity a national population that had never been active, that had remained "defenseless" (inermes) and "without activity" (sin acción).[32] That is, a population which, both unfortunately and fortunately, had been, until that moment, pure potential, not quite because of itself, but because of the poverty of Spanish governance. In this sense, the *Gaceta* conceptualized Mexican labor power as raw material, as a being that could only be revealed and activated when processed through the engine of an independent and national state. On the other hand, the editors hoped that the copiousness of the land would attract European "arms," which, unlike the former, were always-already striving, laboring, and active despite being held captive in the unproductive and despotic horizons announced by the Troppau Protocol. Hence, in this striated panorama of labor, whereas Mexican labor power lied passive because it was untapped, European labor power gushed forth like a geyser, regardless of its governance. Whether the difference between these two lay at the level of ontology or of historicity—that is, whether the difference was a question of the Mexicanness of Mexican labor power, or of its historical circumstance and the fact that it had yet to experience a free government that finally activated it—remained unsaid. Yet, the Empire's stated goal, if we follow the *Gaceta*, was to align these two forms of labor with the catalysis of liberty and abundance. The article emphasized this last point, and re-asserted it: "As it becomes known in that continent that religion, unity, and liberty, sweetly twinned with peace, abundance and moderation, are the pillars of the Empire, their eyes will turn and they will eagerly wish to move to these lands and live as free men, putting an end to being preyed on by the terrible grip of a ruthless despotism."[33]

Thus, Mexico would conquer and "give law" to Europe not only through commerce, but also through example. The goal of these conquests would be, in a sense, to reverse and change the register of the extractivism that had characterized the imperial relation between the Spanish Crown and the Viceroyalty in that, now, the resource to be extracted would be none other than those European huddled masses that yearned to be free. It was through this argumentation that the state, in its public self-representation, arrived at the logic which made of Mexico Europe's telos. In other words, for the *Gaceta*, the Mexican Empire was to be Europe's future in a double sense. First, in that the historical processes that began in the Old World would find their completion in the New, in Septentrional America—the one place, after the affirmation of the Troppau Protocol, where liberty reigned. Secondly, it was to be Europe's future in that it would be populated by and improved through the industry of Europe's own.

The *Gaceta*'s article is noteworthy, then, because it made explicit "aggrandizement" as the economic horizon that articulated Mexico's economic futures; and as a point in a temporal logic which structured the economic imaginaries of independence and early political activity of the Mexican Empire. For the *Gaceta*, the economic futures of the Empire were not only part and parcel of its political futures, but the latter's condition of possibility. The aggrandizement of the territory was precisely that which the nation had been deprived of under the Spanish regime, and which it now proudly claimed as its prize. This language of aggrandizement served as one of the pillars on which the new Mexican art of government was to be established.

If, as Michel Foucault has said, governmental reason (*raison d'etat*) as it emerged in the eighteenth century made of the state its objective, "its foundation and its aim," what we have in the *Gaceta Imperial*'s article is precisely the celebration of the birth of a fully autochthonous governmental reason.[34] This independent *raison d'etat* both prefigures and configures the nation and, more importantly, the state. It frames nation and state as the correct and providential principles of intelligibility of a reality which had been kept garbled and unproductive for three hundred years. As a principle of intelligibility, this autochthonous state-to-come, guided by its own justice, philosophy, and legislative Junta, was to offer, in Foucault's words, a "way of thinking the specific nature, connections, and relations of certain already-given elements and institutions."[35] The whole of the national territory was to be conceived, analyzed and defined through its schema. Thus, even in October 1821, when a cohesive Mexican territory (or, more precisely, a cohesive Septentrional America) was little more than an aspiration with undetermined borders placed somewhere in a largely unchartered far north, the Caribbean, and a foreign and autonomous south, which included Yucatán and Guatemala, the imperial Mexican *raison d'etat* announced in the *Gaceta* nevertheless imagined itself as an absolutely given reality, as an already established institutional whole.[36] The *Gaceta* insisted on what Rafael Rojas has called the Empire's "claim to futurity" despite the fact that its institutions were not yet quite its own.[37]

For the *Gaceta*, the political rationality on which the Mexican Empire sought to imbricate itself stood on three pillars— capitalist organization in the form hereto referred as "aggrandizement," a police state (to be discussed in Chapter 3), and international diplomacy (read: international trade).[38] All of these appeared or would appear summoned in the pages of the *Gaceta Imperial* at one moment or another. Yet, in the article in question, it was precisely the emphasis on aggrandizement that became essential, and which was framed as the principle for the organization that would ensure the new state's future integrity. To put it briefly, aggrandizement here was short for the termination of Spanish fiscal exploitation and monopolies, the apt and productive organization of the Mexican territory and its abundance, the proper instrumentalization of its citizenry's industry, an increase in the size of this population through migration, and, finally, the insertion of the nation into permanent competition with other foreign sovereign states, which would lead to the development of Mexican imperium.[39]

The tenets espoused by the *Gaceta*'s October 6 article were to continue reappearing not only in the pages of the weekly and in speeches and pamphlets, but also as the ideological ground for policy proposals during the brief life of the Mexican Empire (1822–23) and, eventually, the Federal Republic (1823–35) and subsequent Central Republic (1835–46). Yet, unlike the editors of the *Gaceta*, who believed liberty and abundance were enough to catalyze the industry of the newborn nation through the activation of the local populace's labor and the free immigration of European liberty-loving laborers, for most of the political nation—Creole statesmen, *proyectistas*, vernacular economists, and commentators—a more direct and tactical approach was necessary: colonization.

TADEO ORTIZ DE AYALA, POLITICAL ARITHMETIC, AND THE STATE

Tadeo Ortiz de Ayala's name would become synonymous, if not coterminous, with colonización. He would spend the first decade of independence—his last—writing, lobbying, and recruiting to make colonization a reality. A *proyectista* in the eighteenth-century mold, Ortiz de Ayala (1788–1833) embodied the role of the enlightened citizen, alternating from analyst to lobbyist and entrepreneur, always in close proximity to government but never quite of it.[40] His writing alternated accordingly, moving from an analytical to an entrepreneurial mode. He produced two seminal texts, in 1822 and 1832, which analyzed the "conditions" or "statistics" of México, and also wrote a trove of reports, letters, and proposals to government, advocating in favor of colonization policies which, grounded on his own research, left a dent in the economic imaginaries well after his death in 1833. Ortiz de Ayala's decade-long engagement with the question of colonization, and the attention it received from other interested parties who directly or indirectly took up some of his ideas or blind spots, serve as a thorough-line through which to trace the deployment of the colono from independence until its momentary occlusion during the years between the Texas Revolt and the US Invasion.

Ortiz de Ayala's ideas, built on liberal and politico-economic presuppositions, were easily pliable and adaptable to the three forms of government Mexico experienced in its first two decades: Monarchy, Federation, and Centralist Republic. As we will see, Ortiz de Ayala conceived of his colono as a liberal entrepreneur capable of both activating the territory with his (or others') labor and developing a capitalist enclave that would propel a national export economy. The resulting colono would bring to bear the conceptual impasses of the Mexican state's police project, as well as the deeper contradictions vis-à-vis free and unfree labor that plagued liberalism at the onset of industrial capitalist modernity. Ortiz de Ayala's vision of colonization as the engine that would activate the territory, grounded as it was on his analytic work, had a depth and an extension that proved to be foundational. The work was so influential that when the State of Veracruz went on to fashion its own colonization policy toward the end of the 1820s, they did so in consultation with Ortiz de Ayala, noting that "[t]he more the committee has fixed its attention upon [Ortiz de Ayala's] recommendations, the more strongly has it adhered to his ideas. In them are found simplicity, liberality of principles, and practical knowledge. The committee has, therefore, in the main adopted these ideas."[41]

Ortiz de Ayala's colono existed within a Humboldtian worldview. Already in the first analytic document he authored, which introduced him as a champion of colonization, the *Resumen de la estadística del imperio mexicano* (*Summary of the Mexican Empire's Statistics*, 1822), we see him immersed not in the modern discipline of statistics, as his title suggests, but in Humboldt's discipline, a field which throughout the seventeenth and eighteenth century was called political arithmetic. If statistics studied the formation of the state and its contents, political arithmetic set out to calculate and predict the economic and political potential of a polity. It expanded from the assumption that the generative and elemental facts of this potential were given by nature and, thus, available to be interpreted and understood by a state's rational actors.[42] Political arithmetic was not simply a predecessor to political economy. Early proponents of both insisted on the difference. As Mary Poovey has written, unlike political economy, which derived from the moral philosophy of the eighteenth century and, as a result, "contained elements of what we could call psychology, logic, ethics, jurisprudence, history, and rhetoric," political arithmetic was born from the Enlightenment discourse of police, a discourse explicitly concerned with efficient rule.[43] Also unlike political economy, whose proponents "severed the connection between particulars and theory," only to then "recast theoretical statements as descriptive of 'facts,'" political arithmeticians sought to remain grounded in what they conceived of as the particulars so as to harness their actual potential.[44] In that sense, Ortiz de Ayala's *Resumen*, addressed as it was to the new emperor Agustín de Iturbide—out of convenience more than any particular commitment, as his later career would show—offered a summary of what a non-state actor believed should be the foundational principles of a new state reason and practice as dictated by the facts of nature: the centrality of agriculture, the necessity of repopulating and activating the territory through colonization, and the development of commercial ports for exports. At a moment in which the political class worried about the lack of statistical knowledge, Ortiz de Ayala's text provided what its title promised, a digested and updated account of Humboldt's findings, contextualized and processed for a new national government "with the idea of regenerating and giving a boost to all branches of this opulent and vast Empire."[45] The *Resumen* opened with an extended geographic survey of the national territory that spoke authoritatively about its characteristics, going so far as to questioning previous accounts, including Humboldt's, in matters of methodology and arithmetic. The survey came coupled with an exaltation of each region's productive potential as well as with illustrative comparisons with equivalents from Europe and the United States. It was, of course, not a disinterested "scientific" account, for all its purported objectivity and groundedness. Ortiz de Ayala subscribed to the myth of national providential wealth, and believed that the Mexican government was privileged by having within its territory a multiplicity of climates, because these promised endless commercial riches. It was a land wholly available for capitalistic speculation, one in which "man can choose, with the thermometer in hand, the terrain most analogous to his speculations and constitution, surrounded by flattering and innocent benefits."[46]

Surely, because political arithmeticians' ultimate interlocutor and subject was the hypothetical state and not the market, Ortiz de Ayala forewent liberalism's blind trust in the spontaneous interest of the individual. For all his philosophical support of private interest, in practical manners Ortiz de Ayala generally believed that private interest, without strong governmental guidance, proper police, and education, tended to waste.[47] Ortiz de Ayala's political anthropology began from the presupposition that subjectivity was shaped in relation to a government. Precisely because human beings were self-interested creatures naturally predisposed to waste, the imposition of restraints was necessary for the channeling of private vices into public benefits—and these, in turn, to personal liberty. According to him, this was evident to any careful analyst of the national situation in the aftermath of independence. When he took stock of the human landscape, he saw that Mexican unproductivity was not a matter of ontology, but of governance. He went on to explain, for example, that if the middle classes—merchants, miners, and members of the learned professions—lagged behind international peers, it was because they lacked proper direction and, as a result, had remained constrained by regressive institutions. Similarly, if the lower classes amounted to a "dead class," submerged in ignorance and idleness, it was because they had been deprived of property and industry. Finally, if the indigenous had been made "useless," it was because they had been been broken and debased by centuries of despotic tutelage and forced dependence.[48] Each of these cases called for an enlightened and self-interested government, one who knew the wisdom of "civiliz[ing] and giv[ing] an occupation to a miserable multitude, which, like a moth, can endanger public tranquility, because of the vices generated by idleness and destitution, which undermine states."[49] Despite Ortiz de Ayala's later summary dismissal of the Mexican Empire as a despotic institution and his years of direct or indirect service to the Federal Republic (1824–35), the truth of the matter was that his project of actualizing Mexican potential through the efficient colonization of key swaths of the territory could only be carried out through a strong, national state. He said as much just before his death in the 1830s. Seeing the rising winds of a centralist upheaval which promised more direct intervention in the everyday life of Mexico, he called for a stronger administration, one well-advised, informed and "superior to any other [read regional or provincial] power." Only such a state could do what was necessary to "direct society" and its economic aggrandizement.[50]

This affiliation between a strong sovereign state and the colono spoke to the physiocratic undercurrents of most colonization theory in nineteenth-century Mexico, which became explicit in Ortíz de Ayala. As Charles Hale put it, "[t]he physiocrats believed that only land was productive of wealth and that this wealth could only be forthcoming if there existed a wise Legislator to 'discover' [or to enforce] the laws of nature."[51] For Ortiz de Ayala, Mexican economic performance and agricultural output had surely been outstanding in the last decades of the viceroyalty. Yet, this prosperity had been achieved passively, inefficiently; the result of only "a small part of the Imperial territory, with a mid-sized population that was apathetic and lacked emulation."[52] Mexico's problem was precisely that its natural resource production was impressive by any standard and that, even considering governmental inertia, its products were immense, which only further cemented the lack of governmental wisdom. Most in the viceroyalty had been distracted by the riches promised by Mexican mines, yet this emphasis on mineral wealth derived from ignorance. Like others in the first years of independence, Ortiz de Ayala held that the mining industry, which had driven the territory's eighteenth-century boom, had fallen into decadence and needed to be rescued, but he insisted that this industry was not the primary source of Mexican wealth, which was the product only of agriculture.[53] He summarized his position as follows: "The Mexican Empire's true wealth is not based exclusively on metal exploitation, which has little influence on the real prosperity of a Nation; it is founded on the products of the land, which are the basis of secure affluence."[54]

Ortiz de Ayala's account of the national economy was partially correct. It was true that mining had fallen into disrepair and that, even if it were to be rehabilitated, it would not have produced the "true wealth" necessary to propel the new independent state to the position the territory once occupied in viceregal times. As historian John Tutino has repeatedly shown, silver capitalism, which had made New Spain's mines the engine of the world economy and placed the region at the forefront of eighteenth-century globalization, had long collapsed by 1821.[55] By the time Iturbide was crowned in 1822, Mexico had become marginal to a world economy that shifted its axes to industrialization and finance.[56] This collapse of silver had come hand-in-hand with the decay in agriculture Ortiz de Ayala described. As the revenue from silver capitalism dried up and the 1810 insurgency in the Mexican heartland intensified, the government willingly or unwillingly stepped (or was forced) back, and internal and external trade, based on agriculture, shriveled. The decay in farming was not necessarily the result of state action. In fact, one could question whether it was a decay at all. What seemed like deterioration from the point of view of elites and other beneficiaries of the commercial economy of yore seemed a bounty for others. The fall of silver capitalism had hit commercial, profit-seeking farming the hardest. Tutino writes that, while commercial agriculture lagged, "[p]ersistent family farming," by Ortiz de Ayala's apathetic population, "led to ample harvests and low prices."[57] From this, we can gather that, for Ortiz de Ayala, the agriculture that created true wealth, the agriculture in which the colono would employ his labor, and which was the grounds for the state's "secure affluence," was not homestead-centered farming, but the type of commercial farming which produced surpluses and was geared for internal and external trade.[58]

The *Resumen* ended with a brief sketch of how to go about achieving this true opulence through colonization. Seeing as Mexico's population was "unevenly distributed," the state should adopt a policy of populating its vast expanses with colonos which, with time, would draw many citizens to relocate to what would undoubtedly become booming towns. The *Resumen*'s last pages highlighted the potential of Texas and the Californias, but also included the Tehuantepec Isthmus and the Coatzacoalcos River as sites where Mexico's future could be forged through an increase of an industrious population and enlightened management. Ortiz de Ayala would dedicate the next few years finding support for these projects, evangelizing the physiocratic gospel among the Mexican political class and, eventually, become the state's agent in the process.

AN EMPHYTEUTIC COLONO

While the *Resumen* explicates Ortiz de Ayala's worldview and his support of colonization, it was in his political and economic work, in his lobbying and direct engagement with politicians and the government, where his improvisational—and influential—ideas of colonization materialized, and from where they spread their images. The *Resumen* was concluded less than a month after independence, following the *Gaceta*'s article by four days, and was published as a pamphlet in 1822. Shortly after it began circulating, or perhaps simultaneously, its author cosigned a proposal with foreigners Diego Barry and Phillip O'Reilly, in which they offered to transport ten thousand settlers from Ireland and the Canary Islands to the Province of Texas under the condition that they were granted 6,000 square leagues. Ortiz de Ayala's Texas proposal was one among many requesting permission to colonize large swaths of the territory. The proposal itself seems to not have survived, yet the debates it started did. More so than the majority of requests, in large part authored by US citizens, this proposal was welcomed by most members of the Constituent Congress's Colonization Committee. Whether this privilege was the result of Ortiz de Ayala being Mexican, or the fame garnered with his *Resumen*, the congressmen presented it approvingly and enthusiastically to the new Constituent Congress, established in February 1822.[59]

To their surprise, however, it was quickly shot down on June 5, 1822, by one of their own, the committee's sole dissenting member, Veracruz congressman and future Minister of Finance José Ignacio Esteva. Esteva opened his objections by arguing that Ortiz de Ayala had largely ignored the Provisional Sovereign Junta's work in the matter of colonization, especially a work titled *Un programa de política internacional* (A Program of International Policy, 1822), which served as preamble to the Imperial Colonization Law of 1822.[60] That work, he said, through careful consideration, had come to a better understanding of the needs of a newborn state in terms of the economic and political importance of the subjection of its inhabitants and their fiscal duty. For this reason, instead of turning to Ortiz de Ayala's proposal, he believed the aforementioned *Program* should be used and "serve as a guide to the señores diputados" when forming their own colonization plan. Some deputies insisted that Esteva's objections be dismissed, and the government move in support of Ortiz de Ayala.[61] Others, however, came to second Esteva and, with their help, a general critique of Ortiz de Ayala congealed, grounded on the 1822 *Program*. The debate that followed brought forth questions not only regarding the relationship between the state and the colono, and between private and public interest, but also about the role of intermediaries, and the figure of the colono as laborer. In what follows, I will turn to the *Program*, first, and then, return to the debate.

The *Program*, written by Juan Francisco de Azcárate y Lezama, a close supporter and confidante of Iturbide, and cosigned by the Count of Heras y Soto and José Sánchez de Enciso, was an idiosyncratic document, one which emphasized the need for colonization, while underscoring the dangers of free labor.[62] Azcárate y Lezama, like Ortiz de Ayala, believed that a strong state was necessary for the activation of national labor through colonization. Yet, his conception of the state's role diverged slightly. As we will see, for the author of the *Program*, human industry was best motivated and mediated by the market and, because it was the state's task to care for these relations, it should keep a watchful eye over these interactions. The state, then, was to invisibly structure the terms of market engagement and to guarantee its proper operation, its smooth functioning within the horizon of national aggrandizement. If it visibly intervened in the freedom of its inhabitants, it would do so only in a prefatorial manner, to ensure the propriety of the colono's labor and his attachment to local laws. For Ortiz de Ayala, in contrast, the state was the explicit condition of labor; it channeled human activity and made it productive (in a capitalistic sense). It was not simply strong, but forever active. Technically, it would have seemed that Ortiz de Ayala called for firmer governmental control. Yet, as the Texas Proposal seems to have argued, for him, the state was conceived of as an elastic institution, and the only pragmatic way it could satisfy its expectation was through the delegation of its powers to private, enlightened citizens. We will return to this.

In Azcárate y Lezama's proposal, Texas was the locus of Mexico's future aggrandizement. The region beat in all its potential, capable of launching the reinvention of the newfound empire. The territory was "so fertile, with such a benign temperament, so rich in metals and natural productions, that when you read the description that geographers make, it can be believed they speak of Paradise."[63] It thus functioned as the blank, mostly unpopulated slate on which the authors projected their dream of a productive landscape. Fortunately for Mexico, Texas had been largely neglected and abandoned by the Spanish.[64] Peninsulars, according to Azcárate y Lezama, had lacked a coherent approach when dealing with the Northern provinces. They alternated between "thievery" and "liberality" with no discretion, fearing foreign settlers while privileging Spaniards who accumulated all the land grants given to them in "spacious haciendas, many of which are larger than Spain itself" and which produced no income to the state.[65] These large haciendas were largely wasted, and when they were worked at all, they were rented out piecemeal, which further decreased their productivity insofar as "[t]he tenant fears investing [his energies] in its cultivation and improvement so that they are not dispossessed after having worked the lot; the result of this situation is that neither the lord nor the tenant yield the utility they should, and the state deprives itself of a lot of fair revenue, which it would otherwise receive."[66] Azcárate y Lezama noted that, true, Spain had tried to fix their ways in the immediate decades before Mexican independence, but it had been too little, too late. Centuries of poor government had taken its toll and they had been unable to reverse the effect their indirect support for latifundia had on what little population inhabited these regions.

To reverse this, it was necessary to understand, as the United States had, that only private property and effort motivated men: "Man wants and appreciates that which takes him a lot of work to prepare him for comfort and rest afterward; he delights in the work of his hands and wants nothing more than to enjoy it."[67] As a matter of convenience, Azcárate y Lezama proposed the adoption and modification of the US model of land grants of an acre each. Not only was this model already well-known in Europe, but it also benefited the poor, abolishing the arbitrary current practice of renting smaller lots of land not according to their extension but to their estimated yield.[68] The proposed plan was for the Mexican government to give these parcels to colonos—nationals and foreigners—under emphyteutic leases worth six reales to be paid yearly starting only six years after settlement, and exempt from taxes for that same duration. Once the territory was parceled and brought into the realm of production, all would see "how one Province can yield more than what the totality of New Spain did under the incapable hands of their lords of the past, who tyrannized her."[69] With the resulting fiscal revenue, Azcárate y Lezama hypothesized, the Empire would be able to fund its government, its military, and church, and still achieve a surplus.

This emphyteutic nature of the colono's land-grant was the key element that attracted Esteva and others when opposing Ortiz de Ayala's Texas proposal. It was not simply a matter of revenue, but also of security. Unlike many future supporters of colonization, the *Program*'s optimism was not entirely unbridled. Azcárate y Lezama's inaugural colono was not exactly the self-owned, self-determined liberal laboring subject he would soon after become. Despite moving in pursuit of his interest, Azcárate y Lezama's subject was plastic and characterized by a set of customs and dispositions (usos y costumbres) that were derived from his historical relation with geographic space, demographic density, and particular governments. That is, in Azcárate y Lezama, the colono had not entirely been reduced to a flattened and emptied type—universal and abstract—and remained an embedded character. Successful colonization and its positive influence on a nation's aggrandizement resulted from the targeted transplantation of people and the grafting of their customs on a specific and ordained location—in this case, Northern Mexico's prodigal geography. Precisely because the colono was a subject relatively determined by his past environment and not the pure will that characterized Ortiz de Ayala's figure in the *Resumen*, Azcárate y Lezama foresaw problems and did everything he could to control for these.

Azcárate y Lezama's patriotic optimism was kept in check by the current situation in Texas. He distrusted Stephen F. Austin's management of the Texan grant given by Spanish officials in Monterrey to his father, Moses Austin, shortly before independence in January 1821.[70] He thought it unfortunate that the grant itself followed Spanish and not Mexican designs and, as such, short-circuited national attempts of Texan colonization. But it was not simply a matter of the legality and propriety of the grant itself. Austin had begun to lead settlers into the territory a few months before the *Program*, in mid-1822, and Azcárate y Lezama questioned the younger Austin's de facto independence in Texas.[71] More specifically, he suspected Austin's recent attempt to establish a port in the Colorado River, noting that it was not convenient for the Empire that "interested parties are allowed to choose and occupy the land at their whim, nor that they decide and populate the ports, without the presence of Mexicans and the armed forces to defend them."[72] Moreover, the *Program* decried what it considered the unlawful migration of other questionable US elements who were crossing the Sabinas river to penetrate the territory, settling it "at will without order or notice to the authorities; if not all, most of them do not have a passport or any other document that shows their good conduct and behavior; from this, it is to be inferred that they are the most corrupted, [and these] do not fit, nor are they tolerated in a country as free [as Mexico is]."[73]

In light of the situation, Azcárate y Lezama felt the need to address the relationship between government and individual. He wrote that, even though it might seem like an enlightened state did not look directly at the actions of individuals, in reality a government only "acts as if" (disimula) it does not pay attention. The truth of the matter was that "[i]t is impossible for a Government that lives under the most exact police, to ignore the negotiations of particulars."[74] After all, the "private individual interested in a particular business calculates better than anybody his interest, and his observations offer the state a model for what it should execute."[75] That is, an enlightened state was to watch over its citizens with positive intentions. Doing so, would allow it to understand how individuals behaved according to their interest and, then, properly legislate. Say, if individuals found that there was a market for a product, whether nationally or internationally, it made sense that the government should move not simply to tax it, but to encourage the particular trade through formal, practical policy. Likewise, as was the case with Stephen F. Austin's land grant, if a government noticed that its colonos were acting as if they were entirely free from scrutiny, the government should step in an remind them of their commitment to the state.[76]

The US colono, then, represented a problem. He came from a nation that had land to spare, and sought to work Mexican lands moved solely for the pursuit of their private interests, a pursuit that could easily be co-opted by the expansionist intentions of his nation's government. Surely, for Azcárate y Lezama, all potential colonos were inevitably driven by private interest. But, for this reason, he preferred migrants that originated from places affected by demographic and political pressure. Unlike US settlers, these ideal migrants' private interest would be buttressed by the sheer fact of material necessity and lack, and insofar as the Mexican Empire freed them from this circumstance, they would likely become loyal and grateful subjects. Through its pages, the *Program* identified five possible historical sources which, in theory, were not dictated by ideological preference, but by historical contingency and civilizational potential. The *Program's* first source of colonos was determined by their factual mobilization. Families from New Orleans had moved to the region earlier that year under the auspices of Stephen F. Austin's land grant. Insofar as they seemed to be succeeding in setting down roots, it would be possible to encourage them to foster the emigration of their brethren. The second source of colonos was dictated by the promises that led to the attainment of independence. Mexican families should be invited to colonize Texas, sharing the benefits of its resources. Through the catalyst of private property, these Mexican citizens would be rendered industrious and serve as an example for their compatriots. A third source of migrants would be the *Gaceta*'s first: Europe. Azcárate y Lezama explained that the constant wars that plagued that continent, the harshness of its climates, the sheer poverty, and religious strife, had generated a spirit of emigration which, until that moment, had benefited only the United States, resulting in a threefold increase of its population. Among the European nations, the authors preferred the Irish, because of their Catholicism and the fact that they had been persecuted for centuries and yet persevered in their faith. Irish morals, he reported, were known to be impeccable: they were industrious and virtuous. An added benefit was that they were reputed to dislike the British and the Americans. If the Irish were unavailable, Azcárate y Lezama would also settle for Germans, who were not only Catholic, but had also successfully settled in certain Spanish regions.[77] In other words, while families from New Orleans and Mexico were chosen in large part out of convenience—both were close and available and the sheer fecundity of the land would activate their labor—this third wellspring was unique because its value lay not simply in historical contingency or in the quality of the potential laborers, but in the experience of migration itself. This experience showed their commitment and desire for a land to work for themselves. That is, the lengths to which these Catholic European men had historically gone to labor a plot of land—a *proper* plot of land, in which nature reciprocated the labor invested in it, spoke wonders of their commitment to the pursuit of their interests.[78] This commitment, coupled with the profligacy of harvests that Texas promised, could propel the new Mexican Empire forward.

After this triad, Azcárate y Lezama listed two additional potential sources of colonos, but these were hypothetical, and a series of conditions had to be met before they could materialize. The first would be Spain, but only after it recognized the new imperial state. Once it did, the Empire "would admit with *gusto*" those individuals and families willing to transplant themselves to the territories, where they would be treated like any other colono. The second alternate source, which they believed might be more appropriate for California than Texas, was China. California, which was threatened by Russia's American aspirations, remained underpopulated because it was such a remote territory that no Mexican or European family would even consider it.[79] China was, then, the only hope. Imaginable only in the immediacy of independence, when the new Mexican Empire's territory was yet to be decided, China represented an "excellent judgement," positive as long as the Philippines, once part of the viceroyalty of New Spain, remained within the new Empire. Surely, Azcárate y Lezama's justification of a possible Chinese colonization was grounded not on statistical accounts, like their report on US demography, but on an idiosyncratic orientalist register filled with questionable anthropological observations drawn from travel narratives.[80] Whereas Mexico suffered of a demographic shortage, China had the opposite problem. The *Program* noted that Chinese migrants would come to Mexico eagerly, from Canton (Guangzhou) or elsewhere, because "that vast Empire achieves a larger population than the one it can sustain; that is why parents are allowed to kill their young children when their means are not enough to feed them."[81] The Californias, then, offered China's surplus population immense territories that were as rich and perhaps more fertile than those of their native land, and the Mexican government would provide each with a parcel and any help they might need to get their labor started. Being famous for their dedication to commerce and navigation, once settled and in harvest, he wrote, Chinese colonos will surely foster mercantile connections with Asia, which "would activate commerce in an extraordinary and useful manner for our soil."[82]

In other words, according to Azcárate y Lezama's account, Austin's migrants from New Orleans had already lived in Texas and were accustomed to its circumstance; poor Mexicans suffered of "sterile hands" due to the lack of property that derived from Spanish mismanagement; Catholic Europeans had withstood centuries of oppression and pursued their interest with such zeal that they sacrificed everything for a parcel of land, which spoke well of their industriousness; the Spanish were of similar constitution to Mexicans and could adapt quickly, and the Chinese were desperate for land. It was the new incipient state's responsibility to capture the contingent rhythms of global demography and the resulting flows of world migration and transform them into intentional and productive settlement. Ultimately, whatever his geographic origin, the colono's encounter with the providential riches of the Mexican territory would be transformative, both for him and, through the productivization of idle lands and its subsequent positive effects on trade and taxation, for the Mexican Empire.

In light of this, all foreign colonos' interest had to be properly channeled. Constrained, even. The *Program* included a series of provisions for just this purpose, arguing that, while it was likely that foreigners would appreciate the government that offered them citizenship and land, the state should actively foster their patriotism in any way it could, while making sure that these foreign elements be accompanied by national-born citizens and a contingent from the Mexican army to defend and assist them in the unfamiliar landscape, all the while taking advantage of the physical and moral strengths of the new populations.[83]

The *Program* emphasized two preconditions for settlement. First, that the Empire would not offer haven to the "idle, the vicious nor the perverse" and so, "any foreigner that, after three months of their arrival in the Provinces, has not found occupation in a particular task or a known industry, will be exiled from them, or sent to the army."[84] Secondly, it stipulated that foreigners, "by condition, cannot separate themselves from the Province they choose during the first six years of the franchise of their rights.[85] That is, Azcárate y Lezama called for the foreign colono to forfeit, contractually and temporarily, his freedom of movement. In theory, through cohabitation with the Mexican residents of the settlement, mutual influence, and the foreigner's own investment of effort in the improvement of his allotted land, this temporal restriction of movement would allow for the forging of the ties that bind the settler both to the territory and to the humanitarian government that transformed him into a property-owner. Once the six-year period expired, the colono regained his freedom of movement and his power to do what he wanted with the property. But even this propertied freedom was conditional, bound to the state. On the one hand, the colono had to guarantee that his land remained productive. Like all future colonization proposals, the *Program* required for permanent production under the threat of dispossession. On the other, and perhaps more importantly because its inclusion went unremarked, was the emphyteutic nature of Azcárate y Lezama's ideal land grant, which served as the instrument for said potential dispossession.

Its roots in Ancient Greece but popularized in the late eighteenth and early nineteenth-century by Gaspar Melchor de Jovellanos, emphyteusis was a form of long-term agrarian contract which split the nucleus of property into two: *dominium directum* and *dominium utile*, formal possession and use-rights. Anterior to but also contemporaneous with liberal absolute property, emphyteusis opened a line of flight from the "rigidity of ownership." As Rosa Congost and Pablo F. Luna have written, "[emphyteusis] allowed land to circulate and be worked in an economic way, while limiting its use for speculative purposes. Thus, emphyteusis provided a rent to the owner without depriving him of his land and also gave the emphyteutic tenant a long-term [often permanent] right over the land he worked."[86] On the one hand, the owner of the *dominium directum* retained three rights vis-à-vis the land. First, the *pena de comiso* or confiscation," which was "the right to evict the owner of the dominium utile for non-payment of any rent." Secondly, the *laudemio* (laudemium), which referred to the "right to charge a sum every time the use-rights change hands." Thirdly, the *tanteo* or *fadiga*, which granted the owner of *dominium directum* "the first option to purchase back the use-rights of property at the price for which the owner of the *dominium utile* was prepared to sell them."[87] On the other hand, the holder of the dominium utile could sell the property, bequeath it as inheritance, as well as, on quitting his claim, demand the value of any improvement made during the life of the lease.[88]

Gaspar Melchor de Jovellanos, like Azcárate y Lezama and the Mexican elites of the 1820s, had been invested in the aggrandizement of Spain through economic development. In his *Ley Agraria* (1795), he proposed emphyteusis as the device that would allow for the reactivation and productivization of those lands which, in Spain, festered in the "slavery" of entailed estates and mayorazgos. Through it, Spain could colonize its interior and reactivate its citizenry. Yet, unlike Azcárate y Lezama and Mexican Creoles, Jovellanos did not mind the accumulation of property itself, believing inequality to be "the engine of social emulation," and an "incentive to develop one's self interest and undermine sloth."[89] But he did believe that entailment deprived "individuals of the experience of ownership and earthly material comfort while they promote sloth."[90] Emphyteusis allowed for expanding access to ownership without undermining existing property owners. It thus made possible the re-circulation of land and the creation of a class of peasants that were "co-participants of the property," while incentivizing owners of entailed lands through the promise of annual rent. Emphyteutic leases would, thus, make Spanish fields productive and increase colonos' work efforts, seeing as "the right to dominium utile would give them the illusion as well as the reality of ownership."[91]

The *Program*'s emphyteutic land grant differed, though. In fact, it would seem that, by deploying emphyteusis within the horizon of the new Empire's project of interior colonization, Azcárate y Lezama took Jovellanos's device and transformed it into a unique apparatus that accelerated the national accumulation of the territory. It effectively captured, within the realm of the capitalist marketplace, purportedly national territory through the insertion and productivization of lands kept idle, whether by latifundia, *realengo* status, or indigenous occupation. Yet, insofar as emphyteutic colonization split the locus of property in two, it only gave the marketplace access to *dominium utile*—"the illusion" of property, and not property itself—while working as the legal instrument to effectively ascertain the sovereign's claim of *dominium directum* over the totality of the territory. In its brief mention, the *Program* reduced the implication of said procedure to the equivalent of a yearly land tax to be collected after six years. Yet, by doing so, it effectively gave the state direct access to the "private" property of the new citizenry. Put simply, by making the sovereign a "co-partícipe" of all property, the emphyteutic nature of the *Program*'s colonization erased all boundaries between the public and the private and, thus, created a direct, permanent link between the individual and the state, one that cut deeper than any prior affiliation that a foreign colono might harbor.

Unfortunately for Azcárate y Lezama and the other underwriters of the *Program*, while widely read, these proposals failed to make a dent beyond passing references to it, such as Esteva's. The subsequent legislative bodies of the Mexican Empire and the Federal and Centralist governments that followed would come to favor the flashier promises of immediate results of men such as Ortiz de Ayala and Stephen F. Austin, proposals that would most convincingly peddle the promise of the colono and his (police) republic of labor.

THE STATE, THE COLONO, AND THE EMPRESARIO

In the large scheme of things, the objections to Ortiz de Ayala's Texas proposal, voiced by Esteva and others, were an exception. But they were important in how they shaped the proyectista's later successful attempts. Beyond referring to Azcárate y Lezama as a model to follow, the opposing congressmen's critique rested on the propriety of the influence of private parties in the population and settlement of the territory, and the conceptualization of the labor of the colono.

The congressmen's first contention revolved around the size of Ortiz de Ayala's requested land grant, and the fact that his proposal expected to receive it free of charge, on the promise of future taxes to be rendered by settlers. The congressmen noted that, after the land was parceled and sold to interested settler parties, the applicants would generate great personal wealth to the government's detriment. Moreover, the congressmen held that no colono would be humanly capable of working, by himself (or his family), parcels of land of the size in which the original grant could be subdivided, leaving them once more inert, and reproducing the Spanish land tenure system everybody criticized, which had led to immense and unproductive haciendas. The second objection, echoed throughout the following decade, was that the delegation of the task of colonization to a private party could, perhaps, in the course of time, make the latter a threat, "seeing as we do not know what laws or conditions they will impose on the Irish or canarios to whom they give the lands."[92] There was no way to know if these potential colonos would even come to know the benefits and exemptions that the Mexican Empire promised them, "because the contracting party [Ortiz de Ayala and company] will necessarily tax [the settlers]; and, it follows, that none of this revenue will reach the imperial benefactor."[93] Exposing colonos to the arbitrariness of the private interest of empresarios could risk that these new settlers live "in misery, like the unfortunate indigenous people, who generally do not go beyond being day laborers, always working for others for meager salaries that are not enough for them to survive."[94] In other words, the congressmen worried that because the applicants were, indeed, private citizens (and entrepreneurs) who invested their own capital in the migrant recruitment front, they might, whether intentionally or not, put patriotic duty second to personal interest, and, thus, be incapable of pursuing the enlightened management of a colony.

Present in both arguments was the question of the colono's labor. Operative here was the semantic slip contained in the word itself, mentioned in this chapter's opening pages. When these congressmen questioned the capacity of the settler to work extensive lands, the implicated image and narrative of the laborer in question was akin to a yeoman farmer; an autonomous individual who, with the help of his family, worked the land and made it productive. The imagined settlement, in turn, figured as a constellation of autonomous farmsteads whose interrelationship was mediated by the invisible ties of coexistence, collaboration, fiscal duties, and allegiance to a state. For the congressmen, the size of the land to be granted to each settler and the passionate investment of empresarios short-circuited this agrarian fantasy. Whether by the pressures of the extensive property itself or potential debts to the entrepreneurs, Ortiz de Ayala's Texas proposal set the ground for arbitrary hierarchies that would inevitably produce not the settlement of free and autonomous property-owning laborers necessary for the aggrandizement of the nation, but miserable wage laborers, willingly subjugated to private authority and, ultimately, unproductive.

Misinterpreted here, intentionally or not, was the fact that Ortiz de Ayala's colono did not seem to be related to the yeoman farmer. In fact, as we will see later on, his colono was imagined as a liberal, entrepreneurial farmer, embedded in a capitalist horizon of profit, whose land was not conceived of as a homestead, but as an export-oriented commercial operation. A corollary of this was that, insofar as these were commercial enterprises, Ortiz de Ayala's colono was not to work the land himself. If there was to be autonomy or liberty in his Texas, it would be the autonomy or liberty of the capitalist. For the actual work, laborers were needed, whether free men or, as we will also see, slaves. I will return to this point in the next section.

In 1822, the congressmen's solution to what they perceived as the deficiencies of Ortiz de Ayala's Texas Proposal was to insist on the unmediated relationship between state and colono. The Empire, impartial and philanthropic, should remain the sole mediator between the colono and the land. They argued that, because the land in question had been granted to the Mexican government by God, "the sovereign arbiter of the world," the state should not forego their stewardship. They called for the government to distribute the land and recruit colonos itself through a general law of colonization. Finally, they amplified Azcárate y Lezama's proposal for an emphyteutic colono that guaranteed the direct government of the sovereign, calling for a general emphyteusis applicable to all of the empire's provinces.[95]

These arguments had the intended result and Ortiz de Ayala's Texas plan was shelved until Congress had put together a general colonization plan. Before the decision was made, though, Valentín Gómez Farías, who would become president in the 1830s, stepped up to defend Ortiz de Ayala and accused detractors of having misunderstood the proposal.[96] His comments were ultimately ignored, but in the following months he would get the upper hand and become the architect of the basic principles of the General Law of Colonization that they had called for. Yet, at this point of the debate, what is relevant is the acknowledgement that the first Constituent Congress was divided, and a vocal group still imagined Azcárate y Lezama's emphyteutic colono, bound directly to the state, as the model to follow, while the rest began to move toward Ortiz de Ayala's liberal entrepreneur.

The General Law of Colonization, even if drafted a month after Ortiz de Ayala's proposal in July 1822, would remain forthcoming, hampered by concerns over its derision of provincial sovereignty and by politicized procedural complaints that succeeded in undoing it. The task would be inherited by the National Instituent Junta, which replaced Congress after its dissolution on October 31, 1822. But this body would also fail, interrupted by the fall of the Empire after Iturbide's abdication on March 19, 1823.[97] Before this happened, however, a group of deputies of the National Instituent Junta adopted Congress's colonization draft and, taking advantage of the institution's close-to-despotic powers and Iturbide's interest, pushed it through, ignoring the opposition it had been met with. Technically, it was not the General Law of Colonization, but a decree on foreign colonization that that the members of the Junta considered as expedient in light of a series of requests for Texas grants from US colonos, key among them Stephen F. Austin.[98]

The decree, passed by the National Instituent Junta on January 4, 1823, had the stated goal of inviting foreign colonization and of guaranteeing that land was properly and evenly distributed.[99] It nominally placed the central government as the maximum authority, giving it powers to decide the lands to be colonized and to break up any large holdings it deemed necessary. The central government could also expropriate lands left untilled by colonos after two years. These two arrogations, which addressed the question of the reproduction of latifundia, were the closest the body came to assuaging Esteva's and the other former congressmen's objections. Beyond these, however, it mostly defaulted to the empresario-centered model of colonization that Ortiz de Ayala (and Stephen F. Austin) pursued and which survived Esteva and company's critiques and was to become the norm. In fact, the decree promised the empresario additional properties as bonuses for every two hundred families brought, guaranteeing that men like Austin (and, putatively, Ortiz de Ayala) were to accumulate the very same large holdings that the government had the power to break up. In theory, the empresarios' personal holdings could remain whole for a maximum of twenty years, before which time two-thirds were to be sold to the empresario's benefit. The decree neglected Azcárate y Lezama's proposed checks on the liberty of the colono not simply by affirming that each individual was free to leave and sell their property at any moment in time but by also omitting all mention of emphyteusis. Ultimately, insofar as it became the baseline from which colonization was to be thought, the decree effectively struck Azcárate y Lezama's vision of colonization from record and marked its disappearance from any and all following debate.

THE SLAVE, THE VAGRANT, AND THE COLONO

Colonization's fantasy of the free autonomous farmer and its promises of liberty were haunted, from their inception until the aftermath of Texas, by coerced labor. In fact, in the Mexico of the 1820s, it was only within the horizon of colonization that the national commitment to the abolition of slavery was questioned.[100] Despite its limited effect, the abolition of slavery in Mexico had been one of Hidalgo's first insurgent promises in 1810 and continued to be, discursively at the very least, espoused by most members of the political elite. That said, within the horizon of colonization, the argument of the sanctity of the potential foreign colono's private property allowed some elbow room through which to legally make space for enslaved labor. Azcárate y Lezama's *Program* had deferred the question of slavery to a future congress, but the first draft of the General Colonization Law, which came up for discussion in the Constituent Congress in July 1822, a month after Ortiz de Ayala's Texas Proposal, set a precedent on the matter by taking an extremely lenient position. Thus, at a time when a constitution was still forthcoming and, in that sense, an official stance on slavery, the Colonization Committee permitted the exploitation of enslaved labor under the cover of the inviolability of private property. While recognizing that the institution "dishonors the human race" [género humano], they were only willing to emancipate the Mexican-born children of slaves brought into the territory after the law's publication. The offspring, however, would only gain full autonomy after turning fourteen.[101] This was enough for the congressmen, and they believed they had "reconciled [the settler's] right to a property that, whatever its justification, has been respected by past governments and an immemorial custom."[102] Such a policy, its proponents held, would attract the desired foreign colonos.

Some congressmen decried the article in question. One, indignant, declared he had been rendered speechless by his colleagues' willingness to present "slavery transformed into right, and property rights at that."[103] Another countered with a theoretical colonization law that abolished all slavery instantly.[104] Yet, congressman Lorenzo Zavala, expressing the opinion of the Committee and exasperated with his colleagues' constant recurrence to "abstract principles of liberty," called for pragmatism, arguing that, in practice, if all law was to be understood as a restriction placed on natural liberty, there was therefore nothing irregular about making sure that colonization policy respected existing conceptions of property, including that of slaves.[105] He went to insist that Congress was not meant to waste its time in philosophical spiels, "that, ultimately, only bring about revolution," but to give the nation "good laws."[106]

By the time Iturbide dissolved what he considered a recalcitrant Constituent Congress, the matter was still unresolved. The draft in question would eventually make its way to the succeeding Junta Nacional Instituyente in 1823, only to reproduce the same article and the same debates. Again, arguments in the name of human liberty were brought and, again, they were shot down. The sanctity of property trumped individual liberty, and, thus, slavery became wedded to the colono. Interestingly, during these discussions, whenever slavery came up, its supporters were careful to frame their arguments strictly within the horizon of colonization and the colono's property rights. An exception was congressman Salvador Porra's argument, which took Zavala's position even further, shedding all pretention vis-à-vis the relationship between the sanctity of property and slavery. Porras argued that slavery was not simply a matter of property, but a question of labor. If colonos brought slaves it was because "otherwise they would not be able to come, because [they] lacked laborers for their work, considering that there are none in the colonizable provinces, nor are the Apaches and other Gentiles to be employed as day laborers."[107] Slaves were necessary, then, precisely because of the underpopulation of the territories to be colonized, and because what little population existed was unwilling to labor for the colonos. In other words, for Porras, the lack of wage laborers justified the unfree labor of slaves. Embedded in his argumentation was the idea that the free labor of the colonos required by necessity the exploitation of others' labor. Porras notwithstanding, more often than not, deputies argued that the legality of slavery as such was a constitutional matter that should be taken up separately. Ironically, when that matter of slavery was finally addressed by the second Constituent Congress in 1824, its members—many of whom, like Zavala, had participated in the debates two years before—turned to the colonization policy as a precedent that short-circuited the possibility of any complete abolition of enslaved labor in the territory. The question would continue to be legislated well into the 1840s.[108]

In his 1823 *Bases sobre las que se ha formado un plan de Colonización en el Ysmo de Hoazacoalco o Tehuantepec* (Bases on which a Colonization plan has been formed for the Ysmo de Hoazacoalco or Tehuantepec), studied in the next section, Ortiz de Ayala argued that it was necessary to "tolerate" slavery so as to attract, from Louisiana, Florida, and the Antilles "many industrious men with considerable capital in slavery, accustomed to this kind of speculation."[109] He held that only male slaves should be allowed and they should be able to purchase their own freedom after ten or fifteen years of labor. If they were to have children, it would have to necessarily be with the indigenous—Ortiz de Ayala could not fathom any other possibility—and, as a result, they would be born free. With the experience of these industrious men—and the labor of their enslaved workforce—México would be able to exploit coffee, sugar, cotton and cocoa in a competitive manner and overtake international markets. If at this point in time he did not outright support slavery, by the time of his death in 1833, however, whether as a result of his statistical analyses of the international situation or a change of approach, Ortiz de Ayala came to insist that, as proven by the economies of the US, Brazil, and Cuba, actually existing national aggrandizement was to a large extent dependent on the coerced exploitation of black labor. For a political arithmetician, interested in the particulars rather than in the theory of liberal political economy, the benefits of slavery were seen internationally and were capable of skirting, if only for a second, the ideological commitment to free labor. As John Tutino has said, for Ortiz de Ayala "the dilemma plaguing Mexico was how to build an export economy without slavery."[110]

The slave was not the only active figure of unfree labor in the discourses of colonization; there was also the vagrant. In 1823, Ortiz de Ayala's *Bases* tackled the conundrum of unfree labor by adapting current anti-vagrancy policy so as to create a legal avenue for the creation of a constant stream of unfree labor. In its request, Ortiz de Ayala and company petitioned the government for a "certain number" of vagrants and criminals, that the laws currently condemned to presidios, and a small armed escort to guard them. In this scheme, vagrants' labor would be both preparatory and therapeutic. Preparatory because they were there to ready the land, build the necessary roads and housing, for the soon-to-arrive free laborers. Therapeutic because, through the removal from their places of origin, where they would have been imprisoned and processed as vagrants, and their coerced labor, they might be transformed into the industrious and disciplined subjects that the colonia required. Ortiz de Ayala noted that the situation of vagrants in this proposal was closer to an apprenticeship than to a firm penitentiary imprisonment, and he insisted that it lasted only for a period of two or three years. If the transformation were successful, vagrants would become wage-laborers and could even be allowed to become colonos themselves. The opposite scenario, of a failed rehabilitation, remained unexplored, but we can surmise that continuous coercive employment would be the only solution.

In Ortiz de Ayala's scheme, the vagrants' unfree labor would not be a singular occurrence in a colonia's life. It would still be needed after that first establishment of the colonia's infrastructure. Once the inaugural vagrants were rehabilitated into wage-earners or property owners, they would be replaced with others, to be put to work against their will for the colonia's benefit, whether in public projects or in private farms. Unlike other utopian accounts that erased the trace of exploitation that underlies images of "free labor," Ortiz de Ayala recognized however unwillingly the role to be played by exploitation in the implantation and social reproduction of capitalist modernity. The exploitation of unfree labor was meant to permanently coexist with the free labor of the colono. In the absence of the institution of slavery, the police state was to provide, through anti-vagrancy discourse and practice, discussed in Chapter 3, a legal and moral apparatus through which maligned subjects were temporarily stripped of the protections of citizenship and processed so as to provide the necessary labor-power for the sustenance of society—a society of free laborers. Even though it went mostly unaddressed in colonization discourse, the subsistence or family-centered farming of a yeoman-like figure had never been the goal. The industrious colono labored freely, yes, but he was also to have others labor for him. A world without hierarchies or exploitation was unthinkable and probably unwanted in the economic imaginaries of a Creole elite invested in national economic development and aggrandizement. Thus, at the center of Ortiz de Ayala's imaginary network of ever-productive enclaves populated by the free, industrious colono beat, in the form of the immoral vagrant coerced to toil for his benefit and the community, the heart of unfreedom. Its echoes would resound far into the century, emphasizing the reality that the narrative of free work—of the colono's free industry, surely, but also all narrative of free work—was structurally dependent on its opposite, unfree labor.

THE TEHUANTEPEC ISTHMUS AND THE SOLDIER-COLONO

If the 1822 Texan proposal lit a spark in the halls of Congress, Ortiz de Ayala's *Bases sobre las que se ha formado un plan de Colonización en el Ysmo de Hoazacoalco o Tehuantepec* (Bases on which a Colonization plan has been formed for the Ysmo de Hoazacoalco or Tehuantepec), submitted to the relevant committee of the re-established constituent assembly on April 29, 1823, set off a forest fire. Having paid attention to the debates his previous proposal had stirred and mobilizing the statistical knowledge that made him an authority in the eyes of politicians, he conceived of a project that amplified the figure of the colono, taking it farther than anybody ever had in Mexico and leaving an indelible mark on the economic imaginaries of the period. The text's consequences were many, among them Ortiz de Ayala's first stint as an official agent of the state, surveying the lands of the Isthmus of Tehuantepec. He also oversaw the creation of a short-lived province to be developed broadly along the lines he had proposed—the Province of the Isthmus, the foundation of three colonias, the State of Veracruz's general colonization law, and a catastrophic French colonization attempt, to name a few.

The Bases' effect seems exaggerated in retrospect, especially when we consider that the project was not actually ratified in Congress. The text was a simple tripartite document that spelled out a plan written and developed by Ortiz de Ayala, but allegedly conceived along with General José Antonio de Echávarri, one of the founding members of the Army of the Three Guarantees, and lieutenant Mariano Barbabosa. It opened with a prospectus for a colonization plan of the Tehuantepec/Hoazacoalco Isthmus; it moved to the future colonies' foundation and special privileges, and, lastly, expanded on the "General Plan For the Colonization Project of the Isthmus of Hoazacoalco." While these sections worked toward the same end, the creation of colonias in Tehuantepec, in each the terms of debate shifted slightly. The first section presented the proposal as an act of philanthropy; the second established a language that echoed the work already done by Congress, and the third section, the only argumentative one, reduced the foreign colono to a few partial mentions, including the reference to attracting slave-holders from the Antilles referenced in the previous section, and focused on the national colono. Their effect was meant to be cumulative. When the Committee that originally received the Bases went on to present the proposal to the general Congress, it included, as an addendum, an adulatory letter of support signed by no less than a hundred and twenty influential generals, lieutenants, merchants, capitalists, and congressmen. This support made the Bases not simply another proposal amongst many, but the most coherent and cohesive articulation of the ideologeme of colonization.

The Bases' domain of action was not the Northern territories but the Tehuantepec Isthmus, to which Oritz de Ayala referred to also as the Hoazacoalco Isthmus, for the river of the same name. He was not the first person to extol the area, and in his "General Plan" he offered a history of its riches and of Spanish incapacity to exploit these productively.[111] The isthmus was not simply the shortest continental distance between the Atlantic and Pacific, a promising prospect for a system of ports dedicated to exports, but also represented one of the nation's most productive and fertile territories with the necessary microclimates to produce everything from corn and potatoes to cacao, sugar, cotton, cochinilla, among many other export goods (géneros coloniales). For Ortiz de Ayala, the region naturally lent itself to a form of economic development that looked inward and outward; it was a place that called for the development of agriculture and infrastructure, and in turn, a commercial life capable of providing happiness to both citizen and state.

The Bases' influence resulted from how it managed to convincingly make colonization the panacea for all the economic and political problems that kept Mexico's potential interrupted. It is true that, by 1823, colonization was widely held to be a means through which to activate the industry and economy of the newborn nation, yet, in the "Plan General," Ortiz de Ayala basically changed the terms of the debate. He put claims of underpopulation and the question of the foreign colono on the back burner, and framed colonization as the only sensible economic solution to tackle Mexico's deepening economic crisis. The Bases boiled down this crisis to three root issues: the fact that Mexico's coffers were empty, that its standing army was too large, and that its population "lacks property and occupation, is very unproductive, and, for these great reasons, is fully abject."[112] For Ortiz de Ayala, the dire situation of the treasury condemned the government to passivity, incapable as it was of investing in its industries or of implementing reforms that would increase the productivity of its people. What little revenue it generated had to be redirected to pay the standing army, so as to avoid the troops' unrest, or fulfill the debts incurred to pay for the state's obligations. Caught in this spiral, the country was plummeting. The colonization of the Tehuantepec could cut this Gordian knot. Because the Government lacked the funds to jump-start the project, Ortiz de Ayala proposed an entrepreneurial solution, a sort of public-private venture.

Unlike in 1822, this time around Ortiz de Ayala did not turn to the empresario, that profit-driven capitalist individual distrusted by members of Congress. Instead, along with General Echavávrri and Liutenant Barbabosa, he proposed to start a colonization-centered stock company, composed of respectable members of society, which would take upon itself some of the risk of the initial stage of the enterprise (how much remained unsaid), providing the necessary capital so long as the state took up a share of the cost, which they calculated at around twenty or twenty-five thousand pesos. Ortíz de Ayala provided the government with a blueprint of how to generate these funds, analyzing existing streams of federal revenue as well as alternative sources and proposed three possibilities.[113] Whatever was decided, these start-up funds would be funneled through and overseen by the colonization company in consultation with government representatives, who would guarantee the careful and enlightened management of the new colonies. The sum would pay for three settlements, each with a hundred wooden houses, a chapel, and a hospital. It would also go toward the purchase of the necessary instruments for working the land, enough foodstuffs for a year, as well as cover the transportation over land or sea of an estimated three hundred colonos, among other expenses.

With the problem of funding solved and the colonias' cost covered, Ortiz de Ayala moved on to the question of the army. This was a difficult subject. After all, one of the decisive historical factors in nineteenth-century Mexico was the militarized society that emerged from the struggle for independence.[114] Militaries, militias, armed bands, and men with guns abounded across the territories encompassed by the new nation. Whether attached to the central state, provincial governments, or private estates, these extra-legal agents reconstituted both political action and the political itself.[115] By the time Ortiz de Ayala was writing, force, whether as show or outright violence, was quickly becoming inseparable from political contestation and the demand for rights, justice, and restitution. In fact, it could even be said that, already by then, force or the threat of its use had become the bar with which legitimate political speech was measured. As William Fowler and many others have studied and as Ortiz de Ayala would begin to see in his lifetime, the *pronunciamiento*, most often led by army officers, would become the quintessential political practice of the century.[116] Unsurprisingly, the reproduction of these armed agents was expensive, and their allegiance and support was often bound to those who held the purse strings, or those who promised a better management of public treasuries in the form of the timely disbursement of owed wages.

Colonization needed men, Ortiz de Ayala argued, and what were soldiers if not "*hombres de bien* [decent men], but without fortune, or without any income than that which his army offers."[117] In the General Plan, he proposed that the government reduce the army by carefully and gradually transforming its soldiering masses into colonos who, following the example of the "Washingtons" and "Cincinattuses," embraced "the noble and primitive art of agriculture."[118] If a dignified retirement through colonization was implemented, he wrote, these healthy men would be made into "industrious pater familias, and productive and useful citizens."[119] Ortiz de Ayala was realistic, though. Making land productive, even when instruments and seeds were provided for, took time. Thus, the government would sustain the soldier economically for three years, giving him time to get accustomed. This guaranteed limited income had already been factored in the sum the colonization company requested.

In this way that the Bases momentarily minimized the foreign colono-as-entrepreneur (and slave-holder) Ortiz de Ayala had suggested in his 1822 Texas Proposal, and privileged a vanguard of free, industrious, property-owning soldier-laborers, an autochthonous yeoman farmer. This new type of colono, forged through the hierarchical and disciplined existence of the national army, would assuage the fears of disloyalty that had led Azcárate y Lezama to sacrifice the commitment to individual freedom in his *Program*, at the same time as it guaranteed the proper establishment of secure settlements that would, in turn, ease the arrival of both Mexican nationals (thus tackling the lack of employment which haunted the economy) and foreigners, to be recruited in the meantime by the colonization company. In the long run, each colonia would be carefully directed by the colonization company—run by private citizens, surely, but many of these trusted men of the armed forces—and rationally laid out, populated by families headed by about 166 army officers, 27 soldier, 27 nationals, and 27 foreigners; each allotted with six square leagues, a third of which had to be eventually sold, so that, consequently, each colono could, in time, also become a capitalist.

In a sense, both Ortiz de Ayala's argument for the soldier-colono and the soldier-colono himself were grafted into the colonization project. By privileging the army, the Bases were effectively short-circuiting any possibility of opposition within Congress. The justification of the central role to be played by the soldier would have been found convincing by any politician of the time. It both satisfied a political demand—the promise of property for those that fought in the Army of the Three Guarantees—and an economic necessity. Additionally, opposition to the project would have been politically treacherous, godfathered as the Bases were by cosigners Echávarri and Barbabosa, who belonged to the higher echelons of the armed forces, as well as the formidable list of influential supporters who were possibly also interested in participating in the colonization company. Faced with that veritable who's who of elite power brokers, Congress would have been hard-pressed to publicly rehash the argument seen above about the tension between private interest and public duty.

As a group of congressmen wrote later, in their preamble to another Tehuantepec project inspired by Ortiz de Ayala's own and for which he would be hired as prospector, "the idea that a colony offers is that of society in its infancy; simple inhabitants, without more needs than those that are natural."[120] In that same vein, what was fantasized in Ortiz de Ayala's Bases was the mobilization and deployment of surplus population—of the army, of foreign states, etc.—toward the rational self-foundation of society as a police state according to the principles of free labor, private property and export-driven commercial agriculture. His colonization proposal presented the colonia as an industrious utopian enclave, one at first spatially and socially differentiated from the rest of the nation but which, eventually, would expand and transform the entirety of the national territory from within.

When proper legislation for the colonization of Mexican territory materialized during the Constituent Congress of 1824, after the fall of the Mexican Empire (in 1823) and the subsequent establishment of a Federal Republic, the role of the strong state was transferred to the provincial governments. Most provincial representatives argued and would continue to argue that this role had been theirs by right to begin with. The matter would be debated often and consistently through the decades. Put in broad strokes, after 1824, the legislative powers of colonization would remain with the states roughly until 1846, when, in light of the Texas debacle, the central government would claim this right through the foundation of the Dirección de Colonización e Industria, to be discussed later in this chapter, as a federal prerogative grounded on claims of national security and economic necessity. The 1824 law delegated to provincial assemblies the task of legislating how colonization would be implemented in their territories, establishing some basic ground rules which insisted on the invitation to foreign colonos, the necessity of upholding Mexican law, the maximum size of land grants as a thousand square leagues, a suggestion that all colonies have both natives and foreigners, the protection of private property, the privileging of soldiers from the Army of Three Guarantees, among a few other details. The first series of provincial colonization laws came out in the late 1820s and early 1830s. They did not diverge much from the one passed by the National Instituent Junta and the discussions Ortiz de Ayala's proposal had stirred. This was not surprising, though. After his 1823 Tehuantepec proposal, Ortiz de Ayala himself became colonization's point person, and was called on to craft the most influential of these provincial laws.

As we will continue to see, to the extent that colonization was a project of the Creole elite —an elite whose domain of action was, during the first half of the nineteenth century, indistinguishable from the state's project of territorial and capitalist expansion and accumulation—, it called for the complete suppression of the duality of state and society. In Chapter 3, I show how this logic responded to the afterlife of Bourbon governance. As Gareth Williams has written, "Mexican modernity was predicated, not on the principle of self-limitation of government, nor on the quest for the biopolitical regularization of society, but on the consolidation of a police state understood as the direct governmentality of the sovereign qua sovereign.[121] Colonization was an essential element of that "post-colonial quest for a police state capable of creating the good order and sovereign mastery that would allow for the implantation and extension of bourgeois rule."[122] For Ortiz de Ayala and his many supporters, colonization was the tool with which labor would be ingrained in the land and made productive.

THE ACTUALLY EXISTING COLONO

The depths to which colonization discourses developed and were debated in the first five years of independent life were not to be repeated in the foreseeable future. Azcárate y Lezama's and Ortiz de Ayala's work, and the congressional debates they catalyzed, pushed the figure of the colono as far as possible within the economic imaginaries of the time. By the time Ortiz de Ayala's Bases circulated, the grounds of colonization had stabilized, and the righteousness of the policy had become the norm. The following decade, between 1825 and 1835, was one of lawmaking and implementation, rather than theorization. Ortiz de Ayala's colonization ideas remained present throughout. Legislation inspired by his analysis would continue to be authored, his surveys of the Isthmus printed serially and discussed in the press, and his last book publicized widely. But the period would also begin to show fractures in the idyll of a future republic of industrious colonias.

On December 16, 1826, for example, colono and empresario Hayden Edwards, along with the settlers he had recruited, rose in arms and, on December 21, declared the Republic of Freedonia in the Texan town of Nacogdoches, near to which he had received a land grant. The uprising was quickly put down by a force of Mexican soldiers in collaboration with militias from Stephen F. Austin's colony. The Freedonians' revolt rekindled anti-Anglo-American suspicion. Over the next few years, colonos from Austin's settlement would have to insist on their loyalty and on their commitment to the Federal Republic. Yet these settlers' word would be consistently undermined, between 1827 and 1830, by US President John Quincy Adams's determination to negotiate, through its agents in Mexico, for the purchase of the territory between the rivers Sabine and Río Grande. As expected, Quincy Adams's offer alarmed Mexican officials and influenced the Colonization Law of April 6, 1830, which effectively banned US immigration to Texas.

Anglo-American suspicion aside, Austin's colonies, as well as other US colono settlements in Texas, served as the most efficient testament to the successes of colonization. To combat the demonization of Anglo American colonos, Miguel Muldoon, the self-appointed "Parish Priest of Austin and Vicar General of all the Foreign Colonies of Texas," wrote a letter to the *Fénix de la Libertad* on October 5, 1833, which painted Austin's colony as industrious utopia. According to Muldoon, Austin and his supporters had braved the Texan wilds for years—surviving hunger, nature, and Indian assaults—in a feat that could only have been carried out by the will of divine providence, and so "they transformed the horrible wilderness into numerous and civilized towns."[123] Muldoon was in awe: each colonia was equipped with mills, steam engines, buildings, machines for sawing wood, and cotton gins. Each home was surrounded by two square miles of cultivated land, a land he considered the most fertile in the universe. Colonos not only worked their own farms and ranches but also mastered particular trades to the point that Muldoon was acquainted with many respectable settlers who were also high-quality artisans. For Muldoon, every level of an Anglo-American colonia—settlement, house, individual—was directed toward industry. Unlike Mexican settlers in other territories, he observed, most Texan families lived isolated in their respective property, with men working "the land, and women the home and the looms."[124] And yet, all of these independent homesteads formed a community that could come together at a moment's notice. The distance between each family was, in the end, salubrious because it avoided the transmission of vices, maintained each sex properly occupied in the production and reproduction of the household, and, thus, eliminated the possibility of idleness.[125]

The priest's omission of slavery was remarkable for its absence, as evidence of the institution would have been everywhere. In an 1828 letter, for example, General Manuel Mier y Terán had observed that most colonos employed between one and two enslaved men in their households.[126] In most plantations, the number would have been much higher. After all, as historian Andrew J. Torget has written, Austin's colonial enterprise had been built on slave-based agriculture and "the promise of cotton."[127]

Muldoon insisted that the citizens of Austin's colonies had never considered secession. Their interest was to forever "be part of the Mexican territory: thus, by participating in it, they will shine among their neighbors in arts, agriculture and commerce, [whereas] while belonging to the Republic of the North, they totally disappear in the multitude of those outstanding and more enlightened people than themselves."[128] If they sought any separation, it was from the state of Coahuila, but only because they wanted to be enfranchised under the promises of the 1824 Federal Constitution as a separate Texan province. It would not only be just but also wise for the Mexican government to acquiesce these desires, the priest argued, and delivered a threat: "[o]pposing the general vote of the colonists will produce displeasure: if they are harassed at a distance of 600 leagues from a city, who can calculate the result?"[129] Relatedly, Muldoon thought it necessary to note that, instead of religious paraphernalia, these residences had rifles, guns, and sables, and each colono "is a general in his house; all his dependents, including the women, handle the weapons with skill.[130] Threat aside, Muldoon's representation of Austin's colony was the effective actualization of Ortiz de Ayala's Utopian enclave. It represented a de facto self-foundation of society within the Mexican territory, albeit a particularly non-Mexican one.

Azcárate y Lezama, Ortiz de Ayala, and others had believed European and national colonization would be enough to counter Anglo-American expansion. Yet, the decade in question saw both fail tragically, and their downfall began to dent the optimism of elites. Ortiz de Ayala himself attempted to move from theory to practice and, propelled by the success of the Bases, founded a string of colonias in the Isthmus of Tehuantepec between 1825 and 1829—Hidalgópolis, Minotitlán, Allendópolis, Abasolópolis, and Morelópolis. Unfortunately, these settlements quickly fell on hard times. Four factors undermined their prospects, Ortiz de Ayala believed. First, the difficulty of recruiting local hands to labor so as to prepare the territory for future colonos. Secondly, the disinterest of local indigenous communities, who did not jump at the opportunity of being expropriated. Thirdly, the political intrigues of other government agents. Finally, and most damaging, the indifference of federal and state governments.[131] Ortiz de Ayala abandoned the Isthmus before the end of the decade, to take up the position of Mexican consul in Bordeaux (a position offered by then Minister of Relations Lucas Alamán, one of the subjects studied in Chapter 2), where he would continue sponsoring colonization ventures, regardless of his own failure. Before his departure to Europe, however, he served as adviser to a French company that sought to transplant five hundred European families to settle the Isthmus. The company recruited approximately eight hundred French and Swiss colonists. These recruits soon embarked to the Isthmus, unaware that the entrepreneurs had ignored Ortiz de Ayala's insistence on the necessity of preparing the settlements before their arrival. According to an account of the ill-fated project by one of its participants, which, translated into Spanish became popular later in the decade, three hundred died. The rest, forsaken by company and government alike, had to struggle to find their own way back to their homelands.[132] In 1832, Alamán, the Minister of Relations, blamed the failure of colonization policy on the "defective system adopted by empresarios for the distribution of land, and the wrong choice of settlers, who traditionally were [supposed to] have been poor people [acquainted] with working the fields."[133]

In spite of these failures, the colono held steady. His strongest challenge occurred in 1835. What had started as the Texan rejection of the rising tides of centralism in 1830 and, soon after, of Antonio López de Santa Anna's overthrow of the federalist system, transformed into a bid for independence, which ushered an actual and self-proclaimed republic of colonos. In the *Unanimous Declaration of Independence, by the Delegates of the People of Texas*, the Texan assembly proclaimed:

> The Mexican government, by its colonization laws, invited and induced the Anglo American population of Texas to colonize its wilderness under the pledged faith of a written constitution, that they should continue to enjoy that

> constitutional liberty and republican government to which they had been habituated in the land of their birth, the United States of America.

For the assembly, the centralist uprising in Mexico City had broken that promise and had pushed their hand to reaffirm their republican commitments. In their telling, forsaken and betrayed by their host government, these colonos had been forced to assert their autonomy and form their own republic. Yet, theirs would not be the colono republic of free labor dreamed of by Creole elites, but a short-lived state which proudly exposed the heart of unfreedom that Ortiz de Ayala had so insistently tried to hide. The resulting Republic of Texas aspired to be a capitalist republic of labor, albeit not one of laboring liberty, but of enslaved and exploited black labor.[134]

AFTER TEXAS: TENACITY AND CRITIQUE OF THE COLONO (1846–1851)

Despite the traumatic loss of Texas in 1836, the promise of colonization remained strong; its pull unavoidable. The colono was, as we have seen, a protagonist of a Creole narrative of capitalist, national, and territorial subsumption. Had it been made inoperative, another figure would have had to take its place, and none were available that resolved, with such narrative ease, the juxtaposition of a resource-rich land, an "insufficient population," and national economic hardship. Yet, the image of the colono did not come out fully unscathed from the Texas debacle. The event marked an internal shift within its deployment. What had been at stake in the first decade of independence (1821–1831), with Azcárate y Lezama and Ortíz de Ayala at its helm, had been the theorization and dissemination of colonization, its policy, and its subjects. In the immediate aftermath of Texan secession, this theoretical approach was put on hold, replaced by an etiology of colonization's failures, which resulted in its discursive re-activation. As such, by the early 1840s, after a brief absence in which opposing political parties blamed each other for the loss of the territory, the colono began to reappear in public discourse—positively, albeit embedded in a larger reflexive and pessimistic horizon. These etiological accounts were not exhaustive and did not amount to internally coherent positions, but they were effective in convincingly explaining the faults that had plagued the implementation of colonization in Mexico.

For example, whenever federalist paper *El Cosmopolita* engaged with the matter of Texas between 1839 and 1841, its editors argued that its loss had been the result of Mexico's embrace of centralism, its rejection of the federal compromise, and the general abandonment of the state governments by Mexico City politicians, who disregarded provincial needs and fanned discontent.[135] The more moderate albeit liberal writers of *El Siglo Diez y Nueve* agreed with *El Cosmopolita* on the role played by poor governance, but they also thought something had to be said about colonization policy itself, critiquing the existing policy's lack of checks and balances which allowed the Texas debacle to happen in the first place.[136] A third strand, Carlos María Bustamante's, defended the text of existing policy, while shifting the blame to its agents. In his *Gabinete Mexicano of 1842*, Bustamante offered a brief history of colonization in Mexico so as to explain the misadventure. He believed that the attempts to legislate colonization, between 1822 and 1833, had been well-devised and indeed contained the necessary safeguards. Had they been implemented as written, they would have prevented secession. Yet, neither migrants nor the local governments had ever respected or enforced the law.[137] Thus, for him, the main culprits for the failure of Texas had been Anglo-American speculators and slavers, including Austin himself, who intentionally ignored the legislation and began settling families at will. Bustamante lamented that, even knowing that its laws were being broken, the Mexican government had allowed these migrants to enjoy the natural wealth of the territory they settled, as well as the liberties and independence promised in the 1824 constitution.[138] He considered it ironic that the Anglo-American settler ignored the fact that the very liberty and independence he enjoyed in Texas also extended to that of the men he enslaved, for the Mexican constitution decreed, in his words, "that all blacks that flee from any power can present themselves here, and by the single fact of stepping in this land, as in a sacred land, is made free."[139] Thus, for Bustamante, it had been the penchant for slavery, their contempt of liberty, which drove Texas to secession. This single fact, he held, put the lie on the claims of the Texan Declaration of Independence quoted earlier. It also proved that Texas had not been ruined by the colono, for there were no "real colonos" (verdaderos colonos) in Texas.[140] Few had settled the land according to the laws afforded to them or labored them freely, in the manner proper to the figure. In Texas, there had mostly been land speculators, political agitators, slavers, privateers, vagrants, and traitors.

ENTER THE DIRECCIÓN DE COLONIZACIÓN E INDUSTRIA

With time, this rehabilitation of the colono, carried out in newspapers and pamphlets, in the writings of centralists and federalists, liberals and conservatives, set the ground and influenced the articulation, between 1846 and

1851, of Mexico's most concerted colonization effort: the foundation of an institution which Ortiz de Ayala could only have dreamed about, the Dirección de Colonización e Industria (the Directorate or Bureau of Colonization and Industry). The Dirección consolidated all matters related to colonization policy in one central and autonomous office, led by an administrator whose executive capacity made many uncomfortable.[141] The Dirección would go on to draft colonization policy, lobby in its favor, recruit colonos, and administer the establishment of colonies. Its insistent attempt to live up to its charge, albeit its ultimate failure, reanimated the matter of colonization, pushed it further than ever before, and launched a series of debates which, marked by the larger shifts in the political panorama, would lead not to the actualization of the dreamed-about republic of colonos, but to the first sustained critique of colonization as a policy and an ideal.

In order to understand the shifts to be discussed in this section, it is essential to review the historical and political whirlwind which so deeply marked them. After all, much had changed between October 6, 1821, when the *Gaceta Imperial* proudly affirmed the horizon of aggrandizement in the immediate aftermath of independence, and the mid-to-late 1840s, when colonization once more became a central matter of debate, haunted by the long shadow of the Texas debacle and the US invasion. The early economic optimism that underlay the *Gaceta*'s article, Azcárate y Lezama's *Program*, and Ortiz de Ayala's multiple projects, —but which exceeded them and was widespread during the period—had been supple enough to survive the end of the 1820s, despite the souring of the political mood that took place then and which gave way to the series of *pronunciamientos*, coup d'états, and partisan streaks of censorship that characterized the first half of the 1830s. As we will see in the following chapters, in this decade, the general tone of the public sphere shifted, and doubt began to creep into the economic imaginaries of the period. In spite of the growing fear that Mexico's economic futures had been interrupted, the potential of the land remained there, promising the possibility of a return to a providential destiny. The foundation of the Banco de Avío (1830–1842), a development bank funded through import taxes—and the brainchild of Lucas Alamán, the centralist and conservative ideologue who, as Minister of Relations sent Ortíz de Ayala to Bordeaux—rested on such a hope, even if privileging the development of industrialization over agriculture as the avenue that would allow México to regain the road toward aggrandizement. Alamán, the Banco de Avío, and the industrializing designs of the 1830s and 1840s are the subject of Chapter 2. In the same spirit, Vice President Vicente Gómez de Farías's liberal administration of 1833–34 believed it possible to straighten the nation's course through policy and attempted to expropriate Church property with the goal of gaining the necessary funds to pay regime debts and generate the needed capital to spur development.[142] Materially, things were indeed worsening for the national economy. As John Tutino has shown, even before Texas, the militarized conflicts that intensified partisan antagonisms were taking their economic toll, driving costs and debts higher in a context of minimal fiscal revenue.[143] Even if there was a general improvement at the level of family harvests, the scarcity of capital and profits from commercial agriculture and mining were taking their toll.[144]

The Texas Campaign (1835–36) accelerated Mexico's downward spiral. The beginning of hostilities in October 1835 was quickly followed by the abolition of the Constitution of 1824 at the hands of a centralist administration, its replacement in December 1835, in the middle of the conflict, with the *Siete Leyes* (Seven Laws), a conservative body of laws that established the Centralist Republic of Mexico, limited suffrage, and consolidated authority in Mexico City.[145] Yet, centralization proved to be less of a solution than a volley in the ongoing centralism/federalism tug-of-war.[146] The succeeding years would be pockmarked by a series of complicated twists and turns, interrupted in April 1846 by the United States' invasion of Mexico. Technically, the presence of US troops on Mexican soil did not quell internal strife. While battles between the warring parties raged in the northern territories, a revolt finally overthrew the Centralist Republic on August 1846, re-established the 1824 magna carta and inaugurated the Second Federal Republic.[147] On September 15, 1847, the US Army took Mexico City and brought Mexican politics to a standstill.

It was in the middle of the war with the United States that Congress created, by decree, the Dirección de Colonización e Industria (Directorate of Colonization and Industry) on November 27, 1846. In theory, its creation had been legislated, to no avail, as far back as June 1, 1839. But it was not until the return of the federalist regime, which reinstituted the 1824 Constitution, that the new Ministro de Relaciones Interiores y Exteriores José María Lafragua called for its actual establishment, conceiving of it as an independent institution that "acquainted with the field that it focuses on, can work with promptness and intelligence, and can give the Government the enlightenment, policy, experience, and knowledge yielded by research."[148] The Dirección marked a major shift in colonization policy, one which Ortíz de Ayala would have welcomed; it centralized it and reduced the states to the role of collaborators. David K. Burden writes that, "although [the Dirección de Colonización's] line of thought encountered political resistance, it re-emerged as the dominant government policy (regardless of regime) over the next several decades."[149]

The Dirección's *Reglamento* (*Bylaws*), written by the body's director Antonio Garay and secretary Mariano Gálvez and approved on December 4, 1846, claimed all the powers thought necessary for the proper colonization of the territory.[150] These powers were unique and exacerbated by the fact that, even if created by federalist initiative, the Dirección developed its proposals by drawing indiscriminately on all previous legislation, whether crafted by centralist or federalist administrations. The list of these powers is telling and impressive in its scope. The most important of these were, indeed, the surveying and partitioning of the national territory's *baldíos*, on which the whole project rested and which, Garay and Gálvez believed, had never been carried out in a centralized and comprehensive manner. Yet, beyond these, Garay and Gálvez also charged their Dirección with oversight over the public sale and administration of those subsequently partitioned lands (which upon having been surveyed became property of the federal government, if they were not already).[151] In addition, their purview included the recruitment of colonos, their naturalization as citizens, the terms and conditions of the contracts by which these settlers would be bound, the political and fiscal exemptions to be received, the establishment of military colonies and their principles of governance, the foundation of development banks, the creation of regional sub-offices which would execute the Dirección's decisions, and the hiring of recruitment agents abroad, to name those that are most relevant to our discussion.[152] Taking stock of the breadth of these powers, it is possible to characterize the Dirección as a centralist institution with federalist goals. As will be seen, the Dirección sought to override imperfect provincial autonomies, overrun as they were by local and personal interests, with the intention of creating new and more perfect (and liberal) autonomies within each colony. For those paying attention—a war was raging, after all—most of the Dirección's charges seemed abuses of power.

ALL COLONIZATION IS EXPROPRIATION

The earliest reactions to the Dirección came from federalist-liberal quarters, where some were indignant at the new institution's centralist procedures. These early critics directly associated the body's inherent centralism to Garay and Gálvez's prior ideological and administrative commitments. Both men had long served as active figures within many of centralist Lucas Alamán's industrialist designs, studied in Chapter 2.[153] A pair of thorough critiques, by an anonymous Mexico City landowner, followed in the succeeding months, published in *El Monitor Republicano*, which inaugurated a short-lived back-and-forth between their author and Gálvez. As we will see, it was the question of private property vis-à-vis colonization that was at stake in this debate, a matter that had remained unaddressed since Mexican independence.

The anonymous author spoke for the "Sociedad de agricultura" comprised in its entirety of landowners of "the highest standing" (la primera gerarquía), whose interests spanned from the state of Jalisco and Puebla, to Tabasco and the Californias.[154] Identifying himself alternatively as a "member of the agricultural society" or a "poor and Mexican farmer," he argued that the Dirección represented the corruption of the "grand idea" of colonization by the forces of "empleomanía," speculation and aspirantism. These dark forces were, once more, sheltering in the shadow of a "great idea" (gran pensamiento), and exploiting "the sympathies that it attracts, bastardizing it and making it serve their special interests."[155] He held that the Dirección's charter meant that groups such as the author's—the Sociedad de Agricultura, which had been founded by hacendados and farmers as a reaction against centralist developmental policy, so as to create a lobby that would defend their interests—were to submit their domains to Garay and Gálvez, unqualified individuals whose only attributes were their connection to those in powers and who were named to these positions to the detriment of those who belonged to the trades they were to guide: industry, agriculture, development. Exasperated, he concluded: "This is abusive, it is monstrous."[156]

A second anonymous article was published belatedly, on May 19, 1847, in the context of a worsening war and a Dirección de Colonización in hiatus. It responded to a piece published by Gálvez in which he dismissed the Sociedad de Agricultura's concerns and celebrated the institution he represented.[157] Authored very likely by the same landowner, the May 19 text again denounced the Dirección as a standard of "empleomanía," and insisted on the need of a meritocratic approach. More importantly, it directly attacked the idea and implementation of colonization. For the author, aggrandizement as a horizon and colonization as its path had become a wild goose chase.[158] Too much time and money had been wasted in "projects of aggrandizement" (proyectos de engrandecimiento), and yet, like a gambling addict, the nation kept betting on these, even when it had nothing left in its pockets. Thus, looking at the Dirección's charter and reading Gálvez's article, he could only see "a great castle in the sky that conceals a new abyss that threatens the rights and the agonizing private fortunes of every Mexican; nothing but yet another speculation from people eager to become famous."[159]

Even though the article listed dozens of objections, the kernel of its opposition strove on the fact that, according to its charter, the Dirección was not simply responsible for recruiting colonos but with identifying, surveying, and effectively expropriating lands that it considered "baldías," in the name of the foundation of new colonies. For the author, what the Dirección ignored—and consequently, all colonization discourses up until that point—was that the territory that projects of colonization sought to subsume and activate in the name of the modern nation-state had already undergone a process of primitive accumulation and were, thus, already partitioned and claimed (by Peninsular and Creole parties). Moreover, he argued that all colonization projects amounted to the extraction, through taxation and public expenditures, "from this center of the nation, unprotected as it is, [of] a part of its wealth and population, so as to transform them into what they are not, precarious and threatened, out there in the confines of the republic."[160] The truth of the matter was that, in order to pursue its "sinister" goals, the Dirección ignored what for the author was a maxim: private interests work best. This meant that no territorial property in the nation actually remained intentionally idle or unpopulated. If landowners had not developed the vacant lands whose titles they held, it was because these did not promise a return of investment. To do otherwise was folly. As a result, any colonization effort driven by public policy was not simply misdirected because it went against economic principles, but because it did not, in fact, generate new wealth. The transplantation of populations and wealth, from either foreign or national lands, only extracted and siphoned resources from one place to the other. In the process, it dislocated and deflated these resources by plucking them from the interconnected web of relations that was the market.[161] The Dirección, then, "sees progress in the emergence of new creations in the uncultivated soils of the Republic, even if, in exchange, we lose four or six times more in terms of population and industry in those localities that, because of their history . . . are not as interesting to the nation."[162] Put simply, to settle "by force," as was the project of "monstruous Dirección," could only be "a drain, a bleeding of our scarce public wealth, a new tax over our already improductive labors and properties."[163]

It was clear to the author that, in order to colonize, "it is essential that we begin by establishing good government, in whose shadow we would be able to live with absolute confidence and satisfaction, and prosper; without this foundation, colonies cannot form; either they would be very onerous, or barely formed, they would be lost."[164] The Sociedad de Agricultura, for which he spoke, knew this. For that reason, it had to reject both, the Dirección with its abusive powers, and colonization as its object. In fact, he explained that it distanced itself from the supposedly modern maxims which guided the Dirección's policy, and privileged other older and "uglier" principles. Thus, it would always defend "that one hundred active adobe farms, and the hundred old looms that supply them, are preserved" rather than "a great onic or Churriguresque obelisk be erected in any colony in memory of Mr. MG's management; because the modernizations of establishments, with the subsequent and inevitable loss that comes of the transplantation of something, cannot deserve the approval of any calculating man that has something solid and stable invested in the nation."[165]

As can be seen, for the author, there existed no contradiction between the Sociedad's liberal values—such as their privileging of private interest, the free market, and the federalist politics which upheld these—and his conservative commitment to the reproduction of the economic structure and propertied elites for which he spoke: absentee owners of haciendas, landowners, and rentiers. It was precisely this confluence of interests which gave strength to his critique—an hacendado's critique—of the Dirección and the project of colonization. Seen from this perspective, the Dirección de colonización could not be but an agent of dispossession. The author's insistence on property rights, on the fact that the territory that served the economic imaginaries as a stage on which to deploy its fantasies was, in fact and in defiance of all appearances, private property, broke through the romance of colonization and revealed it as nothing else than expropriation. Colonization confiscated private lands for public means and stole away the metropolitan center's accumulated wealth and labor power, and re-distributed it across the territory, all for a misguided political program.

In a sense, this critique prefigured the incisive attacks the Dirección would face in 1848 and represented one of the first moments, if not the first, in which the liberal press published an indictment of the narrative of colonization from the standpoint of property relations and the propertied classes. The hacendado's impressions were, indeed, insightful. As we will see, in 1848, the Dirección would make explicit its commitment, pushed under the cover of colonization, to the type of expropriations entailed by agrarian reform, to a redistribution of wealth, to the lifting of the impoverished masses and the massification of property. Yet, by that time, the political sphere would have been rendered unrecognizable for the hacendado, and in the push and pull of increasing polarization, colonization would become a deeply liberal project, thus limiting appraisals such as this to the conservative press.

AN ENGINE OF LAND REFORM: THE DIRECCIÓN'S 1848 REPORT

In July 1848, the Dirección resumed its activity with increased vigor and produced an expansive report, which ultimately pushed colonization further than ever before. A lot had happened in the preceding six months. The Treaties of Guadalupe Hidalgo ended the war with the United States on February 2, 1848, and ceded half of Mexico's territories to the United States of America. Despite the controversial aspect of the treaties, they led to something very much like a peace, with opposing Mexican parties exhausted by the conflict and the political system in shambles, despite a consensus regarding the necessity of the federal government as guarantor of the territory's security. José Joaquín Herrera, a moderate, was elected to the nation's highest office in June that year and went on to become the nation's second president to complete his full four-year term. This general détente excluded the Sierra Gorda mountain range, where a series of revolts erupted; as well as the Yucatán peninsula, to the South, which was quickly engulfed in a bloody war between Maya communities and the Creole elites, a conflict known as "the Caste War." In this context, the Dirección presented what was then and would continue to be Mexico's most comprehensive and ambitious colonization policy program—a policy that fully embraced the promise of the colonia as the engine for the transformation of society.

The report, *Proyectos de colonización presentados por la junta directiva del ramo, al ministro de relaciones de la República Mexicana en 5 Julio de 1848* (Colonization Projects presented by the directors' board to the Republic of Mexico's Secretary of Relations on July 5, 1848), summarized the institution's labors to date and included a narrative preamble which tied it together. The report's innovations did not lie in its conceptualization of the colonia as productive enclave. In a sense, Ortíz de Ayala had developed the idea as far as it could go and the Dirección's work simply extrapolated from it, improved its execution, while leaving its center untouched. What made the 1848 report innovative was its comprehensiveness. Its two models for colonias—the foreign colono's and the military colono's—were clearly indebted to Ortiz de Ayala's work two decades before. Like the *proyectista*'s, both forms of settlements were imagined as industrious and anticipatory utopian enclaves, spatially and socially isolated, if not economically, from the rest of the territory. Likewise, these colonias were, to a large degree, regimes of exception geared toward labor and the development of the territory. Yet, while in Ortiz de Ayala, these exceptions had been justified on the private aspect of the colonial enterprise, the Dirección's projects were to be public affairs and, as such, the report couched the exceptionality of the military colonia on its belonging to military jurisdiction and the exceptionality of the foreign colono's colonia on its municipal nature.[166] Whereas the former seemed to be self-explanatory, the Dirección launched into a long explanation of the importance of municipal autonomy. Even if at face-value municipal jurisdiction was far from controversial, the Dirección's insistence was necessary because it expected it to serve as a tool capable of breaking through any possible impasse that might emerge between a state's legislation and the exceptional nature of the colonia, founded and conceived of by the federal government but functioning autonomously. More specifically, the municipal exceptionality of the colonia was the cornerstone of the recruitment of foreign colonos and, subsequently, of the Dirección's program of reform. They asked, "[h]ow could the municipal independence regime fail to adapt to new populations, foreigners and especially? The distance to which they will usually have to be founded, the diverse customs, habits and needs, and many other causes, demand local independence for businesses that only touch neighborhoods."[167] The report went on to name the three main exceptions from national law that were necessary for such autonomy: the right to a jury trial, religious toleration, and civil marriages. These three items would make it possible for a colonia's local government to mirror the habits and needs of its specific population, which, when compounded with the fiscal exceptions offered, would open the door for industrious foreign families eager for land.

In order to jump-start the process, the Dirección believed the state should learn from past mistakes and do without empresarios. They wrote, "[m]any land concessions and colonization contracts have been made, and how many new towns are formed? How many lands of those granted are cultivated or used after these long years?"[168] Thus, they argued that "it is necessary to open a wide path, with money from the treasury, for those emigrants who have the will to leave their native country, but not the means.[169] Private interest and capital had failed the state, and, so, the only option was for the state itself to develop the first colonias at its own expense, recruiting poor foreign laborers that had no capital to migrate. Once the state's success had drawn in profit-seeking empresarios willing to invest their capital in new productive colonies, the state would not simply grant them the land, as had been proposed in all previous colonization proposals, but sell it to them.[170] The generated funds would be split between federal and state governments, with one fourth of the amount returning to the Dirección, which was to invest it in more state-led colonization. Through this public-private approach, the whole of the territory—the territory that remained after the debacle that began in the Texan colonies—would soon become productive.

The Dirección did not ignore the Texan debacle, and, for this reason, it insisted that all foreign colonias had to be located in the nation's interior, with the coasts and borders settled through military colonies populated by Mexicans. The Dirección did not delve extensively into the latter colonies and replicated much of Ortiz de Ayala's reasonings—which by then had become the norm. Veterans and active-duty soldiers could request and receive land grants and a series of benefits in exchange for pensions and salaries that were owed to them. Along with these soldiers and their families, the Dirección imagined a community of rehabilitated vagrants. Like Ortiz de Ayala, the report was confident that "the vagrants made colonos would become industrious landowners. This conversion would thus be a good for them and for the republic, which would be purged of criminals."[171] In their view, a system based on the rehabilitation and transformation of vagrants into productive colonos could easily replace the penal system, while purging "the heart of the Republic of the devouring woodworm that tears it apart."[172]

While building on previous models, the report transcended them in that it imagined a Mexico engaged in a multilateral colonization effort, a colonization that was, in truth, many. The report considered the differential needs of a striated national territory and brought forth a specific colono for each spatial configuration. To do this, it deviated from the archive of colonization in a key aspect. Its account of the social situation of Mexico was critical of the palpitating contradiction within colonization discourse: the fact that the population and activation of the territory through colonization ignored a population—the indigenous—that remained actively oppressed and dispossessed.

They wrote,

> [t]he distribution of land with which the new settlers are invited, offering them through liberal concessions, would resemble sarcasm, if at the same time the indigenous people did not deserve, strangers in their own soil, the benefit of the government's consideration. This ancient population must be cared for, so that it multiplies and thrives; and their prosperity cannot be expected, without easy and abundant means of feeding themselves, which for the inhabitants of the countryside, are not possible without productive land to till.[173]

That is, unlike their many predecessors, the Dirección's account of Mexico's circumstance did not tread over the usual tropes that we have seen until now—underpopulation, the feracity of the land, bad habits, and the ill effects of Spanish bureaucracy. Instead, their projects were articulated from a critical understanding of their present context, a context that was not particularly characterized by the effect of the US-Mexico war or the legacy of

Texas, but by the Maya uprisings that were currently shaking Yucatán.[174] Yet, what the members of the Dirección saw when they turned their attention to Yucatán was different from what most other lettered men did. They did not hear of indigenous brutality or the indigenous people's inherent savagery, or even the inevitability of race war in a mixed social milieu. Instead, for them the matter was clear and belonged entirely to their purview and the horizon of colonization: "the disturbances in the mountains originated from land disputes."[175] Surely, these land disputes had given way to bloody clashes, reprisals, and devastation "and what at first had been a war of revenge was turning into a dreadful rebellion."[176] These developments were criminal, of course, and the state could easily proceed to "extirpate" these "evil eruptions" (erupciones maléficas), but doing so would leave untouched the ill, which would inevitably "reproduce with the strength of moral diseases."[177] They wrote:

> If the populations of the sierra were oppressed, tyrannized, and humiliated, if that uprising was born from the fact that the indigenous people wanted to take over the lands of the white owners, due to the need to provide themselves with the means of living, or to recover that of which they had been deprived by indiscreet and illegal expropriations, or by political decisions made under the influence of the wealthy men and powerful landowners, it is not possible to resort to violent repression, but to the remedy of reparations.[178]

That is, the Dirección engaged with the Sierra's population not only as indigenous communities, but as citizens. The Dirección's position on this was, in the context, profoundly idiosyncratic, departing as it did from Creole norm. In the specific case of Yucatán, as David Kazanjian has written, starting in the 1840s (Yucatecan) Creoles spent considerable energy in successfully casting the conflict "as a race war between the centuries-old, essentialized forces of Spanish civility and Indian barbarism, a war that could only be settled by the ever more vigorous 'assimilation' of the races," which would lead to the subsumption of Indians into liberal capitalist civility.[179] In a more general manner, Charles Hale once noted that

> [w]hen the liberals were faced with a stirring of the Indian masses, either in 1810 or in the contemporary Caste Wars, they recoiled from egalitarianism. In this they were no different from contemporary liberals throughout the Atlantic world when confronted with the "social question." Mexican liberals could talk of the need for a society of free property holders or of an "aristocracy of talent" without facing the real condition of two-thirds of the population.[180]

In contrast, the Dirección framed the insurgency as a political uprising against tyranny and oppression and Maya demands not as indigenous demands but political demands. If they "invaded" lands owned by "white landowners" (propietarios blancos), it was done not out of some primitive instinct but out of the sheer need for survival or as an avenue to redress a displacement carried out through illegal expropriation or judicial verdicts corrupted by the influence of rich landowners. The only solution for such a situation was not repression, but reparations. They went on to argue that, in the past, when the government engaged with pronunciamientos and other types of uprisings, it had always tried to meet the demands of the "alzados," granting "concesiones" so as to seek the removal of the "malaise." And yet, these had not been the case with the Yucatán uprisings. The Dirección asked: "Why should this not be done with a large class, which just because of its size deserves great consideration."[181] If these citizens were simply asking for protection, justice, and the possibility of a livelihood, which they lacked due to their deprivation of land, would it not be best to seek the avenues of redress available to democratic regimes? The truth of the matter was that, for the Dirección, what was happening in Mexico was happening all over "America" among the "masses" and in Europe among their working classes. It was a social revolution grounded on the fact that "la muchedumbre" was beginning to want those same privileges that oligarchies had been enjoying for a long time.[182] Governments should move to satisfy their polities' demands and avoid unrest like Yucatán's. For the Dirección, such political redress was difficult in Europe, "where the superabundance of population, and of workers is the origin of misery."[183] In Mexico, however, the government could move toward the satisfaction of such demands, for its lands were unpopulated and fertile. Unfortunately, territorial property was unevenly distributed, much of it in the hand of just a few men, and the majority of Mexican laborers were reduced to serfdom and debt peonage, enslaved to farms much like men were enslaved to other men elsewhere.

The Dirección could only see one solution to the quandary, one feared and predicted by the hacendados of the Agricultural Society, the division and redistribution of property.[184] Agrarian reform, they conceded, was a complicated matter. It was limited by existing law and the bounds of political economy, muddled by the fact that it put the interests of the masses, which sooner or later become unruly, and those of the great landholders, that do as they will, on a collision course. It was also outside of the Dirección's purview. Recognizing this, they decided not to make any great proposals on the matter. But they did proceed to include a chapter within the colonization project which they hoped would serve as a preparatory measure for a future agrarian reform—a reform which they believed necessary for the republic, which promised equality of law, to shed the appearance of aristocracy and feudalism.[185] Titled "De los medios de proveer de tierras a los pueblos que carecen de ellas, y de preparar la división de la propiedad rural" (Of the means to provide land to the pueblos that lack them, and to prepare for the division of rural properties), the chapter included a series of articles that transformed the Dirección into an agent of redistribution. For example, Article 29 allowed the body to purchase lands that it believed convenient for the establishment of new colonias, whether for nationals or foreigners. Likewise, Article 30 created a call for proposals that would reward the best recommendation for a project that could distribute land among the needy without offending property rights.[186] Yet, the most meaningful of the articles, for they were meant to tackle the problem that had launched Yucatán into conflict, were Articles 27 and 28. Despite their small aims and brevity, they were hugely significant for they further developed the depth of the Dirección's colonization project. The first, Article 27, earmarked any funds earned by states from the sale of land to empresarios—a third of the amount, as mentioned earlier—to provide the "pueblos" in need with lands.[187] Article 28 stipulated that these lands could only be distributed to those who were already "vecinos" or denizens (moradores) and could not be sold nor accumulated by a single person in any amount larger than a "caballería de tierra" (around 1800 squared meters). In a sense, the articles in question bypassed the illegality of agrarian reform in the name of its anticipation through the transformation of the indigenous pueblo into colonia, the indigenous citizen into colono. That is, these articles guaranteed that all foreign colonization of the territory went hand-in-hand not only with a national colonization effort, but with the redistribution of lands to indigenous pueblos that had historically been expropriated and dispossessed and, furthermore, established protections to put an end to such expropriation and dispossession.

Ironically, the report in which the Dirección put forth its powerful vision of colonization, included, in its addenda, a measure that announced its failure: the proposal for "colonos medianeros," share-croppers colonos. Relegated to one of its last pages, it was a measure born out of practicality and, perhaps, surrender, written sometime after the rest of the report. From what they said the following month, it seems the proposal was not entirely the product of the Dirección. Even if, throughout the preceding pages, Garay and Gálvez had threatened to quit their offices if the funds they had been assigned were withheld, funds that were primarily to be used to hire land surveyors to identify the nation's baldíos (unoccupied lands), the proposal for colonos medianeros faced up to the reality of an empty budget and implied a conceptual splitting of colonization, the effective separation of the colonia and the colono. The proposal, an olive branch to landowners such as the one discussed in the previous section, was welcomed by Congress because it allowed for a more flexible approach to the activation of the territory. The measure invited hacendados and landowners to request the Dirección for colonos to work their existing properties. The Dirección would take their request and recruit industrious foreigners and bring them to the country at the landowners' expense. In exchange, the landowner had to assign the immigrant sharecropper a piece of land. These colonos would work both the hacendado's primary hacienda and the granted lot and, after a decade, have an option to purchase said lot through permanent emphyteusis—a concession to motivate landowners to active their idle properties. If emphyteusis, as proposed by Azcárate y Lezama, had meant to tie the colono to the state, it now did so to the landowner. The share-cropping colono undermined the grandiloquent aims of the report, yet Garay and Gálvez trusted that they could fold this figure into their larger project. The measure, they argued, would attend to the development of already existing yet unproductive haciendas, while also, with time and the prosperity of the established colonos, promote the other forms of colonization mentioned in the report. In their account, the splitting of colonia and colono could serve as a new atomized approach to the matter with the potential to completely transform the imaginaries of colonization. The share-cropping colono did not necessarily cancel its multilateral approach. As presented in the addenda, each element would work toward the same horizon: each industrious share-cropping colono would serve as the anticipatory seed that would transform and modernize existing haciendas; each colonia—military and foreign—an enclave and model of an industrious republic; each indigenous pueblo an apparatus for the industrious uplift of the indigenous Mexican masses.

A month after the report, in August 1848, the Dirección began to fear that their assigned funds were not forthcoming, and that their proposals had largely been ignored. So, they decided to further develop the measure in favor of *colonos medianeros*, seeing as it had generated some interest and was implementable. Their "New Project for colonos, landowners, sharecroppers, renters, and wage-workers" (Nuevo proyecto de colonos, propietarios, medieros, arrendatarios y asalariados) was a humbling admission of defeat—"a testimony of the docility with which [the Dirección] is willing to adopt the conceptions that are not its own"—that placed the Dirección at the mercy of landowners and hacendados.[188] Directed not at Congress, but at a newly formed "Agricultural Commission" (Comisión de agricultores), the Dirección tried to move beyond the previous months' iteration of the measure so as to explore other avenues that would give teeth to this form of colonization. So, in the "Nuevo proyecto," they argued that not all potential colonos were the same. Just as there were poor European emigrants that would surely take up the offer to work a landowner's lands in exchange for a land grant and a salary, there were also those with vast fortunes who might be interested in purchasing and working their own lands, and those with humbler means interested in renting property to work. The Dirección could match these interests to those of a diverse landowning class in Mexico, where there surely were many who wanted to rent or sell their lands, and others who would simply benefit with the hiring of talented and vigorous laborers.[189]

Even if it was a creative attempt to carry out their charge in the face of obstacles, the "Nuevo proyecto" transformed the Dirección's role from their previously imagined function as the engine of the reform of the nation to a simple middleman between possible colonos and the Republic's landowners interested in hiring colonos or "colonizing" their properties.[190] The Dirección's 1849 report listed the "Nuevo proyecto" as the body's only action toward their assigned goal. It represented the culmination of a movement in which colonization went from being an imperial concern, to a localized matter, only to then be centralized by a strong federal state and, finally, privatized, passed on to the landowning elite as an option for the development of their own private property. While it may not have been immediately clear to anybody involved, the Direccion's admission of its defeat and its submission to landowning interests and their influence over political matters represented nothing short of the material exhaustion of colonization. So, for the first time in the history we have explored in this chapter, the dream of the productive subsumption of the nation's territory was explicitly cut short not by bureaucracy or historical contingency, but by the collective interest of that social class which claimed ownership over said territory.[191] Colonization had never stopped being invested in private property; in the transformation of idle land, of commons, into productive, private property. And yet, private property had, unbeknownst to the preachers of colonization, always been its limit. Yet this could only come into view after the country lost half of its territory—what then became California, Nevada, Utah, Colorado, Arizona, Wyoming, New Mexico, and Texas— and with it, the extensive lands that had, for two decades, been the object of the colonizing narrative, lands that had belonged to indigenous communities whose rights, unlike those of the Creole elite, could be legally ignored. Put differently, it was only after Texas and the Treaty of Guadalupe Hidalgo, on the eve of the creation of the Dirección, that colonization's inward turn became a concern for the propertied classes of Mexico. As it drew closer to home, propertied elites could only see in colonization its expropriating drive—made explicit by the Dirección's projects—and the threatening possibility of autonomous colonias and a free industrious citizenry, organized rationally and responding not to established hierarchies and traditions but only (in theory) to private interest and the dictum of the market. It was as if, after Texas, the dream of Mexico's territorial plenitude came to a dramatic end, and what was left in its stead was the accumulated private property of the Creole elite and other landed interests, assailed by indigenous insurgence in Yucatán and the Dirección de Colonización in Mexico City. In this context, the colono suddenly found himself without a future.

A CONSERVATIVE CRITIQUE OF COLONIZATION

Colonization's ideological exhaustion came shortly after. Between 1848 and 1849, the matter was debated constantly and consistently. The number of pages dedicated to it by papers such as *El Siglo Diez y Nueve*, *El Monitor Republicano*, *El Universal*, and *La Voz de la Religión*, to name a few, attest to the readership's interest and its attraction in the newsstands. Surely, the colono had been a staple in the spheres of public opinion since independence. Yet, during these two years, engagement deepened, moving beyond the adulatory call for the necessity of colonization, to more in depth and, often, critical accounts.

The new fervor with which the matter was engaged was directly related to the Dirección's initial impetus. But it also responded to a changing political panorama. During the Herrera presidency, the political sphere began to stabilize and to tenuously reformulate itself along new party and ideological lines. In a context in which it seemed that all that was solid was melting in the air, the certainty of colonization had re-emerged at the hands of the Dirección, if only momentarily, as a catch-all policy capable of grounding a liberal vision of the world. In the aftermath of the 1848's reports publication, liberal papers took up most of the Dirección's 1848 proposals and, by and large, extolled them. By 1849, however, their position soured in the face of legislative inertia and the Dirección's later passivity. Yet, the ideological exhaustion of colonization did not take place in their pages, where critiques of the ideal focused mostly on what we could call procedural differences. Despite their eventual frustration, liberals still held that "[c]olonization is for [the nation] the only hope of social and political progress, and we dare say that it is the only condition of its future existence."[192]

A deep critique could only be articulated from a new conservative position and the papers it spawned in the second half of 1848, such as *El Universal* and *La voz de la religión*.[193] These conservative papers reacted to each and every liberal position and slowly, but thoroughly identified their blind spots, their historical failures, and their contradictions. In fact, *El Universal* spent its first six months surveying and exhaustively analyzing the main tenets of Mexican liberalism to the point that, eventually, it proudly stated that they had "proven [liberalism's] irrationality almost mathematically."[194] The result of this inquiry had been that "[t]his emphatic list of citizen rights is a trick, a deception, a hypocrisy of the so-called liberals, to deceive and seduce the unhappy pueblo."[195] Freed from "theories," the conservative ideologues of *El Universal* pledged allegiance only to the "realm of facts."

Colonization was but one of its targets. Now politicized in the eyes of the conservative press, the matter was approached as yet another liberal hoax.[196] *El Universal* began its frontal assault on November 19, 1848 and did not let up until March 1849. In its first editorial on the subject, they recognized that colonization had become one of the key political demands on which the nation's future revolved, and that all of the thinking men of their generation had included it in their political programs as a necessity. While admitting that, in the abstract, it was truly a powerful tool for the aggrandizement of nations, they believed it was plagued with problems. These problems were not simply of a political or procedural nature. They ran deeper than that.[197] For *El Universal*, proponents of colonization were incapable of any self-assessment, caught as they were in a circular logic according to which they "presented as a principle that which was the matter of dispute."[198] They argued that the relationship between population and aggrandizement, for example, had become political dogma, taken for granted by "quick men."[199] For the editors, "the very sad condition of the classes of our society, is the radical principle of the backwardness [atraso] of our population," and the discourse of colonization's haphazard engagement with the actually existing Mexican population and, consequently, with the reality that the majority of said population was indigenous, revealed its insufficiency.[200] With the exception of the Dirección, proponents of colonization had barely addressed the Indian's condition and had, in fact, abandoned him to the dustbin of history.[201] Calls for colonization could be heard from the earliest days of independence, but what had been done, since 1821, with regards to the indigenous? Nothing, the editors answered. In fact, it would seem—and the editors wrote this ironically—that Mexico's "misfortune has consisted of the fact that we were unable, as in [the United States], to make the indigenous race disappear."[202] Only the sudden disappearance of the Indian pueblos or a spontaneous genocide could explain the lack of post-independent indigenous policy. For the editors, this nonexistence resulted from the shortsightedness of the theories and models with which liberals engaged with the world; with the fact that "we did not have European models to handle the Indians stranded in unsanitary terrains, as we have them to imitate customs; our misfortune, in short, has consisted of the fact that our political lens can only perceive an area of a very short and ruinous extension."[203]

Here, then, the editors shifted their focus. If, as its proponents had held for decades, colonization had to do with labor, the activation of the population, and the nation's aggrandizement, the question of the Indian and his participation in the national economy had to be addressed. *El Universal* acknowledged the Dirección's attempt to account for the indigenous in the 1848 report yet believed its approach to be short-sighted. For the paper's editors, the Dirección's understanding of the reasons of indigenous struggle in Yucatán—which they had attributed to indigenous exploitation in haciendas, plantations, and farms—was mistaken. Like other liberal and urban Creole letrados, held *El Universal*, the Dirección's administrators extrapolated from the circumstance of the "indios" of Central Mexico, who lived in cities or neighboring towns and who worked in the region's haciendas. These indigenous communities were not the issue in Yucatán. It was not the exploited Indians in haciendas who were rebelling, insisted the editors. In a sense, these communities were productive, and *El Universal* did not feel the need to question or deny their dismal working conditions. That was not their concern. After all, indigenous day-laborers had already been subsumed by the Creole economic apparatus and were fulfilling their function. The trouble came from those communities that still managed to stay clear of it, from the "pueblos that, far from considering themselves as slaves, are beginning to understand, beyond the sentimentality, shyness, and suspicion that tend to make the Indian smart and bloodthirsty, the principles of their sovereignty and independence."[204]

According to the editors, if the abstractions of liberalism were abandoned, and the subsequent politicization of the Indian bracketed, it became obvious that the problem was not the indigenous person—as could be proven by those that labored in haciendas—but indigeneity in itself; the culture, customs, and form of life that comprised indigenous existence and continued to limit their embeddedness in the nation. Liberals had consistently blamed the Spanish Empire for Mexico's maladies and for what they considered indigenous apathy, but they had ignored that viceregal authorities had at least engaged with indigeneity in what the editors, Creole supremacists after all, believed a productive manner. To improve the stock of the Indian, viceregal authorities had established missions in Indian towns and prohibited indigenous languages, two measures which, among others, facilitated the commerce between the civilized and uncivilized. These had been steps in the right direction. To expand on their position, the editors addressed three key elements of indigenous sociality: their relationship with the market, with the political, and with religion. Beginning with the economic aspect, *El Universal* argued that indigenous market activity could not properly be considered commerce, for there was no attempt to achieve a surplus: "What does society gain, then, from commerce with the Indians? A mere exchange of poor products, and the spectacle of a degraded and vicious race."[205] Perhaps, were it possible for them to engage in (Spanish) conversation, in Creole culture, they would see the benefit in creating more complex commercial relationships and enrich themselves.[206] Indigenous languages, then, were one of the main obstacles for the formal and commercial subsumption of the Indian. If their commercial relations remained "simple," so did their political relations. Culturally, it seemed that the only political engagement the indigenous were interested in took the form of litigation over boundaries and land. This short-sighted obsession with land further cemented what for the editors was indigeneity's anti-social sociality, which foreclosed the possibility of fraternity and collaboration, and made of all others—whether "hombres blancos" or other Indians from other pueblos—an "enemy" and possible invader. When coupled with a simplified mode of commerce obstructed by language, this jealous conceptualization of land short-circuited all politics, which resulted in their complete indifference to any form of organized government, and a complete lack of any demand beyond the desire to not be taxed.[207] The third and only positive element of indigenous sociality was their commitment to religion, which fostered their ties to the "white race." The Catholic faith, threatened by the Dirección's attempt to introduce religious tolerance in Mexico, represented their only link to proper civilization and to the Creole state. It was faith which kept them in check and in their place.[208]

El Universal held that the solutions to the problems faced by Mexico would not be found through the establishment of colonias or through the mythological amalgamation of the races which *El Siglo Diez y Nueve* was beginning to float. Indigeneity, understood in this context as the non-economic bartering of products, the antisocial attachment to land and a language that interrupted the possibility of equivalence, short-circuited the foundation of so-called free labor on which the aggrandizement of the territory depended. The solution proposed by the editors was the further development of the religious involvement of the indigenous and the pursuit of the slow but effective road of primary education.[209] It was through civilization that indigeneity could be eliminated, and the indigenous person brought into the fold of the national economy. Would it not be wiser, they seemed to ask, to enrich the nation through the uplift of the population, instead of colonization? Once "civilized," these formerly indigenous men would productively jump-start the desired demographic increase.[210]

For *El Universal*, colonization's questionable anthropology of labor was a corollary of this incapacity to understand the cultural materiality of Mexico's indigenous population. The quest for immigration and population-increase had gone unremarked since the *Gaceta*'s October 1821 article and little attention had been paid to how its proponents tended to present facts that belonged to the realm of anthropology as ontological—such as the vigorous industriosity of the European. For *El Universal*, this resulted from a structural problem within liberal logic: the undue emphasis it placed on the human will and its capacity to remake society. The commitment to "the abstractions of the ingenious system of that poor crazy-man Juan Jacobo [Jean-Jacques Rousseau]"—which the editors used as shorthand for a particular strain of voluntarism, the belief in popular sovereignty, and social contract theory— had led to a misinterpretation of the relationship between the individual and the social which forgot the simple fact that "man did not enter society, he was born in society."[211] If they brought this up in the context of colonization, it was because it led to the erasure of the predetermined nature of men—predetermined, they believed, by God, history, and geography. Only through this erasure was the colono transformed into a tabula rasa, a pure will driven only by interest, emptied of all culture, political attachments, or psychology. *El Universal* provided, as an example of this emptying, an argument they attributed to *El Siglo Diez y Nueve*. Like many before them, *El Siglo*'s editors explained that the arrival of active and enterprising foreigners would spur Mexicans to emulate the recently arrived. This would, in turn, lead to a national transformation. For *El Universal*, Texas put the lie to this assumption. The arrival of useful foreigners was not eased simply through lands grants and liberal promises. Colonos were men and, like all men, they were moved by passions and interests. The editors wondered why, if such foreigners were to arrive, should they pledge loyalty to Mexico? Was it not possible that rational and enlightened men, moved by their own interest and threatened by the chaotic political panorama, decide to pledge loyalty to the United States instead; a state capable of protecting their wellbeing? Or, what if they decided to stay faithful to their own manners and mores and, as a result, preferred to secede, like Texas had done?

History showed that "the greatest and most difficult sacrifice of the human heart is obedience and voluntary submission."[212]

Moreover, beyond the question of prior loyalties, liberals also ignored two additional facts about colonization. On the one hand, if colonization were to be accomplished following existing laws, which invited foreigners to settle regardless of class and origin, chances were that the arriving migrants would not conform to the dream of the enterprising bourgeois yeoman. It was more likely that the desired colonos would actually be either poor foreigners (and therefore, for the editors, intellectually degraded), conniving charlatans (as was seen in Texas), or, eventually, freed Black Americans—and they referred to American articles that talked about the future and necessary relocation of freedmen abroad.[213] On the other hand, even if the idealized colono-entrepreneur came to Mexico and submitted themselves to local laws, their colonization "will surely produce the development of the elements of prosperity and wealth that the Republic contains; but all of that wealth and prosperity will not be . . . for the nation's children, but for the settlers and the generations that come from them."[214]

Ultimately, *El Universal* believed that the problems that colonization addressed obliquely could be tackled directly. It was not that they ignored the breadth of the territory and its riches, the numeric incapacity of the existing population to exploit these, or the fact that local customs were far from the perfection that a nation should aspire for, but that they believed and stressed that the state should focus on "increasing the population while benefitting the existing population; on exploiting the elements of wealth that our soil contains, with the benefit of the owners of that soil; on perfecting customs, without enslaving those whose customs it is intending to perfect; and, finally, on illustrating reason, without misleading or hallucinating us."[215]

As we can see, *El Universal*'s thorough engagement with colonization unveiled both its foundational blind spots and the discursive omissions through which it was defended. And yet, despite their constant examination of colonization's origins, history, policies, and despite their "destruction" of its "fundamentos principales," the editors were dismayed that people continued to rally in its defense. They asked, what do proponens of colonization do when challenged by rational argument? They "[s]hout in a masterly tone: colonization, colonization!."[216] In light of this, there was nothing left to do for *El Universal*, but to turn to a popular refrain which, for them, captured the liberal insistence of hiding colonization's aporias behind grandiloquence and false promises: "to be white [and without stains], something has to be done!"[217] That is, if colonization's proponents were truly serious about their project, they would tackle the intrinsic limits and defects that *El Universal* had pointed out. Instead, they shouted and repeated their truims, ignoring the emptiness at the heart of the colono. *El Universal* eventually abandoned the matter and shifted their attention to other liberal myths and promises. By then, it became obvious that Congress, either convinced by their arguments or unwilling to invest in the project, had indefinitely postponed any action on the Dirección de Colonización's proposals.

CONCLUSION

Colonization had been and would continue to be, as *El Siglo Diez y Nueve* disappointedly wrote, "one of our dreams and, at the same time, the nightmare of good patriots."[218] In this chapter we have seen how colonización swung from dream to nightmare, from an instrument that, through the influx of an industrious populace capable of harnessing the providential riches of the territory, would herald the rise of an economically powerful Mexican Empire to a self-inflicted wound which put the nation's very existence in peril. After Texas, the colono re-emerged once again, at first timidly, cautiously, having learned from experience, only to quickly take his throne as an explicit state-project, as an engine that would reform Mexican society from above. Yet, increasingly tied to liberal politics in the radical polarization of the late 1840s, the colono soon came under an acidic critical scrutiny that stopped it in its tracks.

As mentioned in the chapter's introduction, colonization was never quite a coherent, closed concept or idea. The itinerary of deployments we have followed attests to how its borders remained open, shifting so as to maintain its explanatory capacity burning. The *Gaceta*, Azcárate y Lezama, Ortíz de Ayala, the 1822–1824 congressmen, Carlos María Bustamante, the Dirección de Colonización, and *El Siglo Diez y Nueve*, among so many others, turned to it because, despite recognizing existing challenges, the figure offered a path forward. Colonizaciónt made sense in that it offered a narrative frame for the intentional self-foundation of society, a self-foundation that was to be carried out in the image and likeness of Creole capitalist modernity.

The Dirección de Colonización e Industria was not dissolved until 1853. Yet, by 1850, two years after its promising 1848 report and policy proposals, it was obvious that all of its plans had been shelved. Congressional inertia was mainly to blame. Lawmakers' disinterest was, in large part, a result of the pressure exerted by propertied interests and the widespread opposition to religious tolerance. By 1850, even a disillusioned *El Siglo Diez y Nueve*, once its most ardent supporter, was calling for the Dirección's elimination.

Nevertheless, the dispersal of the impetus of 1848 did not quite amount to a dismissal of the idea. Recognizing the difficulty of federal action, liberal and moderate papers now called for private initiatives, for the propertied classes to take the matter into their own hands—and lands. Small legislative gestures kept the fantasy alive. In 1853, Congress passed colonization as a concern to a newly established Secretaría de Fomento. This was followed in 1854 with that body's creation of the figure of the colonization agent—a bureaucrat-cum-diplomat charged with, in the style of Ortiz de Ayala's diplomatic forays of the 1830s, the international recruitment of empresarios. Interestingly, the first of these agents would be none other than Rafael Rafael, *El Universal*'s publisher. No significant progress was made by Rafael Rafael as agent. Another attempt followed in 1856 and 1857. Under the helm of Secretario de Fomento Manuel Siliceo and Mexico's most liberal government, colonization would once more be centralized and taken up as a national concern, only to be interrupted by the War of Reform (1858–1860), a civil war that shook the nation and ultimately cemented liberalism as the political language of the Mexican Republic.

It is useful to think of colonización as a fantasy. In its psychoanalytic usage, a fantasy is not, as Horacio Legrás has written, "a stage where a preformed actor displays his or her potentials and limitations. Rather, a fantasy builds a world where there was none before."[219] Put in this manner, colonización did not simply satisfy or realize Creole desire for an industrious population capable of harnessing the proverbial riches of the land; it staged "desire as such."[220] *El Universal*'s conservative editors saw this and put together a critique that briefly amounted to the traversing of this fantasy, the "unveiling [of] the structuring function of lack" of colonization itself; that is, the revelation that colonization, like all fantasy, was anchored "in a region that is outside and beyond any positivity and that no number of images can placate."[221] Yet, as we have seen, despite their attempts, the fantasy of colonization proved to be tenacious, capable of resisting all setback, and would continue to stage its productivist Creole desire well into the nineteenth century.

When colonization re-emerged as a substantial political concern and topic of debate and reflection during Porfirio Díaz's long presidency (1876–1911), it did so very much in the terms that we have discussed throughout this chapter; the discursive blind spots pointed out by the Mexico City landowner and *El Universal* remained unaddressed. If there was a major shift in the discussion in the last third of the century, it was the growing racialization of the project. The discursive strand which emphasized race had begun to take shape in the shadow of the Caste War and, during 1848 and 1849, had made a series of brief appearances in *El Siglo Diez y Nueve*, but only solidified into a full-blown position in the aftermath of the War of Reform. Yet, the centrality of race within colonizing discourse, so brilliantly studied by Joshua Lund and often-remarked by the historiography, did not translate to the racialization of the totality of the ideologeme of colonization or the policy itself, which throughout the second half of the nineteenth-century would continue to place equal importance to Mexican nationals, European migrants, and the repatriation of Mexicans from the United States.[222]

CHAPTER 2

The Artisan

Industrialization, Labor, and the Modernization of Customs

The men employed in the factories, those engaged in workshops, those who work at home, either under the dependence of an employer or now freely, those in need of cooperation, and the wanderers who are driven by the rhythm of their will in an inconsistent manner, all of them verge on idleness to a greater or lesser extent and their derangements can be corrected, to a greater or lesser extent.

Guillermo Prieto, *"Artesanos y obreros V"*

The artisan, with his identity and form of life defined by his labor, should have figured as one of the standard-bearers of the economic imaginaries of post-independence Mexico. Yet, for most of the nineteenth century, despite being the most readily available urban figuration of industriousness, he remained undesired by the Creole elite. More often than not, he was found to be lacking; playing the role of suspect, rather than ally. The artisan was too real—roughly thirty percent of Mexico City's population was involved in artisan labor: weavers, shoemakers, hatters, tailors, carpenters, etc. He was too present, too historically embedded, and ubiquitous to be idealized as the industrious salvation of the territory. Unlike the colono, imagined as an increasingly productive and productivizing human engine introduced into the body politic, the ever-present artisan evidently labored but not enough, strove but did not transcend. He remained limited by his social and biological circumstance, by his manners and customs, by an anachronistic and unproductive form of labor that did not yet differentiate between the spatialities and temporalities of life and work; haunted and pre-determined by the presentism of the market, by the harsh realities of supply and demand, by a decapitalized urban geography and economy that often could not or would not provide a full day's worth of employment. As a figure, the artisan embodied the potential and burden of labor, but also the possibility of its interruption and corruption. An example of industriousness's fragility, the artisan was always a vagrant-in-waiting, as we will see in the next chapter. Thus, more so than the settler or the vagrant, the artisan brought to the fore the question of the proper formation of the citizenry, not so much for their own sake, but for the transformation and modernization of the customs and manners of the people in the name of national aggrandizement.

Contempt for the artisan built on decades of self-righteous politico-economic critique of the guild structure. The power of guilds had once been based on the monopoly of labor, market, and craft knowledge, and, starting in the 1760s, the main stalwarts of the Spanish Enlightenment—Bernardo Ward, Pedro Rodríguez de Campomanes, and Gaspar Melchor de Jovellanos among other members of the elites—launched a consistent assault on the guild which emphasized its obstruction of national industrial development and its opposition to two fundamental conditions of capitalism: the freedom of work and the right to work.[1] These writers called and argued for the suppression or radical re-articulation of the guild, in spite of the fact that they were not necessarily well-acquainted with the realities of the world of the artisan, its conflicts, or even with the guild's actual incapacity to effectively maintain its privileges.[2] They were, with time, successful. As the eighteenth century came to a close, the legislation of the Spanish Empire, first, and then, that of the newly independent American nations began to undo and put the guild's privileges to rest, working toward the extinction of the artisan. Yet, as we have seen in this book so far and as Sonia Pérez Toledo has emphasized with regards to the artisan, there existed a distance between legislation and compliance.[3] "This distance," Pérez Toledo goes on to write, "is mediated by customs and traditions that are part of a world that follows slower rhythms of change."[4] Notwithstanding the economic and legislative transformation of the world of labor and the concomitant political elimination of the guild as a corporation of privileges, workers' lives were and continued to be crisscrossed by its customs, habits, and relationships, all of which were tenacious and resistant.[5] This tenacity guaranteed, at least in the first half of the nineteenth century, a certain half-life for the artisan guild of yore.

In the immediate aftermath of independence, though, the negative figuration of the artisan had to contend with the hard fact of artisan participation in the process and war of independence itself, and in the republican discourse of the nation's first decade. Artisans were the first to hear the grito de Dolores on September 16, 1810. It was to them that Miguel Hidalgo y

Costilla turned to as he launched his midnight insurgency; it was them he armed first and foremost.[6] Eventually, as the war intensified, artisans and skilled laborers were to become a significant element among the insurgent forces—"overrepresented" in terms of occupational categories among rebels, according to the calculations of historian Eric Van Young.[7] These once-mobilized artisan masses did not instantly fade away after independence. During those first post-independent years, they remained an influential presence in local and national politics. So, months after the end of the conflict, for example, in one of the first proposals for the structure of the new nation's constitutional congress, soon-to-be-emperor Agustín de Iturbide imagined a gathering of legislative representatives from the nine groups that, he believed, made up the new nation's polity. Artisans were one of these, along with miners, rural landowners, merchants, lettered men, the aristocracy, the audiencias, the university, and the *pueblo*.[8] After the fall of Iturbide's Empire in 1823, the new federal government affirmed the principle of popular sovereignty, further empowering the artisans that made up large numbers of the now-politicized urban masses.[9]

It could not have been otherwise. As it happened elsewhere in the Age of Revolutions, republican discourse made of artisans one of its most important political protagonists, a model and representative citizen for a republic built on industry, virtue, and progress.[10] It was the closest the figure had come to reclaiming the social standing it had lost in the last decades of the eighteenth century, with the rise of the languages, images, and ideologies of political economy. In the 1820s, pamphlets and political papers confirmed this role, and often offered artisans as rhetorical stand-ins for the virtuous "people." For example, in a pamphlet published shortly after Iturbide's proposal, in 1821, author "JMR" offered a dialogue between a "friend" and an artisan. In what would increasingly become a trope, the text began when a politically informed citizen walked up to an artisan to ask for his opinion about a particular decision or proposal made by a governing body—in this case, the Junta Provisional Gubernativa, the nation's first legislative body. The artisan apologized for not being up to date; he had been too busy, "held by a job so laborious and mechanical, that when [he is no] carrying it out, [he] miss[es] it."[11] But the friend went on to give him (and the reader) a quick summary of the situation anyway, and the artisan, after yet again apologizing for not being too informed, delivered the author's favored position. In this and many other texts, the artisan embodied the ethically and politically correct argument, and the enunciation of this position came structurally and discursively tied to an explicit critique of the unproductive and unemployed.

Surely, the apparent specificity of the artisan as category was only a mirage. Behind it, fanned a wide heterogeneous slice of the population, differentiated from within itself by craft, level of specialization, hierarchical position within the workshop (master, journeyman, apprentice), recognition, and social prestige. As E. P. Thompson historically put it, "[t]here were great differences of degree concealed within the term, 'artisan,' from the prosperous master-craftsman, employing labour on his own account and independent of any masters, to the sweated garret labourers."[12] Within the "artesanado" of the first half of the nineteenth century, then, there were those who could easily be thought of as capitalists and entrepreneurs, and yet the large, impoverished majority toiled in poorly remunerated small workshops, or rented out their labor and sold their craft outside the structures of these shops for however much they could get.

The artisan's republican dignity in labor, with which the figure was charged, would dissipate throughout the century, as Carlos Illades and Adriana Sandoval have shown.[13] The dissipation was already evident in the 1820s. Despite the preponderance of the artisan as a positive figure, the free-market policies and the economic imaginaries which abounded in the aftermath of independence consistently undermined the workshop in practice. Some respite was offered to artisans by the 1828 Acordada Revolt, a popular uprising which resulted in the overturning of that year's presidential election results, the raid of the Parián market, and the presidency of populist Vicente Guerrero. Guerrero condemned the "sloppy application of liberal economic principles and the inconsiderate latitude given to foreign trade," and called for "wisely calculated import bans," which could allow for the prosperity of the nation and its workers.[14] The turn to prohibitive measures, though, was short-circuited by a series of obstacles, key among them an empty treasury and the Thermidorian reaction which expelled Guerrero in 1829. After the 1830s, it became ever more common among the Creole elite to understand that, even if independence had freed the artisan from what liberals saw as the oppressive clutches and deadening structures of the guild, the figure continued to represent a holdover from the past. Across the political spectrum of elites, the life of artisans was deemed to remain too constituted by the guild structure, too embedded in the unproductive customs and habits partially responsible for the disappointing circumstance of the public economy.[15] The artisan as a figure, then, was taken to be beholden to a striated concept of labor that belonged to the stratified society of yore; a concept of labor that was stringent in its differentiation of one craft to another. Even if it was argued from different positions, the consensus was that this differentiation interrupted capitalist disposition toward the flattening of labor, toward the realization of the market truism that "all forms of labor have in common that they are labor."[16] Artisanal insistence on the "qualification" of labor—that is, on a trained examiner's certification and regulation of the craftsman's ability to properly produce their product—created an obstacle for the abstraction of that particular craft, to a mediation that was better left to the market; and, as a result, it interrupted the artisan's subsumption into the ideal figure of capitalist labor: the individualized subject, freed from political constraints to labor and to adapt to the dynamics of the market.

This chapter focuses on the artisan as object, rather than subject, as a persistent source of anxiety in the economic imaginaries of independence. As we will see, the period between 1830 and 1846 saw the initial optimism of independence peter out, and the consistency of political instability and economic scarcity marked a move away from inclusive narratives of economic well-being and republican discourses of liberty. In what follows, we will analyze the attempts and arguments that sought, but failed, to either eliminate or modernize the figure of the artisan and what it represented in the horizon of national aggrandizement. In other words, this chapter approaches the figure of the artisan from the position of its adversaries. The chapter is split in half. In the first part, I study the displacement of the artisan in the works and policies written by conservative stalwart Lucas Alamán and industrialist Estevan de Antuñano between 1830 and 1846. In the second half, I center the Junta de Fomento de Artesanos, an official body that sought to reactivate the figure of the artisan within the horizon of national aggrandizement. Through both sections, however, we will see that what was often at stake in discussions regarding the figure of the artisan was not simply the question of labor, but the expansion of capitalism and its concomitant ethics, as well as the matter of the modernization of customs.

INDUSTRIALIZATION AND PERPETUAL DEVELOPMENT (1830–1846)

The relationship between Lucas Alamán, Estevan de Antuñano, and Mexico's artisans was, to say the least, adversarial. The two men represented, for many, not only the elite class interests that sought to erase the principles of popular sovereignty that had given the artisan its voice, but also the economic and political forces that wanted to displace artisan labor and its forms of life so as to bring about a modernized system of mechanized industry and unqualified labor. Both men were participants—intentionally for Alamán, unintentionally for Antuñano—in the Thermidorian reaction of the decade. Alamán and Antuñano were protagonists in the narrative of Mexico's first industrialization. As per the context, by industrialization, Alamán, Antuñano, and their contemporaries meant the development and mechanization of the cotton textile industry. Taking advantage of the political power granted by the centralism of the administration that ousted (and, soon after, executed) Guerrero, Alamán and Antuñano worked toward the articulation of the economic imaginaries of independence with a new language of capitalist modernization and technology absent before their interventions. Like Ortiz de Ayala, studied in Chapter 1, both Alamán and Antuñano were more than mere ideologues. Both were personally and financially invested in the transformation and mechanization of Mexican manufacture. As Charles Hale once put it, "[a]s men of enterprise, [Alamán and Antuñano] were closer to the continental type of the aristocratic entrepreneur, in contrast with the English industrialist who typically formed part of a new social class, having few ties to land, family traditions, or to older activities like mining."[17] More explicitly than any of the figures we have seen in this book, throughout the 1830s and 1840s, these men would argue that in order for Mexico to be truly autonomous, the nation had to be economically independent, and such independence was only possible through the enjambment of national aggrandizement and what they held was the "perpetual development" of capitalist technology.

Lucas Alamán (1792–1853) was one the most influential Mexican statesmen of the first half of the nineteenth century. Remembered as a conservative reactionary, as an accomplice in the execution of President Vicente Guerrero, as founder of the Conservative Party (1849), as a foremost historian, and a latter-day monarchist, he was also the main supporter and ideologue behind Mexico's first industrialization. As we will see, it was Alamán who inaugurated the argument according to which Mexican autonomy depended not simply on the recognition of foreign governments, but on the economic independence of the territory—an independence that was only possible through industrialization. The argument was not simple dogma. It was the spirited drive behind a dramatic change in policy that survived his administration and remained influential until the US invasion in 1846. Alamán would not be alone in his industrial pursuits and aspirations. His associate, Estevan de Antuñano (1792–1847) was to modern industry what Tadeo Ortiz de Ayala was to colonization. The self-avowed father of Mexican industry, Antuñano was, in his own time, Mexican modernization's organic intellectual. He emerged somewhat suddenly at the beginning of the 1830s as an idiosyncratic spokesperson for many of Alamán's policies and began to preach for the need of an industrial transformation of the nation. Antuñano penned dozens of pamphlets and articles to this end, while at the same time investing all of the financial resources he had accumulated into his own industrial enterprises. The inauguration of his La Constancia Mexicana, Mexico's first water-driven cotton mill, made possible by Alamán, only confirmed Antuñano's centrality. Unlike Alamán, who largely ignored the contempt he generated among artisans and other opponents, Antuñano believed that animosity to be unwarranted, and saw himself as one of the few individuals capable of guaranteeing the industrial survival of the artisan. Yet, for him, in order to save the artisan, it was necessary to remove him from the center of industrial production.

ECONOMIC INDEPENDENCE AND ALAMÁN'S INDUSTRIALIZATION

Between 1830 and 1845, either as Ministro de Relaciones or Director General of Industry, Lucas Alamán delivered six reports ("Memorias") to the nation's legislative authorities. These reports gave extended accounts of the economic life of the territory and recorded his observations, expectations, and industrial designs. Beyond Alamán's tenure in power, these reports were widely influential, and served as the lodestar for Mexico's early industrialization. Precisely because of their depth and reach, a reader might be struck, though, by the gaping absence of the artisan. When the figure was indeed mentioned, Alamán mostly referred to foreign technicians and machinists involved in the establishment of modern industry.[18] On the rare occasions he specifically addressed the Mexican artisan, he did so negatively, gesturing not at an industrious figure, but at a problem; a figure qualified not by the nature of his labor, but by his condition, whether "unemployed" or "miserable," always the future object of state action.[19] In contrast, men employed in modern factories, mentioned as sparsely, but in a descriptive and unqualified manner, Alamán called *jornaleros*; that is, wage-workers. By a writer as careful as Alamán, the language was not accidental. It buttressed the displacement of the artisan not only from Mexico's industrial future, but from the political language itself. Wage-labor, for Alamán, was certainly understood as in Marx; that is, as the productive relationship between the free, unqualified labor of man and the freed, undifferentiated wealth that made of rich men, capitalists. The wage relation was the tool for the formal subsumption of both into the capitalist mode of production. Wage labor was not simply an economic relation, though, as we will see. Both Alamán and Antuñano believed it also served as a police mechanism, and as a technology capable of modernizing the customs of the people. Granted, in Alamán's reports, the wage worker was not even close to being a protagonist of economic discourse and played a minor role. If there was a subject implied in the narrative that wove together Alamán's six reports, a narrative of the quest for economic independence and industrialization, it was most certainly not an individual; it was the state, conceived of as an active and centralized government, moved by its self-serving logics.

For Alamán, the only way Mexico could be truly independent— economically independent—was through industrialization, the basic conditions for which were, unfortunately, unavailable. The obstacles that hindered the technological transformation of Mexican labor, in Alamán's 1830 report as Ministro de Relaciones Interiores y Exteriores, were of economic and cultural nature; one had to do with policy, the other with police. On the one hand, the "purely prohibitive system" of previous administrations did nothing to foster the material conditions necessary for industrial success; namely, capital investment and adequate machinery.[20] For Alamán, the first decade of independence, plagued as it had been by administrative disorder and political restlessness, had exhausted international goodwill and the credit extended upon independence by foreign governments in general, and British investors in particular, and had led to the decapitalization of the national economy—worsened by the expulsion of what wealthy Spanish population remained in 1829—and the mishandling of government revenue.[21] This circumstance made it impossible for private individuals, if they were so inclined, to access the necessary money markets to cover the high front-end costs of establishing a machine-powered modern factory. On the other hand, the local population was deemed lacking. The underpopulation of the territory undercut the labor market from which such factories were supposed to recruit their workforce. This lack of a reserve army of labor was further undermined by the relationship between local custom and the two more readily available "industries," mining and agriculture.[22] Mexican laborers, Alamán believed, would be scared away by the intensity of factory work, seeing as they could otherwise "find their subsistence more easily," whether in agriculture or in mining, both blessed by the fertility of the land. Surely, he wrote, "whoever can extract silver directly [from the land], does not occupy himself in doing other things through which he can procure it."[23] That is, reproducing older tropes, Alamán suggested that the ease with which nature provided the possibility of plenitude led to a decline in work-effort, which in turn affected industrial development because it thinned the available workforce and led to a lack of demand and consumption of local products, which consequently weakened internal markets.[24]

Matters of the economy and the population, of policy and police, were not strangers to each other, as we have seen already. In fact, such questions fell directly under the purview of the Secretaría de Relaciones Interiores y Exteriores (Ministry of Interior and Exterior Relations), which Alamán helmed. The Secretaría was charged not only with the nation's diplomatic apparatus and trade policies, but also with questions of internal affairs such as "public tranquility," local militias, freedom of press, the population's mobility through the granting of passports, economic prosperity, health, local governance, and the education system, among others. Later, when he returned to political office in the 1840s, under the auspices of Santa Anna's dictatorship (1841–44), he would occupy an equally powerful position as Director General of Industry. Between the 1830s and the 1840s, then, Alamán would take advantage of these bureaucratic offices and their capacity to intervene in the social fabric to override said obstacles. From both positions, he would insist that the industrialization of Mexico should not be neglected, even if it seemed to face unsurmountable challenges. For Alamán, a show of administrative strength was necessary. It was not simply a matter of preference, but of survival. He wrote that "[a] people must have in mind not to depend on others for anything that is essential to subsist, and therefore, legislative measures must have as their object the provision of what is lacking, while following the gradual order that facilitates everything."[25]

Alamán's idea of economic independence sent shockwaves through the Creole elites. In one fell swoop, it broke with what had been taken as economic dogma since the establishment of the Republic; that is, the idea that to be economically independent meant to participate as an independent nation in the free, global market and to thus enter in direct relation with other free nations in a constant and persistent exchange which, through competition, fostered development and improvement. Despite his critics, Alamán did not oppose international markets—he was a protectionist, not a prohibitionist—and, as his Banco de Avío proposal proved, his plan for the industrialization of Mexico depended precisely on the taxation of imports, not on their elimination. Against the position of many merchants and liberals, who fashioned policy inspired by Ricardian concepts of comparative advantage, the ability to produce goods that other nations could not, Alamán's developmentalism echoed what in the twentieth century would come to be called import substitution industrialization, the concerted effort to use trade policies, national loans, and subsidies to create internal markets and develop self-sufficiency. Alamán's narrative of economic independence was, on the one hand, a call for a coherent and cohesive national program of economic development. It insisted on the active guidance of such development by a rational and powerful central state—granted, one which was under his sway—free from the influence of agiotistas and the compulsion of regional merchants. On the other, it was an attempt to rethink and re-articulate the economic life of the territory after what he believed had been the decadence of the first post-independence decade. Surely, a corollary of this narrative was the implication that post-independence governments—Iturbide's Mexican Empire and the federated republic of the 1824 constitution—had cut ties with Spain only to submit the nation to new albeit informal masters. Ultimately, for Alamán, industrialization would not only, with time, invigorate and guarantee the national economy vis-à-vis regional and international interests, it would also effectively transform the territory and serve as an instrument to improve its population and guarantee political stability.

Alamán's program of industrialization was a response to the economic history of the previous decade. His reports as Ministro de Relaciones between 1830 and 1832 contrast with those he delivered during the Republic's inaugural years in 1823–25, when he first occupied the office. For the Alamán of the early 1820s, Mexico's economic future had depended on the rehabilitation of the mining industry. He explained, "[m]ines are the source of the true wealth of this nation, and everything that speculative economists have said against this axiom has been victoriously rebutted by experience. Thus, we have constantly seen agriculture, commerce and industry follow the progress of mining, progressing with them and decaying in the same proportion."[26] The centrality of mining to the territory had been an item of faith for many members of the Creole elites. During the second half of the eighteenth century, silver had made the Bajío—the lowlands of Central Mexico—the richest and most economically dynamic region of the Americas and had fueled global trade all the while incentivizing commercial cultivation and textile production, and leading these to their historic peaks.[27] Alamán himself came from a dynasty that owed its wealth to that silver boom, and so his early policy and economic thought had revolved around this idea of the necessary recuperation of the silver economy. As a young minister in 1823–25, he had little reason to question the belief that mining was the natural industry of the land. In fact, he had argued that, precisely because of the profligacy of the territory and the ease with which the minerals could be extracted, the mining economy, unlike others, presented the benefit that it called for the employment of a massive workforce to cover all the stages of its production, from extraction, to refining and transportation.[28] Thus, in the aftermath of independence, he had believed that a reasonable return to a silver economy was necessary for the aggrandizement of the new nation. Mining had been and should continue to be the engine of the territory economy. Unfortunately for the Alamán of the 1820s, despite his dealings as Minister and his early successes in recruiting

British finance and capitalists to, first and foremost, fund the federal government, and, secondly, to revive parts of the mining industry, the prosperity of yore did not follow. At a national level, old mining regions like Guanajuato, devastated by the insurgency and civil war, did not flourish for decades, while the ones that did manage to recuperate in the mid-to-late 1820s, like Zacatecas, retained their revenues in local treasuries, out of reach of the federal government, unlike in the past.[29] This incapacity of the government to access revenue, whether from mining, taxes, or customs, aggravated the already tenuous reality of the federal treasury. The funds loaned by the British to the first republican government, through Alamán's efforts, were quickly exhausted and soon became delinquent, pushing the nation to the brink of bankruptcy. At an international level, the multipolar commercial capitalism that had preceded the nineteenth-century, of which Mexico's silver capitalism had been an essential part, collapsed between 1790 and 1825, pressured by international wars, regional revolutions, internal territorial strife, challenges to the sugar and slave economies, and the emergence of England as an industrial, mechanized powerhouse.[30] This reorganization of the capitalist world system led to the concentration of power and production in the hands of the British (and later other nations of Western Europe and Northeastern North America) and the constriction of the rest of the world to the role of suppliers of raw materials.

By the time he returned to power in the 1830s, Alamán found a state mired in penury, indebted to local *agiotistas* (speculators, usurers) and the British institutions he himself had once upon a time called on. The narrative of economic independence offered itself as the symbolic alternative to the discourse of recuperation (of the silver economy) he, like many others, had espoused in the immediacy of the territory's separation from Spain. Alamán accepted the irretrievability of a silver economy as a national horizon and, concerned about a fraying social fabric that tended toward political conflict, proposed mechanized industry as an alternative around which to build a national economy. In the 1830s and 1840s, Alamán would come to argue that the modern factory was meant to occupy the place left vacant by the eighteenth-century mining industry, and like the latter, it would serve as the material support for the articulation of a new, industrial sociality. What mining and industry had in common, unlike agriculture, was that they were generative matrices; that is, in order for either to be successful, they had to develop a whole apparatus of adjacent industries. He wrote, "one of the great benefits produced by industry's progress is to relate all branches [of the economy] to each other, to make profitable for one what was lost for the others, and to give value even to the most despicable things."[31] Yet, modern industry was superior to mining. For Alamán, industrial labor and production liberated the economic life of the nation from its subjection to nature. That is, whereas mining "does not depend on the will of man" and was, instead, dictated by and limited to nature in its quantity and location, modern factories were of "perpetual duration" and, thus, provided the other branches of the economy with "permanent development [fomento permanente]."[32] In other words, Alamán distanced himself from the physiocratic dispositions of certain strands of the economic imaginaries of the period—embodied, as we have seen, in figures like Ortíz de Ayala. For Ortíz de Ayala, but also for the many liberals who espoused versions of comparative advantage, there was a providential aspect to a nation's economic activity, predetermined by the abundance of particular natural resources. In Alamán's telling, modern industry, by its very essence, liberated the economic aggrandizement of a nation from these impositions. Mechanized factories, established by men of means when and where they pleased, promised a form of unlimited production that required neither a particular environment nor constant technological upgrade. They simply required an increase of labor in the form of the number of hours worked.[33]

Economic independence through industrialization, then, freed the nation not only from foreign influence but also from natural determination. Alamán's attempt to sever these ties did not represent a denial or lack of adherence to the myth of Mexico's proverbial riches. In fact, industry's "fomento permanente" depended precisely on the profligacy of the land. Alamán's industrialization put Mexico in a different path from other already industrialized nations. Unlike national economies built around a single natural export commodity, or industrial economies that depended on the importation of raw materials, both of whose prosperities were threatened by the very scarcity that generated their wealth, a national economy built upon the permanent engine of mechanized industry, fed by the territory's proverbial wealth, with its unlimited potential, was capable of grafting itself into the inherent temporality of modern technology and guarantee economic growth's "perpetual duration." For the fate of the artisan within this machinery of permanent production, let us now turn to Antuñano.

ANTUÑANO, ARTISAN PLIGHT, AND TECHNOLOGICAL REPLACEMENT

As we have just seen, the displacement of the artisan in Alamán was affirmed through omission. Estevan de Antuñano, however, never one for subtleties, put it front and center. The Antuñano of the 1830s, who indirectly served as idiosyncratic publicist for Alamán's industrialization projects, was certain about one thing: the economic aggrandizement of Mexico required the technological replacement of artisan labor. Yet, before going on the offensive, Antuñano celebrated artisan tradition. In his first big foray into the public sphere, 1833's *Manifiesto del Algodón*, he affirmed the historical tenacity of the Mexican artisan. Artisan labor, he wrote, was responsible for Puebla's historical fame and wealth. Up until 1810, before Hidalgo's insurgency spread through the territory, "Puebla's artisans enjoyed a long age of employment [ocupación] and all the happiness, [theirs was a situation] compatible with the state of colonos; [that is, they had] enough [work] to keep usefully busy, and an abundance of money."[34] According to Antuñano, this period of industrial plenitude, which lasted for at least a century, was a testament to the ingenuity of the artisan class, who had flourished not because of Spain, but despite its metropolitan burdens. Puebla's artisan genius had been such that, at its height, its production had not only satisfied local demand, but managed to profitably export its surplus to the Internal Provinces (the northern frontiers of New Spain, Sonora and Sinaloa, Nueva Vizcaya, the Californias, New Mexico, New Santander, León, Coahuila, and Texas; today Southwestern United States), and to other American territories, such as Perú and Guayaquil. Unfortunately, in 1833, at the time of writing, what little remained of this splendor, could not "be considered but as the scattered fragments of a great building, and an honorary monument to the ingenuity of the people of Puebla."[35] Taking up a prophetic mode that would soon after become part of his rhetorical repertoire, he noted: "It seems that the Almighty, knowing the future, wanted to end all that was old in our customs and understandings, to dress us in new clothes, clothes that were analogous to the great role that we were to play from the time of regeneration, which was already near."[36]

To be clear, Antuñano did not believe that the 1810 War of Independence, fought by many "weavers who, throwing aside the tools of their trade, embraced the rifle, induced by a fanatical enthusiasm that blinded them," was directly to blame for Puebla's decadence.[37] For Antuñano, the Grito de Dolores had been the beginning of an awakening. Before it, he believed that "because we knew little, there was little we desired, we lived contently, confined to a sphere of half light, comfortable in our fanaticism and our scarce knowledge about the generality of the sciences and the arts.[38]" Thankfully, independence—and this meant Iturbide's independence of 1821—had "removed their cataracts" and made it possible to see that what they had taken for industrial glory in the viceregal past had been a mirage. Puebla's splendor was surely to be celebrated, he held, but the truth of the matter was that the very same artisan success he applauded had been accomplished within and because of an "unnatural" system that had limited competition and had kept Mexicans ignorant of the latest developments of industrial technologies. That is, the wealth and plenitude brought about by the artisan guild had been the tainted and unnatural harvest of an oppressive and despotic system. In Antuñano's view, this was the reason why, as the Spanish Empire fell apart and Mexican independence coalesced, the natural regime of the free market ravaged the territory's industry—and Puebla's in particular. Cheaper and better industrial products, hailing from Europe, flooded Mexican markets, "and made beggars of our artisans, who less skilled, could not preserve their existence, already miserable."[39]

Antuñano echoed the artisan's plight, to a degree. While the first independent governments had understood that Mexican industry (and agriculture) were unprepared to compete, and had, thus, tried to rescue national production through prohibitionist measures, these had ultimately been empty gestures. As many defenders of the artisan had argued, politicians had been short-sighted and had subsequently allowed exceptions, created loopholes, and granted concessions to the great merchants. Assailed by cheaper products from abroad, the local workforce "had lost the hope of finding useful employment, and of escaping their misery; and the people as a whole, the hope of prospering."[40] That said, Antuñano believed that insisting on protectionist measures was only half the battle. There was another truth that had to be accepted, however hard it might be: "[t]he ancient way of spinning and weaving is incompatible with the liberal institutions of the nation and therefore rationally impracticable, and it is also at odds with the policy that should be observed with friendly powers, and proper decorum."[41] He continued: "Mexico is now independent and free, and it is powerful and rich, due to the abundance of its soil, and the courage and ingenuity of its children: it has entered the rank of a civilized nation, and it must adorn itself with the clothes that correspond to it, or risk contempt and perhaps slavery."[42]

Mexico, for Antuñano, was caught in a death spiral. In the *Manifesto*, he diagnosed the 1830s as follows:

> the only and true reason for our misery, for our scant enlightenment and for our domestic dissensions [is] the lack of useful employment for the majority of Mexicans [which results from the fact] that everything has to come from outside, nothing has to been made here. There being no useful employment [ocupación], how are there to be profits? Without these, whence abundance?

> Whence marriages? Without these, whence population? Whence virtues? Whence peace? Whence national strength? . . . Necessity breeds all vices; she is the legitimate daughter of idleness; thus, as long as there are unemployed men in Mexico, we will not be able to get out of the pitiful state that are are now.[43]

In other words, Antuñano narrowed Mexican economic despondence down to one factor: that the industrial products consumed by most Mexicans were not locally produced. As a result of this disposition toward foreign goods, there was a lack of employment in industrial production, which led to the unemployment of this same majority. Lacking a steady income, in turn, this population could not afford current industrial products made locally (in artisan workshops, which employed some of the population) and were forced to purchase cheaper, imported products, thus speeding the spiraling to the point that it threatened the very life of the citizenry and the republic's survival. For Antuñano, there was only one competitive and realistic way to interrupt this degenerative cycle: the nation would have to do away with the traditional artisan workshop and its expensive products, and establish modern, mechanized factories to produce affordable alternatives.

Artisans opposed this solution, Antuñano acknowledged, because these mechanized factories merely brought home the threat that haunted them from the outside and because every machine capable of mass-producing their handicrafts represented the progressive disentailment of their labor.[44] Antuñano did not deny any of these allegations. They were true. Whatever was left of the traditional workshop survived not because of artisan labor, he argued, but despite it. Should a republican government privilege the well-being of a small workforce of weavers and threaders over the plight of masses of citizens who suffer abject poverty? Antuñano raised this question in his *Manifiesto*, and then dramatized it in the *Ampliación*, published the same year and geared toward a popular audience. For Antuñano, the republican context in which the very asking of the question was possible suggested that the only answer that could be given was negative. The question furthered his emphasis on the anachronistic nature of both artisan production and artisan discourse. The plight of artisans appealed to a form of government that, in 1833, was long gone. The only tenable republican position was to put the interest of the many over the few and, so, to turn to the technological transformation of industry to provide for its polity. By its very nature, modern production faced the masses. Modern factories employed multitudes. They also made possible the low prices that improved the livelihood of all, including the "more than three hundred thousand" peasants that, earning so little, had to sacrifice a significant portion of their earnings, which is not even enough to feed them properly, to clothe themselves.[45]

Artisan opposition to technological improvement was illogical, too, held Antuñano in the *Ampliación*. In their contempt for machinery, artisans ignored the fact that their workshops already depended on technology that, once upon a time, had been new and had displaced the indigenous *otate*, a former instrument which they now considered obsolete. Antuñano seemed to argue that, in their ignorance, artisans had forgotten that their whole identity and form of life had been formed under the auspices of a new technology that displaced old instruments.[46] Would the craftsman, then, in his rejection of progress, prefer to return to the former method? Industrial backtracking would lead to the disappearance of many goods demanded by the present market, because the technology in question was incapable of their production. "A man could work until he bursts day and night and would never be able to get out of his underwear and camisa de manta. No, sirree, it would be nonsense to go back to the times of the gentiles," riposted Antuñano's fictionalized artisan.[47] In the face of modern technology, artisan instruments were now as antiquated as the *otates* had been in the past, and as incapable of satisfying the needs and demands of the present moment. Were all modern industrial product banished from Mexico, artisan production "would not be enough because there are many new objects to be desired, and that have already formed a need in us."[48] The mere expression of these anti-modern concerns externalized a larger problem, one that had to do with customs' belatedness, with "the mark of despotism that has not yet been erased for those of us who were born under his empire."[49] We will turn to this point later, but in the mean time, let us go back to Antuñano's quarrel regarding artisan technology. In his *Ampliación*, the industrialist stopped short of drawing out the logical conclusion of his arguments: that if the artisan workshop had always had technology at its center, the celebrated fact of qualified labor had always been but supplementary to a process dictated by state policies and market forces that had led to Spanish adoption of handlooms in the first place. All industry, all labor, had technology as its axis, Antuñano implied. Modernization, in that sense, was synonymous to the progressive development of technology, a development that was constitutive and subjectivizing.

Without much subterfuge, Antuñano argued that his factories would improve the industry of artisans through the destruction and replacement of their means of production. Surely, he suggested, the replacement would be progressive, and it would give master-artisans and workshop owners time to adapt. In the *Manifiesto*, he reminded his readers that the three or four factories that he had established or proposed were not enough to meet the whole nation's needs and demands, as many believed. For a time, modern machines would co-exist with the artisan workshop. The complete transformation of the nation would need, at the very least, three hundred factories to meet existing demand.[50] Antuñano estimated the process would take between six and eight years. First, early adopters (his factories, in particular) would have to prove themselves to be successful, so that their example and profits incite new capitalists to invest in similar enterprises and, only then, the nation would reap "an abundant patrimony."[51] This period of adaptation, he explained in the *Ampliación*, would give artisans the opportunity to accept the necessity of modernization, upgrade their own instruments and, so, transform their workshops. Either way, the result was the same: in time, former artisans would benefit from their work in factories and their lifestyles would improve. More importantly, so would the lives of "thousands" of unemployed citizens who suffered because of the burdensome reality that there were not enough productive opportunities available for the masses—a lack of opportunities that artisan workshops were incapable of satisfying.[52] The benefits would also trickle down to the peasantry, seeing as

> a million people would have to be employed in cultivating [cotton], and this number of citizens would directly have a more comfortable life: they would advance the education of their children, and from there, the nation would earn the goods it lacks; public benefit would keep on growing; our coastal population would be busy in the cultivation of this plant; and many would be enriched directly by these enterprises . . . and, we would reach the height of power, of wealth, of happiness.[53]

The *Manifiesto* summarized the author's position in one of the many slogans he would go on to pen, forever the businessman: "To new times, new customs."[54] The "clothes" and "customs" that corresponded a free, independent nation, for Antuñano, were those cut in what, referring to factories, he called "the modern style" (estilo moderno).[55] By the "modern style" of factory, he meant a factory structured not around the qualified labor of the artisan, but around the limitless potential of modern technology. Put simply, for Antuñano, the means of industrial production in Mexico—the artisan workshop— were at odds with the rising tide of the world economy, which called for the wholesale adoption of properly capitalist enterprise. This adoption would lead to nothing short of an industrial regeneration. The modern style would not simply modernize the industrial process, but, with time, it would lead to a transformation of the very customs of the Mexican polity. Industrial, technological modernization would inevitably lead to the production of a new, modern worker; one constituted by the capitalist social relation and, as such, inherently productive.

CUSTOMS IN THE AGE OF ANTUÑANO'S MECHANICAL PRODUCTION

In the following years, Antuñano would insist that the removal of the artisan from the center of the means of production never entailed the erasure of the worker. In a very strong sense, the worker continued to be at the heart of his concerns. When he wrote "To new times, new customs," he referred to both the means and practices of industrial production in the nation, as well as the customs and habits of the people.[56] For Antuñano, a polity's production was commensurate with its material state. Thus, because the instruments "that Mexicans use for production are scarce and dull, it corresponds that their state is likewise poor."[57] This state was worsened by the fact that "the healthiest and most important elements of the people [preserves] always those customs that the colonial system gave them," and, as such, it was up to legislators and industrialists to "improve customs to bring them to the level of our admirable institutions."[58] The quickest avenue, then, for the improvement of the masses' customs was the adoption of modern, mechanical factories. Such factories were the most adequate measures to "civilize and unite our classes, as required by our system."[59]

Without a doubt, all labor was positive and moralizing. Antuñano recognized the importance of agricultural production in this sense, but believed industrial labor to be superior. "[I]nsofar as the arts' operations are softer than agriculture's," he wrote, "they moderate the character of man."[60] Unlike the peasant, who works the fields either by himself or along others like him, the factory floor necessarily called for the cohabitation of social classes, of the worker and the enlightened administrator, and this intermingling was beneficial for the latter because of the availability of a model and a figure capable of disciplining him.[61] Moreover, the machine itself worked on its operator in that "to run smoothly in their progressive operations, [machines] allow neither delays nor distractions."[62] Structurally, factories were places idleness was impossible and workers were incapable of separating from their tasks. Modern industry, for Antuñano, refined workers at every level by virtue of its operations, organization, and instruments. By removing the instrument from the artisan's hand, the modern factory effectively reversed the hierarchy, putting the artisan in the modern instrument's gear, and, so, the artisan was transformed into the collateral production of the industrial process; a production which was essential for the industrial regeneration of Mexico preached by Antuñano.

Antuñano's industrial regeneration did not only depend on the subsumption and transformation of artisan labor. True aggrandizement entailed the democratization of employment. When Antuñano celebrated modern machinery's capacity to employ the poor masses of the nation, he did not simply mean unemployed artisans, or even men. By replacing "qualified labor," machinery effectively made possible the formal subsumption of the whole population into the workforce. As Antuñano noted, "machines, to work well, do require neither too much learning nor, commonly, too much force."[63] That is, machines were indifferent to the worker's specificity, be it skill, background, gender, or age. The industrialization of Mexico, then, expanded the definition of, and made possible for the first time, the republic of labor that so many had preached. Through technology, such a republic would be one in which all were usefully and productively occupied, be them men, women, or even children. An effect of this democratization, for Antuñano, was the capitalist's potential co-optation of extra-economic social relations. In his 1837 pamphlet, *Ventajas políticas, civiles, fabriles y domésticas que dar ocupación tambien a las mugeres en las fábricas de maquinaria moderna* (Political, Civic, Industrial and Domestic Advantages gained through the Occupation of Women in Modern Factories), the expansion of the laboring body's definition meant, first and foremost, the productivization of the family unit qua unit within the factory. To this end, Antuñano argued for the benefits such a move would reap both the worker as well as the factory owner. On the one hand, if every member of a household was gainfully employed in a modern factory, their general well-being, economic security, and prosperity would increase in that they would all be earning a wage, which in turn benefited the nation as a whole. On the other, "[o]nce all the individuals of a family are put in a factory, utility mandates that, although made up of small portions, [profit] grows without having to increase individual wages, [and, in turn] this will result in that the [cheapness] of the workforce of our factory will protect us from the ruin that industry [as a whole] is exposed to by having to be put on a stricter budget [because of higher wages]."[64] In other words, by hiring entire family units, made up of men, women, and children, and paying each the going rates, which were lower for women and children according to Antuñano's appendix to the pamphlet, a factory owner made significant savings while populating his workforce.

These economic benefits, however, were not necessarily at the center of the pamphlet. As its title preached, the advantages yielded by such practices were, first of all, political and civic, and only then industrial and domestic. For the industrialist, "everything directed to the instilling of good morality on workers, is immediately opportune for civil and religious morality, for industry in general, and for the owners of the establishments."[65] As he would go on to show, the inclusion of the family unit into the means of production brought with it the extra-economic ties and duties that bind husbands to wives and parents to children. It made these ties productive for everyone involved. Keeping a family united in the factory floor meant an added layer of discipline and moral surveillance. Antuñano wrote, for example, that "employing women also [in the factory] yields the advantage that the males are more subjected to the place and to their civil, industrial and domestic obligations."[66] If the father of a family were tempted to abandon his post, his wife and children, interested in keeping their own jobs, would "contain him." The same would happen to children who were normally exposed to "becoming lost" (extraviarse) and neglecting their duties when their parents were at work; now at their side and busy, those risks would be lessened. Women would also benefit. If something were to happen to their husbands, they would not be left despondent, having both their own wage and their children to sustain the household. Moreover, employment would remove young women from the danger they were exposed to at their own home, where they would otherwise be idle and alone. Nothing would be safer than spending the day "in a busy place under the sight of her relatives and cared for by the factory administrators and master-craftsmen, who commonly have to be people of judgment."[67]

In all of these calculations, Antuñano took into account the fact that modern factories like his own were usually established outside the large urban populations from where its workforce originated. It was logical, for him, that capitalists should provide housing so as to attempt to shorten or eliminate the commute, full of risks. An added benefit would be that the line between household and workplace would be blurred. This indifferentiation of the spheres became easier once the family unit as a whole was transported to the new location. The proximity not only eliminated the temptations and dangers of life in urban centers, but also allowed for a better control of the workforce. It also promised a small profit for capitalists. Once a whole family was employed and residing in factory housing, the capitalist could conveniently charge them a moderate rent. In other circumstances this would have negatively affected the livelihood of a worker by draining their already low wages. Yet, in the new context of the modern factory the expense would not be as resented because the family unit depended on more than one wage.[68] Ultimately, Antuñano wrote, "[t]he more resources these people have to subsist," the more likely was that they would improve their habits, their health, and decorum; and "the less they are likely to steal, which has been frequent in our workplaces. It is easier to avoid this vice, as well as drunkenness, in people located near the factory."[69]

La Constancia Mexicana, Antuñano's main factory, was held up as a model of the "ostensible benefits that are already being produced for the general industry and public morality."[70] In any given moment, a visit to the establishment would give testament to the three hundred Mexicans it employed, split between day shifts and night shifts, all of whom "gladly go to work, even on holidays: drunkenness and robbery have been banished from that mansion; all people are willing, and are completely free to enjoy themselves after working hours: new habits are becoming established, such as cleanliness on holidays and a dignified character.[71] He added: "[T]he workers of La Constancia Mexicana are giving the lie to all of those accusations which are rendered on the Mexican character."[72] La Constancia's benefits went well beyond the factory workers themselves. By selling its produced fabric directly to artisan workshops and, directly buying their products when made, La Constancia guaranteed employment to the suffering artisan workshops of Puebla. He estimated that "more than four hundred families in Puebla and other localities find their subsistence through knitting the thread produced by La Constancia."[73] Beyond Puebla's neighboring regions, La Constancia also spurred a cotton plantation in Veracruz from where Antuñano got most of his primary materials, and the twenty families that cultivated cotton there. All in all, he surmised, if one counted its own workers, the carpenters and blacksmiths that built the buildings, the artisans that bought their fabric, the peasants that grew and worked the cotton, those involved in the transportation of goods to and from its premises, etcetera, more than fifteen thousand people were benefited at any moment by La Constancia's activity.[74] In short, La Constancia, like all future modern factories, was an engine of production, both of profit and customs. By putting the machine at the center, the industrialist managed to insert men in an endless chain of production that, because of its sheer intensity, activated all other national industries, from mining and agriculture to commerce, while at the same time establishing the necessary, economic conditions for the creation of the new customs that a new Mexico called for.

THE STATE, THE BANCO DE AVÍO, AND MODERN PRODUCTION

Later, in an 1844 letter to Alamán, a less exuberant Antuñano spelled out his dream of a perfectly integrated republic of labor, the horizon toward which his existing and working factories were geared. It was a thoroughly modern landscape, one which offered the harmonious and productive articulation of the entrepreneur's projects, nature, mechanic force, and a new Mexican artisan-laborer, one whose life has been wholly channeled into constant, productive activity. He wrote,

> For years I have thought about the establishment of a valley of Mexican industry in the beautiful gorge of more than 9 leagues where, on the banks of the Atoyac River, 9 of my farms (Santo Domingo, La Noria, Cusinaloyan, Apetlachica and La Uranga) stand; such a valley would consist of 10 or 12 factories powered by hydraulics, and 10 or 12 villages of tenant farmers that work the majority of the unoccupied land of said farms, so that having both a place of their own and rural property, [these tenant farmers] would also be the most moral of artisans, alternately attending to the fields and the factories of their demarcation for which effect the towns would be designated in the appropriate way.[75]

Antuñano's frankness was no doubt sincere. But it was also strategic. Like in most pamphlets he wrote, absent in the reverie itself, but framing it, were additional players—the most important of which was the State. The letter's addressee, Alamán, was at that moment serving as Director-General of National Industry (1844–46), a newly minted position that allowed the latter the power to resume the work he had begun as Minister of Relations with the foundation of the Banco de Avío in 1830. The letter to Alamán captured the audacity with which Antuñano had, from the very beginning, voiced his grand, industrial fantasies; and which had garnered him not only fame as an industrialist, but also the state's favor. A second player omitted from the letter, but whose presence was closer to a haunting, was the group of financiers and investors whose loans fueled Antuñano's enterprises, but whose usury, he believed, concomitantly promised their ruin. He would argue, on multiple occasions, that such figures' blind interest in profit disagreed with the ways of modern industry. The payment terms of the loans these financiers gave were too short to account for the particularities of modern industry—the purchase of machinery abroad, its transportation, its establishment, the sourcing of primary materials, etcetera. Even worse, these loans could only be obtained in exchange for collateral in the form of mortgages on real estate, a trend that forced industrialists to necessarily become landowners instead of investing their liquidity on more profitable sectors.[76] This exasperation with financiers emphasized a historical reality: merchants of the period avoided risk and were largely disinterested in "capitalist" enterprises, preferring instead the accumulation of capital through diverse commercial undertakings (proper to a "comprador bourgeoisie"), the extension of short-term credits, speculation with public and private debts, and the purchase and accumulation of land.[77] For Antuñano, then, if there was to be modern industry, the state had to intervene (so as to help industrialists such as him). Otherwise left to its own device, the market would consistently undermine the industrial transformation of Mexico, a transformation which was to bring about, for the first time in its history, as Alamán had proposed, the nation's economic independence.

In Antuñano's view, there was no contradiction between state intervention in this regard and his criticism of artisan glory as having been the product of an unnatural system. The unnatural conditions under which artisans flourished, for Antuñano, had been prohibitionist and, in that sense, profoundly autarkic. Unlike those, the intervention he called for was protectionist, surely, but, more importantly, preparatory. The state's role was simply to set the ground for the implantation of industry, to make up for the colonial isolation which had salted the possibilities of Mexican industry. Against supporters of laissez faire, he held that the market for loans was only free when seen from a distance. In reality, it responded to the established interests of the same powerful Mexico City and Veracruz merchants who benefited from imports and who were unfazed by paeans to national aggrandizement.[78] Even though he did not spell it out, for Antuñano, these merchants were complicit with the continuation of Mexican industrial dependence. In that sense, the merchant-financiers were as marked by despotic conditions of the past as artisans were. The market which they ran had to be replaced, modernized, and rebuilt, because were it for the workings of its invisible hand, no modern factory would ever be established.

Enter Alamán and the Banco de Avío para Fomento de la Industria Nacional (Industrial Development Bank). Antuñano's gospel of the technological transformation of Mexico depended on Alamán's interventions and the larger theoretical framework for industrialization which I addressed earlier. In the broadest of terms, the Banco de Avío was established in 1830 under the aegis of Anastasio Bustamante's government (December 1829–December 1832), an administration intellectually led by Alamán that had come to power by means of force. As Robert Potash has shown, the earliest piece of legislation that made possible the Banco intended the institution to alleviate and assist the small artisan workshop.[79] Yet Alamán, its first director and the administration's ideologue, "acted as if he had been given much larger resources and a specific mandate to carry out the industrialization program" he had presented elsewhere.[80] His 1831 report as Minister of Relations outright denied the significant urban presence of an actually existing artisan (manufacturing) industry, while at the same time seeking to bypass hesitant financiers. In it, Alamán explained that, up to the previous year when his administration created the Bank and other related instruments, government had wavered between policies, more often than not adopting prohibitive measures that, for him, were ultimately pointless. These measures were meant to protect industries by staving off harmful competition, but were incapable of creating them where they were nonexistent—and for Alamán, as we have said above, artisan workshops did not count.[81] Upon coming to office, he wrote, it had been clear to him that "[i]t was therefore necessary to think about the creation of that capital, and apply it to the promotion of industry, giving it the appropriate direction."[82] Moving beyond the letter of the law, but sheltered by its loopholes, Alamán launched his program and only then had Congress ratify it.[83] Thus, a state articulated on the presupposition that the first decade of independence had been excessive in its liberties and its concessions to the popular masses, broke with the laissez-faire practice (if not law) of the preceding period, and acquired "an instrument for influencing the rate and direction of economic development," one whose emphasis on modern manufacture "was a deliberate effort to alter the existing pattern of economic activity."[84] Through the Banco, Alamán's program sought to generate industries, industrialists, venture capital, and an internal market where he believed there were only seedlings. Only by doing this constructive work, would industrialization be possible. In a similar fashion to the import substitution industrialization programs of the twentieth century, the state would tax the imported textiles (made in modern factories abroad) that were drowning artisans, and which made local modern factories untenable, and, thus, raise the funds necessary for the Bank to be able to financially assist—or, more precisely, create—local industrialists.

The Bank was attacked from all flanks. From the more liberal side, it was condemned for opposing the propriety of the free market and for "erecting itself into an inspector general of manufactures."[85] Alamán himself was charged with being a mercantilist, seeking to separate Mexico from the concert of nations.[86] The artisan classes and their benefactors argued the opposite, that the Banco subordinated domestic industry and its workers to the will of international merchants.[87] Alamán ignored these criticisms. According to him, such actions were necessary. Put in a somewhat figurative manner, the Bank allowed for the heavily taxed introduction of the very disease that was wreaking havoc to national industry in a sort of inoculation program that, with time, would create the conditions for the spread of industrial immunity. Surely, artisan workshops would suffer, as they were already suffering from the omnipresence of foreign textiles, but their sacrifice would be worth it because in the meantime the nation would be developing the necessary antibodies to, eventually, stop the reproduction of industrial dependence: a national modern and mechanized factory system.

As mentioned earlier in the chapter, Alamán's role as Minister of Relations of Anastasio Bustamante's government [1830–32] gave him the power to carry out these designs. In its expansive powers, the Secretaría inherited the potential to activate both the modes of Bourbon governance that will be described more thoroughly in Chapter 3, and its concomitant police logic; that is, the Secretaría had the power, on paper at the very least, to deploy the strength of the state so as to administer and police the social realm in the name of public happiness, understood as economic prosperity and political stability. As José Enrique Covarrubias has written, "[i]nstead of submitting its management to the federal and republican spirit of the Constitution [of 1824], which would have implied the public life of institutions," Bustamante's government, led by Alamán, put the emphasis on administration, giving the state the tools to directly engage in the economy.[88] It would be from this very same Secretaría that, in 1834, the expansion of anti-vagrancy policy would be launched, as we will see later in this book. A decade after leaving his post as Minister of Relations, he would return to a position that granted him similar powers as the chief officer of the Director General de Industria Nacional (General Directorate of National Industry, 1840–1842). During his tenure in both positions, and as the main ideologue of the Bustamante regime between 1830 and 1832 and the Santa Anna dictatorship of 1840–1842, Alamán would take advantage of the availability of these bureaucratic instruments and their capacity so as to intervene in the social fabric and, thus, override what he considered were the obstacles to Mexico's modernization.

Lorenzo de Zavala, a politician deeply associated with the populist republican bent of the 1820s, believed the bank to be but "one more instrument created to increase governmental power in the Republic."[89] Alamán would not have denied it. Through these offices, he pushed for the materialization of the governmental reason that had been celebrated by the *Gaceta Imperial* back in 1821. As explained in Chapter 1, in the effervescence of its time, the *Gaceta* had believed that with separation from Spain the territory had begun to witness the birth of an autochthonous *raison d'etat*, one which made of the state—built on the pillars of aggrandizement, police, and international diplomacy—its objective, foundation, and aim. For those early publicists, this *raison d'etat* would finally reactivate and productively organize the population's industry and the territory's abundance in the name of Mexican imperium. For Alamán, that dream had gone unrealized, as confirmed by the fall of Iturbide and his Mexican Empire and the eventual downturn of the Federal Republic. From the point of view of Alamán and other members of the Bustamante's reactionary regime, that *raison d'etat* had increasingly been made impossible by the federation as a form of government and the stubbornness of the particular interests of the regions, as well as by their commitment to the abstractions of popular sovereignty and the concrete forms it took—populism, demagoguery, and what they saw as the tyranny of the majority. When they decided to overthrow Vicente Guerrero in 1829, they did so to take control of "the abandoned machine of the state," in the words of José Maria Tornel, so as to revive it and give it the (centralist) authority that it had lacked.[90]

Once in power, Alamán could deploy his office and its institutions in the name and benefit of a state whose sole interest was its own existence as the vehicle for its aggrandizement and public happiness. It was an active state, subjected to neither the will of nature—remember that industrial manufacture, for Alamán, freed man from merely exploiting what was given to him—nor its constituencies, which would have forced the administration to listen to the plight of the artisan. Had it been for Alamán, and had Congress been more lenient, the Banco would have gone beyond its main role as a financing and incentivizing operation to becoming a state trust and holding company, launching its own enterprises, managing its own factories, etcetera.[91] Be that as it may, for Alamán's industrial designs to be successful in the long term, the state needed entrepreneurs. Alamán's echoed the figure proposed by Ortiz de Ayala in 1822, discussed in Chapter 1, despite the marked differences between the two men, especially in matters of philosophical commitments. Ortiz de Ayala was nominally a liberal, whereas Alamán was not, but Ortiz de Ayala's empresario was a private citizen who served as the state's enlightened intermediary (in colonization projects) and who ultimately depended on a strong government's policing of the people and the territory. The same could be said of Alamán's. Alamán was surely unfazed by the anxieties Ortiz de Ayala's empresario had generated among members of the first Constituent Congress, who believed the figure was charged with an inordinate amount of power over his subalterns in regions out of the reach of the State. In fact, as we will see later, Alamán expected the industrial entrepreneur to take an active role in the shaping of the lives of others. Interestingly, the figure of the individual industrialist or entrepreneur, in 1830s Mexico, did not generate the gravitational pull that a figure such as the colono did. Antuñano was surely celebrated and recognized as its personification, but he remained an idiosyncratic figure, influential but not paradigmatic. In this, Ortiz de Ayala and Alamán also differed. While Ortiz de Ayala stressed the individual entrepreneur (whether it was an actual individual or a corporation), Alamán was more interested, in the 1830s, in the formal articulation and association of multiple individual industrial entrepreneurs; on the creation of what eventually, in the following decade, became an industrial lobby. So, from his Ministry in 1830–1832, Alamán invited citizens of means to join together and create stock companies that, organized locally and regionally, could partake in potential industrial ventures across the territory. In this, Alamán was successful, and the effects of such moves would have a greater effect in the following decade. At the time of his 1831 report, he reported the establishment of one such stock company in Mexico City—in which he himself had personally intervened—and shared news of others well on their way in different regions. These others were still in the early stages, he reported, and would require time to raise the necessary funds and be assisted by the Banco de Avío.

Antuñano would be one of the first industrialists supported by the Banco in 1830 and, by the next year, had become one of the institution's priorities. Unlike many of the bank's first investments, which did not pan out, the development of Antuñano's factories showed progress, however slow, from the beginning. His factory, La Constancia Mexicana, would be inaugurated in 1835, and become the first water-driven cotton mill in Mexico, a success for its owner, surely, but also, for the Banco. As Aurora Gómez Galvarriato has noted, Antuñano's mill appeared "around the same time that the Lowell mills were built [in Massachusetts, launching the industrial power of New England], and only twenty years after the first mechanized mill was established in the United States."[92] *La Constancia's* accomplishments launched a veritable growth in industrial enterprises across the territory, which further confirmed Antuñano and Alamán's industrial bets. Before this happened, though, Antuñano had taken up the pen and begun writing. The 1833 pamphlets we have already studied, in which he addressed artisan plight, were, in many ways, a defense of Alamán's designs at a moment when they were under heavy fire. Antuñano's message would largely be consistent through the rest of his life, and, very early on, resulted in the fact that the industrialist became the face of an industrialization program that was, in large part, made possible by Alamán. Antuñano's "purposive energy," as Potash has called it, also had the effect that the Banco and all future administrations continued to privilege his projects, whether they did well or not.[93]

The Banco aspired for 1832 to be the year when the first modern factories would be up and running. But, despite Antuñano's drive and the institution's own push, politics intervened. The Bustamante government had faced consistent military opposition since it rose to power by a revolt of its own in December 1829. In the year 1830, as the bank itself was founded and Alamán's industrial projects began to gain adherents, the government launched and emerged victorious from a military campaign to pacify the territory. The succeeding peace of 1831, of which Alamán and the Bank took advantage, had come at a steep price. Through a conspiracy, the Bustamante government captured Vicente Guerrero, who it had deposed as president, and summarily executed him by firing squad on February 14, 1831.[94] Guerrero's death dissolved what was left of the opposition, but remained a lasting stain not only on the administration's history, but on Lucas Alamán, considered by many to be directly responsible for the decision. For Potash, Guerrero's execution "was a moral and political blunder; it merely numbed the opposition, it did not destroy it. Moreover, the national conscience was shocked that a Mexican government would resort to treachery to destroy this great patriot of independence."[95] So, 1832 saw, instead of the Bank's first industrial success, the fall of the port-city of Veracruz into the hands of the opposition and, with it, the latter's control of the institution's funds, until then safely stored in the city's custom houses. The Bustamante government would hold on to power until December of that year, but Alamán's tenure would end months earlier, in April 1832.

The Banco would survive, though. It would only be dissolved in 1842, after having weathered the fall of Bustamante and Alamán, as well as the next succeeding decade of political instability, spanning nineteen different presidencies and two additional constitutional arrangements. Yet, before that happened, the governments that followed Bustamante's, whether they were ideologically akin or alien, would follow the Banco's lead and continue the implementation of Alamán's plans. Antuñano, as the most visible of the entrepreneurs, would benefit from the Banco during its decade-long activity, and his successes would both remain a testament to Alamán's original proposals as well as launch a wave of industrial manufacture in the territory. In Alamán's absence, Antuñano became the main representative and spokesperson for industry's perpetual development in the 1830s and 1840s. That said, once Bustamante and Alamán were out of the picture, the Banco went from being, in the words of Potash, a "semi-independent agency" to a "consultative body" and lost much of its power, to Antuñano's dismay.[96] Both its projects and its funds would depend on the president, and would be held to the office-holder's whims. In this, it would indeed break with Alamán's designs. For Alamán, the industrialization of the nation held precedence over politics insofar as political independence hinged on the nation's economic independence. The following administrations, more out of historical contingency than ideological positioning, would submit the economic to politics.

THE STATE, THE DIRECCIÓN DE INDUSTRIA, AND THE ECHOES OF BOURBON GOVERNANCE

The Banco's dissolution, though, would not spell the end of Alamán's industrial designs. As soon as the Banco was unmade, it was replaced by the Dirección de Industria Nacional (the Directorate of National Industry). The Dirección was an executive organ established by acting-president Nicolás Bravo on December 2, 1842, which effectively functioned as the Banco's inheritor and its expansion. The Dirección served as an industrial guild, patterned on the organizations of yore, with obligatory membership for owners, managers and administrators of large factories.[97] Technically, it was to be organized across regional Juntas—successors of those originally summoned by the Banco—but directed from Mexico City, with a centralist and vertical bent. Its establishment finalized the articulation between the government, supporters (and debtors) of the Banco, and a private association of large textile manufacturers called the Sociedad para el Fomento de la Industria Nacional (1839–1842; also confusingly called the Junta de Industria). The Sociedad's goal, since its own foundation in 1839, had been to wrest control of industrial economic policy from the hands of a distracted state and, so, take the reins of the industrial development started in the 1830s.[98] The Sociedad's manufacturers had done their share of work to influence the succeeding administrations between 1839 and 1841. In reconstructing its meanderings, Potash has shown how the Sociedad's manufacturers supported Santa Anna "in his bid of power [in 1841], hoping thereby to obtain a government that would be more consistent defender of their interests," and, afterward, acted as if theirs had been the crucial role.[99] They would indeed exert influence over Santa Anna and governmental policy between 1841 and 1846. Yet they never quite managed to override Santa Anna's personal interests and his opposition to the formalization of the Sociedad into an official body. They had to wait for, and take advantage of, Bravo's interim presidency between October 1842 and March 1843 to see their plans realized.

Many of the members of the Sociedad owed their existence, both symbolically and literally—for it had funded their enterprises—to the Banco de Avío, and what they sought through the process of institutionalization was precisely the power to administer industry in a coherent and rational manner, impervious to political whims and tumults. Accordingly, the members of the Sociedad agreed that the best choice for the new role of Director General of National Industry was none other than its mastermind—and member of the Sociedad—Alamán. Through this office, Alamán would continue the work he had begun as Minister of Relations, pushing the industrialization of Mexico as far as it could go. The following year of 1843, in his first report as Director General, a triumphant Alamán celebrated the successes of the associated industrialists. He did so not by celebrating their prowess and spirit of enterprise, but by acknowledging and emphasizing that "these developments, although marvelous, would have been unsustainable, and the fate of Mexican industry uncertain and vacillating, had the individuals who run it remained isolated; if their efforts had not been directed to the same end; put simply, if a corporation had not been formed, that would give them unity and stability."[100] In other words, even as the head of the associated large-scale manufacturers of the territory—and as an entrepreneur himself, having started his own textile factory in the late 1830s— Alamán remained steadfast in his belief that, despite his opponents' paeans to the free market, the agent and subject of industrialization was none other than the state.

John Tutino is right when he writes that "Alamán's nation was led by industrial and landed entrepreneurs, not by villagers, estate tenants, or factory owners."[101] Yet, it is important to emphasize that, while industrial and landed entrepreneurs were indeed the main beneficiaries of Alamán's "nation," its subject and guiding force continued to be the active state modeled on the foundational logics of Bourbon governance. Surely, for Alamán, the state's aggrandizement was isomorphic to industrial and landed entrepreneurial interests. Ultimately, what the leading members of the Sociedad sought, through the creation of the Dirección, was precisely to coalesce each and every industrial enterprise, to allow for their subsumption by the state apparatus so as to function through and be mediated by it, coherently. For Alamán, and by extension for Antuñano and the willingly associated large manufacturers (and those unwilling, too), it was up to the state to guarantee the economic independence of the nation, which could only be carried out through its direct implantation not only of properly capitalist, mechanized industry and its "perpetual duration," but of a market which could, with time, grow an invisible hand.

The Bourbon undercurrents of these ends were made ever more explicit in Alamán's 1845 *Memoria* as Director General of Industry. There, Alamán subscribed a report and recommendation by Pedro García—director of the Junta Industrial of Dolores Hidalgo, in the Department of Guanajuato—in which the latter proposed "compulsory means" to allow for the immediate creation of an internal market capable, in turn, of generating demand for the products of mechanized factories.[102] Before sharing García's proposal, Alamán offered a prologue. He argued, like he had before, that the general prosperity of the nation depended on the creation of a strong internal market (for industrial products). For this to be possible, it was necessary to "introduce habits of greater comfort, and inspire the taste of certain needs and conveniences to the general mass of the population."[103] Again, the obstacle for the implantation of industrial production was of a cultural nature. The creation of taste and desire for comfort among the masses was essential. Seeing as "the social order is a chain in which all the links are intertwined, the improvement of customs that follows from here would promote the arts and farming in a thousand ways, and these, in turn, providing cheaper effects, would facilitate a greater number of enjoyments to that part of society that now lacks them."[104] The question for Alamán, then, was how to go about the creation of this demand, of this cultural change. Antuñano, with his fantasy of factories as republics of labor, had offered a model of how to modernize the customs of a given enterprise's workers. García moved beyond the factory floor and offered an answer for how to affect the whole of society. He confessed that the Junta he represented did not have the necessary knowledge to develop or explain their proposal "with finesse," but decided it would be beneficial to share their ideas.[105] Alamán agreed and reprinted it.

The Junta de Industriales de Dolores Hidalgo's recommendation was simply that "[the lack of consumers] would be overcome by means of a ruling that would force the class that is being talked about [the poor], to appear in public always dressed and in proportion to their faculties, correcting them in some way when they failed to satisfy this precept."[106] In other words, the state could drive the creation of an internal market and of a consumer society by imposing a dress code on the poor, and by punishing any deviance. In the viceregal twilight of the 1810s, José Joaquín Fernández de Lizardi, one of the most important polemicists of the 1810s and 1820s, had insisted on the utility of dress codes in the inculcation of work habits.[107] For Fernández de Lizardi, if all individuals had been made publicly identifiable by their trade through their manner of dress, the problem of the opacity of the social would be solved, and the possibility of vagrancy, idleness, and unproductivity diminished through a combination of shame and enforcement. A dress code, in this sense, had been strictly a matter of police. García's emphasis was, putatively, first and foremost economic. He held that the measure would result in "an expansion of consumption in all classes, which for this reason would nourish the rapid progress of the miserable artisans, who are still very necessary and useful people, whatever state they currently find themselves in."[108] García recognized the viceregal roots of the proposal and acknowledged that "[t]here was a time when the Spanish government provided that the middle class and even the very low class were forced to wear [specific] clothes.[109] He surmised some would inevitably resent such a move by the government, and would object that it was cruel that such a "miserable people" be forced to "incur in an expense that exceeds their capabilities."[110] To these, he replied: "that not all members of the lowest class are as miserable; in fact, there is a large part that manages to save without harming their subsistence, and these even have leftover reales, of which their families only see a small part and which are wasted on vices; seeing themselves forced to purchase the appropriate dress, it would be easy to diminish their crapulous life, and gain moral advantages and comfort."[111] He continued, "fortunately, ours is a docile people; and in a very short time, growing accustomed to comfort and shelter, would soon stop considering this environment oppressive, and would bless the hands that made it possible."[112] That is, for García and the Junta he represented, most members of the "clase ínfima" were in fact working poor and, as such, wage-earners. The proof of such income was none other than the vicious life led by so many. The imposition of the dress code, then, would secure this wage and channel it in a manner more appropriate and productive for the State's ends. The wage would be made productive in a double sense. On the one hand, it would increase demand for locally made industrial products. On the other, it would encourage the circulation and accumulation of wealth by reducing moneys wasted on vices. Beyond fomenting and strengthening the internal market, this measure would raise the standard of living of the working poor (against their will), and improve their moral circumstance. The wisdom of the measure was undoubtable, García figured, because it took into consideration the whole organism of society—the "chain" referred to by Alamán. After presenting his case, García confessed that neither he nor other members of the Junta were aware if the original, viceregal impetus of the measure had been "the moralization of the people, or the protection of commerce from foreign goods that it monopolized."[113] Yet, it did not really matter because "whatever intention it originally had, both one and the other seem to be well-calculated, and would likewise render beautiful and useful results for us."[114] For García and the Dolores de Hidalgo Junta, the wisdom of viceregal policies such as the imposed dress code—and anti-vagrancy policy, we can safely guess—was its overcoming of liberal demurrals in its pursuit of a holistic approach to economic intervention.

Unlike most reports that Alamán summarized in the *Memoria*, the extensive space he granted García's fanciful proposal, and the fact that he did not paraphrase it but quote it verbatim, is noteworthy. Equally notable is the fact that, after the sizeable fragment, Alamán dropped the matter and moved on to consider other measures of a more moderate and pragmatic character which could bring about a similar effect, such as the establishment of a savings banks, which we study later in this chapter. Of course, viceregal nostalgia was not unheard of, and a year later, as the US invaded Mexico in 1846, it would become ever more preponderant. Nonetheless, the proposal struck a discordant note within the text. Let us remember Alamán was a careful writer; one whom had been accused and branded since the 1820s of being retrograde, oligarchic and, more importantly, a Bourbonist. He denied the latter, and as Van Young has shown in his recent biography, he was most certainly not nostalgic for the Bourbon monarchy itself.[115] Yet, if we were to uphold the accusation, we would have to insist that Alamán was a Bourbonist only in the sense that, for him, the state could and had to mold the character and aspirations of its subjects in its pursuit of what had once been called public happiness, but which he now framed as economic independence. If he did not paraphrase García's unseemly proposal, it was precisely to avoid giving more ammunition to his many enemies. He included it, nonetheless, and with it, like a ventriloquist, he gestured not at the actual utility of imposed dress codes, but at the existence, among industrialists, of a recognition of both the necessity of direct, unmediated state intervention, and the welcome continuity between economic policy and police, production and custom.

THE LIMITS OF INDUSTRY'S PERPETUAL DURATION

Even if it went largely unacknowledged, industry's "perpetual duration," for Alamán and Antuñano, ran on the instrumentalization of Mexico's proverbial natural wealth. Both industrialists had believed that the development of mechanized industry would inevitably activate commercial agriculture, benefit mining, and generate overall demand for products and labor, which would spread well beyond the horizon of the factory. For this reason, they worked in tandem with cotton producers, through the Banco, in their private lobbying, and in the press, to push for protectionist measures which limited the entry of both raw cotton and cotton-based products. The second half of the 1830s proved Alamán and Antuñano right, and profits swelled both for a new generation of industrialists as well as for cotton growers. Yet, toward the end of the decade, as the number of manufactures increased, inspired by Antuñano's success, and mass consumption of locally made products expanded (that is, as Alamán's industrial designs began to pan out), industry's growth stumbled. The problem did not emerge from the consumer-side, which Alamán had privileged, or the production front, which Antuñano focused on—or even at the level of Mexican labor. Its location preceded production altogether: it was a matter of resource availability, of scarcity. Neither Alamán or Antuñano had considered this contingency, invested as they had been, willingly or not, in the myth of the proverbial wealth of the territory. With the secession of Texas in 1836, the cotton-growing regions had been reduced to Veracruz and Oaxaca and, by 1838, the national cotton crop proved to be insufficient to supply the rising industrial demand from an equally rising number of established factories. Between 1839 and 1842, as Eric Van Young had written, Veracruz cotton harvests fell about two-thirds, "with the 1843 harvest in total collapse."[116]

As Mexican cotton became insufficient, now-independent Texas's cotton grew exponentially, dwarfing the cotton-producing US regions of Mississippi and Alabama. Cotton's price sky-rocketed, due to both its national scarcity and the financial speculation of merchants. Demand had grown fast at the international level, too. In Mexico, as Gómez Galvarriaga writes, "manufacturers had to either stop production entirely, or shorten daily production in an effort to continue, waiting anxiously for the arrival of new crop."[117] Antuñano, who in the previous years had argued for the heavy taxation of foreign cotton so as to incentivize the local crop production, took to the pen to argue for the opposite, the liberalization and importation of cotton. Even if it remained unaddressed, this cotton would have come from slave operations in Texas and the United States. He would spend years writing publicly and privately to the higher echelons of government on the matter. As Potash has written, "[t]he situation brought about the first break in the previously united front of manufacturers and farmers."[118] Cotton-growers opposed liberalization and were seconded by many industrialists, whose businesses were safe because they had expanded their concerns and established their own cotton-growing operations. The problem did not stop, but effectively slowed down, industrial development. Despite Alamán's influence on then-president Antonio López de Santa Anna, his efforts were hindered by the president's opposition to the relaxation of prohibitions. Santa Anna pushed back against liberalization because he himself might have been involved in the cotton-growing business and because, coming from Veracruz, his main supporters were too committed to and dependent on the ban.[119]

Ultimately, the truth of the matter was that the economic independence idealized by Alamán and Antuñano, an economic independence built on the perpetual growth of national modernized industry and dependent only on itself, had been impossible from the start, and could not have been carried out even through the employment of all artisans and idle citizens, the impression of all vagrants into work, and the inclusion of women and children on the factory floor. Alamán's dream of industry-powered perpetual growth was, indeed, a fiction. Surely, it was an impersonal fiction, a key element in the West's own economic imaginaries, one whose authorship went beyond him and his compatriots. It was the fiction of an Industrial Revolution that begun, as Edward E. Baptist has put it, in the Lancashire textile industry; one which made modern machinery and steam-power the protagonists of a narrative of capitalism's insurmountable potential and its eventual transcendence of the economic and developmental constraints placed on nations by natural scarcity and the limits of human potential.[120] If the narrative offered human labor a role to play, it was in its transformation into a cog in the machine. The narrative, though, ignored the whole realm of labor which produced the primary materials fed to the machinery in the first place. Baptist writes that the invention of "the cotton gin still left two significant choke points in the production of raw cotton. This meant, therefore, two bottlenecks for the nascent textile industry as well, and here they were: growing the plants and harvesting the fiber."[121] These choke points were not transcended through technological ingenuity, or through the search for greater efficiencies by industrial entrepreneurs, as Alamán, Antuñano, and most others would have argued. Focusing on Britain, Baptist notes that had British industrialists tried to replace cotton, which it could not grow, with wool, they would have had to devote more than all of the country's agricultural land to this sole object.[122] In other words, for these natural constraints to be transcended, cotton-growing regions—the United States chief among them—had to turn to a classic, manual instrument: the whip. In the first two decades of the nineteenth century, then, "[c]otton made by people enslaved on the United States' southwestern frontier [became] both the world's most widely treated commodity and its most crucial industrial raw material."[123]

Neither Alamán nor Antuñano raised any qualms about lobbying for the importation of cotton produced through enslavement. Through diverse yet common fronts, they argued, again, that such importation should be allowed in emergency conditions, such as the shortages faced by modern industry between 1838 and 1846. To do otherwise, was to risk the ruin of such industries, and with them to risk the destruction of a true republic of labor, one which offered the potential of full employment and economic independence. Here, like in the case of Ortiz de Ayala's colonization fantasies, the implication was that all purportedly free labor was, at one moment or another, structurally dependent on its opposite, unfree labor. If Alamán and Antuñano's 1830s call for the entry of slave-grown foreign cotton began to gain ground in 1844 and eventually succeeded in 1846, it was in no small part thanks to the Dirección de Industria Nacional, led by Alamán himself, which spent years working to form a united block of manufacturers. The unlimited entry of foreign cotton was finally permitted in 1846.

This victory was short lived, though. On the one hand, it was too late for Antuñano. By then, he had become deeply indebted to the *agiotistas* who either owned cotton-producing lands or who speculated through the purchase of the available supply of the specie. Between 1844 and his death in 1847, his industrial emporium began to fall apart, sold piecemeal, or mortgaged in order to pay the debts acquired because of the scarcity of raw materials. By the 1860s, La Constancia would fall into the hands of the French merchant who owned much of the Antuñano debt. On the other hand, it was also too late for the rest of the manufacturers and for Alamán's industrial designs. On May 1846, four months after allowing for the importation of Texan and American cotton, the United States invaded Mexican territory. Alamán, who as Director General of Industry aspired to avoid explicit involvement in politics, was dismissed from his post in October of that same year.

The country that would emerge from the war would once more shift gears, leaving behind the dreams of the perpetual duration of modernized industry and returning to the fantasy of the colono. As studied in Chapter 1, in the aftermath of the loss of half of the territory, the Dirección General de Industria would be dissolved and replaced by the Dirección de Colonización e Industria, the most concerted colonization project to date, and one which looked, yet again, to commercial agriculture as a way forward.

THE INHERENT MORALITY OF ARTISAN LABOR (1843–1846)

After a decade of artisan erasure and opposition, President Santa Anna moved to acknowledge the tenacity of artisan labor in 1843 by recognizing and instituting an organization, isomorphic to the industrialists' Sociedad, dedicated to artisan protection. The Junta de Fomento de Artesanos (Artisan Development Junta), officially established on December 27, 1843, but decreed by the president on October 2nd, sought to reactivate and restructure the stewardship and direction which had once been the artisan guilds' charge. Until its founding, its members believed, "the manufacturing artists of Mexico, who in a long series of years have seen with pain the destruction and disappearance of the Republic's industry, groaned in the interior of their deserted and abandoned workshops, burdened with the immense weight of misery."[124] But no more. Directed by artisans themselves, the Junta would protect their interests and their members from an ever-more hostile environment; it would work toward the recuperation of what Pérez Toledo has called the "sense of [artisan] moral community" that had once coalesced around particular guilds; it would push forward on the education of the artisan class, and, finally, would revive and publicize the dignity and moral superiority of qualified labor.[125] The Junta's work, its board of directors was quick to clarify, was patriotic in spirit and not corporative. After all, they were sure that "[t]he protection of manufacturing [industria fabril] is one of the most necessary branches [to the nation], as it is the source from which domestic and public happiness can emanate. Without this support, the human race would always be staging ever more tragic scenes, replete with misery and anarchy."[126] Its members prophesized that industry—artisan industry, specifically—was the key "to remove [the nation] from the abjection in which it has been preserved for so many years."[127] The Junta abstained from engaging—either criticizing or even mentioning— modern, mechanized industry, much in the same way Alamán had omitted artisan labor in the 1830s. Insofar as the Junta spoke for its members, and worked toward their own benefit, they had no reason to grapple with industrialists explicitly. In fact, the Junta's interests coincided, in broad terms, with the Dirección's emphasis on the industrial future of Mexico. Like the Dirección, the Junta lobbied and pushed against liberal models of extractivist, exportable economic futures, built on agriculture and mining, and dependent on foreign imports of manufactured goods. In its stead, they proposed an economic national horizon built around the artisan workshop. The Junta served, of course, as a form of co-optation by the state, but it was also an official recognition of the material and industrial interdependence of modes of production in the first half of the nineteenth century. In other words, despite Alamán and Antuñano's industrial dreams of artisan displacement, of the subsumption of all industrial production by the modern factory, the artisan workshop held its ground and survived the nineteenth century. Their tenacity proved that if economic independence, in the form dreamed of by Alamán and Antuñano, was to become a reality, it would have to be done by taking advantage of all of the nation's productive capacities. Through its years of activity, the Junta lobbied in favor of the artisan class and its efforts yielded dozens of concessions from the State in the form of commercial and fiscal protections which, at the very least, kept some part of the working-class artisan employed. The Junta's labors also resulted in the foundation of the Fondo de Beneficiencia Pública, one of Mexico's first mutual aid societies, which veritably benefited the lives of the common artisan.

The Junta and the Dirección coexisted in the 1840s, if not amicably, at least in parallel. In the 1830s, sectors of artisan labor had resisted Alamán and Antuñano because they believed that, were the two men's industrial plans actualized, the handicraft industry would cease to exist. Alamán and Antuñano, in turn, attacked artisan labor because they knew that certain of its representatives actively worked against the establishment of new forms of manufactures (and of the new government), and because they believed that artisan prejudices were a cultural obstacle for modern, industrial enterprises. By the 1840s, however, the animosity had been dialed back. Modern factories had taken root in Mexican soil and, in spite of difficulties, had flourished; yet they had not managed to extricate the artisan workshop. In a way, both forms of industrial production spent the decade guaranteeing their own survival and focused on the articulation of an industrial horizon against that of commercial agriculture. In fact, their educational projects and economic concerns often coincided. The Dirección's lobbying, for example, against the contraband of prohibited foreign textiles benefited artisans, and Alamán's calls for the creation of savings banks, more on which later, were often seconded by the Junta. Surely, had both survived the 1840s, their projects would have found themselves on a collision course. Yet, for the time they actually coexisted; historical contingency had taken the steam out of the conflict. This did not mean that, at the level of discourse, they had abdicated for the defense of the particularity of their particular form of labor. As we will see, the Junta, of course, would insist on the inherent superiority and morality of artisan labor.

THE SEMANARIO ARTÍSTICO AND THE CUSTOMARY MORALITY OF ARTISAN LABOR

The Junta de Fomento de Artesanos was the State's vehicle for the artisan's effective subsumption. It spoke for them and to them in specific: "And you in particular, appreciable and worthy artisans, who are going to be the founders of the aggrandizement and prosperity of the most powerful of the republics; the nation's fate depends on you."[128] For this purpose, shortly after its founding, the Junta launched the *Semanario Artístico* (Artistic Weekly *or* Artisan Weekly), a publication which, as its subtitle proudly announced, had as a goal the "education and development of the Republic's artisans."

It was the first publication in independent Mexico made by artisans and directed exclusively at them. It privileged practical, moral, and political education while preaching the values of work and of technical innovation. While the Junta was founded by presidential decree, the publication was independent in that it was not subsidized by the government, like many other public papers, but by the organization's membership. Its closest model was a short-lived paper titled the *Semanario de Industria Mexicana* (Weekly of Mexican Industry, 1841–42), which focused on mechanical innovation, moral education, and was published by the Sociedad para el Fomento de la Industria. As such, the *Semanario Artístico* was meant to satisfy one of the key articles of the Junta's constitution, which stated that the body "had resolved to take charge of the instruction and propagation of the topics that should enlighten artisans, [so as] to regularize their ideas, organize their methods, familiarize them with reading, and inspire them a love of letters and a love of the arts."[129] As expected, the weekly put forward ideas belonging to the Junta's board, which was not composed by common artisans, but by prosperous workshop-owning master-artisans and entrepreneurs; a group that jealously watched over the strict procedures and high fees limiting access to the organization. Yet, despite this fact, as Pérez Toledo has shown, the *Semanario* played an important role as a "tool of socialization," establishing connections and conversations across the different strata of the trades that addressed artisans as a whole and, so, constituted them as a diverse, yet cohesive collective.[130]

As we will see in the next chapter, after the exhaustion of the republican passions of independence, the 1830s and 1840s saw an increasing return to a moral understanding of the political and the economic that came hand-in-hand with the worsening circumstance of the material and political reality of the nation. The *Semanario*'s push for the moral education of artisans and for the improvement of their customs, echoed this return, and reaffirmed the generalized acknowledgment that an engagement with economic matters was indissociable from moral forms; that the moral and economic universe existed within an undeniable continuum regardless of the changing circumstances and the supposed separation of the spheres preached by modernizers. In fact, the continuity between moral and economic imaginaries, and especially the defense of a "moral economy" against the despotism of the market, was an essential aspect of artisan socialization.[131] Through its articles dedicated to "moral education," the editors sought to offer a model of the artisan that was radically different from that of the individualized modern worker; a model that presented the figure as a laborer for whom work was not simply a form of life but also an inherently moral form. In this sense, the *Semanario* aspired to be a bulwark against the negative figuration of the artisan, rampant in the press of the period, and against the consistent harassment of the artisan by anti-vagrancy raids.

For the editors of the *Semanario*, morals structured man's pursuit of happiness. Unfortunately, the Mexican population, a significant portion of which was composed of artisans, was "given to ignorance and enslaved to worry and routine, and ignores the principles of sane morality, does not know of its importance and cannot even glimpse its influence in the art of being happy, which is nothing but knowing and fulfilling one's duties."[132] The *Semanario*'s edifice of morality was thoroughly marked by its industrial ethos. For its editors even in the most civilized countries, the efforts made by religion and "sane reason" to charge politics and morality with the capacity to combat the population's vices had failed.[133] Reason, the call of duty, and the interpellation of the individual's conscience were useful in keeping bodily appetites and passions at bay, but were not enough to impact the habits and customs of the majority of citizens. The only avenue for such a transformation was labor. Only through the multiplication of working opportunities and the employment of the majority of the population could customs be improved.

According to its articles, manual labor was an inherently moralizing activity—perhaps the only one available to man. Against the human inclination toward idleness, labor protected the working artisan physically, materially, and psychologically from distractions and deviance by forcing upon him a "habit of regularity," and by pushing him to "continually master himself, to frequently struggle with a thousand difficulties, and perhaps to suffer a troublesome privations."[134] Labor thus strengthened the artisan and challenged him with an increasing difficulty that nourished his will and granted him a vigor available only after a "long perseverance." To create, then, the proper conditions for the renewal of national customs it was necessary to interweave the "common benevolence of all agents of production," with an explicit moral education that, by building on virtuous habits, could lessen the undeniable burdens of labor and make it even more productive and even pleasurable.[135] A coupling of both, labor and education, could guarantee man's happiness in all aspects of life, and, in turn, social peace and order.[136]

To emphasize the moralizing nature of work, and specifically artisan labor, the editors turned to a French article by a Monsieur Fregier, which they translated and published on March 4, 1844.[137] According to them, it offered "the most beautiful of sketches (el más bello cuadro) of the customs of artisans in general," one which could be of influence to "our Mexican artisans;" to all those "who want to duly deserve the title of honorable, noting that the habit of doing well (obrar bien) is indeed a natural thing in those who by their profession are so prepared to exercise the Christian and moral virtues without effort."[138] The text itself offered the artisan as the standard-bearer of a "primitive virtue," founded in labor, and a sort of proto-republican civility, which was the by-product of the shared condition of those who work. The artisan was frank and humble, "ready to be useful," helpful to his colleagues and respectful and loving to his master-artisan or employer. He was charitable and often joined with others from his workshop to either lessen the work of those artisans who were ill, or to pool funds and resources to assist the families of others incapable of working temporarily. Even if an artisan committed a crime and was jailed, the others would offer a "beneficent hand" (mano benéfica) to keep him and his family afloat. This solidarity often extended beyond those of his class, and the artisan "alleviated," as much as he could, all who surrounded him. It was a "way of being (modo de obrar) [that] is uncommon in other social classes," the author wrote, because "it is the reward of a benevolent character and a habit marked by good practice (buen proceder)." That is, the "way of being" of the artisan was characterized by both manual labor, inherently moralizing, and the workshop as a mode of production which organized work as a collective (even if hierarchical) endeavor which generated a certain *esprit de corps*. This labor catalyzed the emergence of a primitive form of virtue that was communal, a form which preceded the modern individual subject of the liberal imaginary and political economics.

To artisan-readers of the period, these appeals to collective virtue must have harkened back to the abolished corporativist sensibilities of the craftsman's guild. In this sense, the *Semanario*'s program of moral education also answered to a particular survival within the artisan workshop of the customary morality of the guild structure; a customary morality that, by the 1840s, had been abolished for at least a generation. As we have mentioned before, and as E. P. Thompson has clearly evinced, the artisan's life had once been striated, structured by repertoires of manners and mores, laws and norms, celebrations, and processions, all of which were particular to each trade and each guild and were ultimately mapped out along the hierarchical axis of the workshop.[139] The guild structure's undoing did not end this panoply of customs, habits, and moralities. It simply led to their becoming opaque to "gentry inspection," as Thompson puts it.[140] Pérez Toledo has underscored this survival, and argued that in practice and the everyday life of the population, and particularly within the artisan class, guild practices were still active.[141] As an example, she notes that "[l]earning a trade began, as in the colonial past, when the apprentice being handed over by his parents to a master-artisan, who was in charge not only of introducing him and training him in the trade, but also providing him with food and clothing."[142] The *Semanario* turned to this "opaque" survival so as to offer an ideal figure of the modern artisan, one which rivaled the denigrated version found in the press and which could serve as an alternative to the modern liberal subject, isolated by his individualism and motivated only by self-interest.

So, insofar as the editors spoke for the master-artisan, they must have had a better understanding—or, at the very least, an understanding—of the tenacity of artisan custom. They must have also been personally acquainted with the rhythms of the actually existing workshop and the present incapacity of many of these to employ their apprentices and officers for a full day's work. In light of this, they built their moralizing program around two elements they drew from that customary repertoire of the past. On the one hand, as we have seen, while celebrating the artisan's identification with his labor, they took what was in fact the perseverance of an aspect of the corporate solidarity of the guild and transformed it into a private virtue. On the other, they invoked and affirmed the paternalist ethos of the guild structure, the master-artisan's responsibility to serve "as the moral custodian of apprentices and officers, entrusted as he was with the care of the proper behavior and customs of his disciples as well as their dedication to the learned trade."[143] Despite the similarity of its effects and its near-identical form, this moralistic paternalism differed from that of other Creole elites' in that, as can be expected, the master-artisans and/or those that staged the master-artisan position of the Junta and its *Semanario* participated in what Marx once called the "the filial relationship" of the workshop, a relationship which gave masters "a double power," in that it established both a bond of exploitation and one of a more personal or affective type.[144] As we saw before, Antuñano had hoped to access this "double power," which he believed would put a restraint on the mobility of his workforce, but lacking the capacity to appeal to the customary morality of the artisan, sought to find a similar liaison through the hypothetical employment of whole family units.

These appeals to the master-artisan's paternalist custodianship allowed the editors to call for stricter control of the worker by the employer. The latter, after all, could intervene in the life of the artisan in time to interrupt the formation of certain vices—alcoholism and an addiction to games of chance, in particular—which threatened his health, his labor, his family and society at large.[145] Granted, the editors also advocated for the workers, but not to call for, say, the abolishment of physical punishment; instead, they urged master-artisans (and parents) to lessen the brutality with which they attempted to "correct" the behavior of their apprentices (and children), because these "corrections" were often known to be "too severe and humiliating, and instead of achieving amendment, they sometimes lead to the loss of shame."[146] Surely, the worker's life was of concern to all elites. Yet, when said concern was articulated from the position of the master-artisan, of the actually existing workshop owner and employer, instead of the abstract economic imagination of lettered men, journalists, or politicians, the porosity and partiality of the working day became a matter of explicit concern precisely because it was not simply a matter of calling on the artisan to work more or work longer, like other elites did, but of protecting that part of the artisan's day which the present Mexican workshop and the master-artisan were incapable of productively occupying. This part of the artisan's day had to be kept safe from deviance—and anti-vagrancy raids—and in standing reserve for that moment in which the shop's workload picked up and the Junta's industrial future materialized. Surely, whether we take the Junta's concern for the poor artisans at their word or not, its direct interest in the artisan's material circumstance cannot be denied. The *Semanario*'s educational project was an attempt to improve the customs and quality of life of the poor artisan by instilling values that would, in the view of master-artisans, guarantee the subject's general well-being and domestic happiness—as defined by the group's elite. From a more critical perspective, if internalized, these values and new customs would at the very least keep the poor artisan out of the reach of anti-vagrancy raids which could impair a workshop's capacity to respond, at a moment's notice, to the whims of the market.

Beyond these explicit calls for the direct and immediate involvement of the master-artisan in the lives of his workers, the truth of the matter is that, unsurprisingly, the paternalism of the master-artisan position structured the whole of the moral education section of the weekly. For this reason, along with the elements we have seen until this point, we also often find, couched within the running conceit of the priority and foremost importance of the artisan's welfare, an anxiety regarding the deleterious effect of social mobility on the harmonious existence of the workshop. This anxiety took the form, on the one hand, of a celebration of the humility of the artisan; and, on the other, on an assault on any social striving. As we have already shown, for the editors, "[t]he life of the artisan is a true moral education" because labor itself was taken to be a moralizing activity.[147] But, labor, they also insisted, "is the school of resignation: it teaches us our dependence, reminds us what we owe to others: it corrects and punishes our vanity, and reminds us that human life is but a time trial."[148] In other words, beyond the moralizing effects of work on the body and mind of the worker we saw above, another element of work's pedagogical aspect was the fact that it revealed the material dependence of the worker on, surely, others like himself, on raw materials and nature, but more importantly on the employer who provided him with the opportunity to educate himself through his effort. Awareness of this dependence, the editors suggested, was not simply a matter of what we could call phenomenological description, but a recognition of the laborer's debts and obligations. The editors insisted on this recognition in article after article. In a particular text from June 22nd, 1844, they briefly did away with the niceties and subtleties that characterized their tone, and adopted a categorical and unambiguous stance. I quote in extensio:

> What artisans lack more than anything—and this applies in general to all poor classes—is a true knowledge of their situation, and enough strength to settle for it; it is knowing how to usefully manage the resources they acquire through their work. It is not correct to push against necessity, but to know how to suffer it and adapt life to it. Without denying that it takes a lot of courage and resignation to endure poverty in its bad days, the writer of this is convinced that this same laborious and economic poverty can in ordinary times provide for the necessities of life and even enjoy many of the benefits and the comforts created by civilization. In no society can all desires be satisfied; what the worker lacks the master also lacks, and what seems desirable to the latter is an object of envy for the director of a workshop. The measure of what is necessary changes according to the individual's condition, and the same happens with the measure of the superfluous, and they must change simultaneously because no one is happy with his fate. Furthermore, poverty will always be the more or less limited expression of what is necessary, according to the conduct of the individual, the state of the circumstances and the number of members of his family.[149]

For the editors, then, the virtuous artisan did not have to strive or struggle, but work and embrace his circumstance, his "laborious poverty." This poverty was a providential and given state of scarcity, fixed in the nature of the social—where desires could never be wholly satisfied—and unmovable, impossible to transcend. With the exception of the "bad days," the poverty of artisans was self-regulating and, "in ordinary times," yielded what was necessary for survival, if not always what was desired. For the artisan to assert this circumstance and to let it guide his actions was to be virtuous because it implied his acceptance of his "sole subjection to the designs of

Providence."[150] The proper and virtuous artisan, then, gave his everything to his work, which was made possible by the master-artisan, mandated by Providence and regulated by nature, because it gave him everything; a moral education, a purpose, and, yes, a modest salary. Put simply, for the *Semanario*, the end of the moral education of the artisan—of the improvement of his customs—was to make the burden of labor more palatable and accepted, not less burdensome.

From this point of view, desires for social mobility, understood both horizontally, as the free movement and displacement of the population, and vertically, as the climbing of the social ladder, bordered the immoral. What could the origin for such desires be but greed, envy, and a general dissatisfaction with Providence? Another article put it transparently: "[f]or those classes in unfavorable positions, it is extremely dangerous to try to escape from their circumstance through reckless steps, such as through their children's education, marriage, or placing them beyond their station."[151] While these wants were damaging to "all poor classes," as we have seen, in the particular case of artisans it was all the more so. An artisan who aspired to improve his circumstance beyond what was possible in his place of employment was bound, on the one hand, to fail, given the economic realities of the 1840s and, by doing so, put the workshop, himself, and his family at risk.[152] On the other, were he to succeed, it would imply turning his back to the moral debt he accrued with the master-artisan as well as abandoning the interconnected webs of artisan solidarity already described. These aspirations had the potential to flatten artisan labor, to make it indistinguishable from all other forms of modern labor and, so, rip it from the sphere of influence and patriarchal reach of master-artisans. Social mobility, in other words and in the end, was an unnecessary risk; one that disregarded the inherent morality of proper artisan labor and existence, as well as the fact that such labor was not an interchangeable vehicle or instrument, but a form of life.

Had the Junta and the editors of the *Semanario* been capable of manifesting the figures they preached, the artisan that would have materialized would have been a prudent, austere laborer whose life was limited to the workshop and his personal residence, and whose desire was thoroughly circumscribed to the improvement of his moral countenance and the well-being of his family. It was an apolitical economic figure, thoroughly moral in that he labored for labor's sake, having given up on aspirations of mobility and being deeply content with his place in society. He was also a socially and geographically embedded figure, preferring to stay close to his place of employment and active in the well-being and general betterment of his community. Against images of the liberal and modern free worker, self-interested and sovereign, the *Semanario*'s artisan emerged as an alternative, a figure whose form-of-life was dictated by, and circumscribed to, his labor, understood not only as an activity, but as a striated constellation of inherited customs, practices, and relationships that both pre-existed and transcended his individual self.

This imagined artisan was a self-serving fiction. It was a figure which allowed the paternalist master-artisan to claim the moral authority over workers' well-being, while relinquishing all material responsibility to them. It yielded communal welfare to the private charity of self-organized artisans and neglected to recognize master-artisans' direct power over the "modest" wages of the worker and his poverty, both of which were presented as natural or given by invisible forces. As E. P. Thompson has written, "[t]he masters disclaimed their paternal responsibilities; but they did not cease, for many decades, to complain at the breach of the 'great law of subordination.'"[153] Yet, as Thompson also noted, "[p]aternalism as myth or as ideology is nearly always backward-looking."[154] Accordingly, as we have said, the Mexican master-artisan of 1843's patriarchal claim was severely limited by the historical reality—the political abolition of the guild structure, the dire economic conditions which impaired the capacity of most workshops to fully employ their workforce, and the material fact of artisan poverty and geographic mobility and displacement.

Despite the fact that the ideal reader of the *Semanario*'s articles on moral education was the novice artisan and journeyman, it is possible to argue that, in practice, the actual target of the publication became the master-artisan himself—the alphabetized owner of a workshop who read the paper not only for the news on the progressive expansion of the Junta's mission throughout the national territory, but for the purpose of self-affirmation and reification. While ideally the weekly would have reached the lower levels of the workshop and, through its consistent droning, lead to the transformation and re-foundation of its customs and manners, in practice it served as an echo chamber in which master-artisans found affirmation and articulation. This affirmation, in turn, inserted the master-artisan, who had been pushed aside in the previous decade in favor of the industrialist's potential, into a national horizon, into a project charged with a moral and political drive that went beyond the deepening of their private fortune.

THE INSTITUTIONAL MODERNIZATION OF MANNERS

Whatever was left of the master-artisan's paternalism was also generative. The *Semanario*'s and the Junta's moralism underwrote their efforts to establish and publicize the creation of the Fondo de Benefiencia Pública (Public

Charity Fund), an institution which allowed for the refunctionalization of certain aspects of the "corporative mentality of the guilds" as well as the institutionalization of the very same practice of "spontaneous" charity among artisans celebrated in the Moral Education section of the paper.[155] The Fondo, a mutual aid society or "caja de ahorros," was intended to remediate "the general scarcities," "public misery," and "private necessities of the majority of [the nation's] inhabitants" by providing tools that would allow individuals to overcome the sort of contingencies—marriages and baptisms, illnesses and deaths—that drove the working poor to outright penury.[156] The Fondo had been one of the Junta's flagship projects since its foundation. An independent organization, it would depend not on the Junta or the government, but only on the weekly fees paid by its voluntary membership. In its functions and inner-workings (and despite its secular nature), it echoed the cofradías (confraternities) of the past: socio-religious associations that, along with the guild, had once structured artisan lives and communities, and which revolved around the devotion of a patron saint. The similarity was not simply a question of shared goals, but of many explicit parallels in fees, rules, regulations, and practices.[157] The institution's effects were both immediate—more than three hundred people subscribed to the Fondo in its first three months— and long-lasting.[158] According to Pérez Toledo, the creation of a formal vehicle, in the post-guild era, that allowed for artisan articulation influenced the foundation, in the 1850s, of a new form of associations that resembled the Fondo, but originated in the self-convocation of artisans rather than the officialist position of the Junta.[159]

The *Semanario*'s editors saw the Fondo as an institution essential to its project, a harbinger of the inculcation of the morals it preached and the subsequent transformation of artisan custom. For them, a moral life required, as they stressed over and over again, a productive administration of that providential poverty mentioned earlier. Were the artisan's "modest" salary given "a wise direction, appropriate to the worker's true interests," he would soon meet his happiness, while also freeing himself from those vices that tended to dissipate these earnings and lead to debt and worse.[160] The Fondo offered the artisan this direction, while also guaranteeing "timely help in the most frequent of life's necessities," and instilling the "habits of a well-understood economy founded on the love of work."[161] The Fondo worked against outright charity, which "to a certain point, degrades and humiliates [the poor], feeds their laziness and ruins the nation."[162] Instead, savings banks "elevate and support the morality of the poor, because they themselves are their own saviors and alms-givers: in gratitude, they extend themselves and their labor is excited with the promise of its rewards."[163]

Motivated by the promised benefits, workers reduce what they spend in meals and liquor, and "persuade themselves that it is necessary to economize while they are young and can work so that they save some money for when they are old and sick."[164] These institutions, the editors concluded, were "antirevolutionary in essence" insofar as they gave workers "with its own labors and without dispossessions" a part in the pleasures of wealthier classes, while embedding them into the social and economic fabric of the nation understood as national economy.[165]

The *Semanario*'s celebration of the expediency of the Fondo echoed and was echoed by Lucas Alamán, as well as other industrialists. Savings banks were not unknown at the time. News of their utility in London had been circulating since at least 1826, and their procedures were similar to that of cofradías, as we have mentioned.[166] Yet between 1839 and 1841 the idea of cajas as tools for social uplift, as well as for subjectivization and subjection of the populace in general, and the artisan in specific, gained ground among participants in the manufacturing industry.[167] Between 1841 and 1842, the editors of the Sociedad para el Fomento de la Industria Nacional's *Semanario de Industria Mexicana* extolled, across multiple articles, the cajas for precisely these reasons, all the while making note of the establishment of similar funds by foreign artisans established in Mexico, and publicizing the creation of a caja by Próspero Legrand and Felix Mendarte, directors of the Cocolapán textile factory in the Veracruzan city of Orizaba.[168] Yet, it was Lucas Alamán as head of the Dirección de Industria who most influentially pushed for the utility and necessity of cajas de ahorro in the 1840s. In his 1843 *Memoria*, he reported that, during its first year of existence, the Dirección had put resources into researching the potential benefits of "bancos de ahorro," because the relevant literature showed that these were "one of the most convenient measures to improve the customs of the artisans" in that they provided artisans "the avoidance of moments of vain prodigalities and to build themselves a peculium for their needs and for aid in their old age."[169] The result of the investigation, authored by Mariano Galvez, the Dirección de Industria's secretary and future director of the Dirección de Colonización, was included in an addendum. There, Galvez celebrated the proven success of such institutions in England and France, their convenience in light of the same contingencies that the *Semanario artístico* would address in 1844, their capacity to diminish the number of indigents, and their adequacy to provide "people of little fortune the pleasant satisfaction born from property."[170] In England and France, Galvez reported, two thirds of those indicted by tribunals or the authorities were vice-ridden men, given to gambling, lotteries, and drunkenness, whereas people who participate in similar banks have never been found in such circumstances.[171] Savings banks, for Galvez, functioned as generative instruments that hindered bad habits while simultaneously forcing the worker to prudential or provisional acts. If established in Mexico, he wrote, their beneficial effects would be even greater.[172] He went on:

> Our workers suffer from the same spirit of unpredictability and have the same dissipating tendencies for which this class is unfortunately recognized everywhere. They need, for the same reason . . . the benefits that depositors get from cajas . . . They need cajas to deposit in them the small sums that they have left [after guaranteeing their livelihood], because they are very prone to waste when the temptation of pleasure or caprice arises, and these temptations go away when savings are not at hand because they have placed them cajas; and, once they make their first deposit, they continue doing so, because the only person that does not save and economize is he who has not started saving and economizing."[173]

According to the secretary, the Mexican working class, like all such classes, suffered from an impulsive drive toward dissipation, which could be curbed through the (temporary and self-imposed) removal of the means which made possible such waste. By subjecting himself to external constraints, the worker began a process of subjectivization to transform such constraints into habits and these into a new custom. Indeed, these results benefited the worker, but more importantly they benefited the state. Such a citizen inevitably began to prefer order to disorder—so as to not risk the status of his savings. He also served as example for others, all the while contributing, through the formation of "small capitals," to the wealth of the nation.[174] Ultimately, for Galvez, cajas de ahorro had the potential of elevating the well-being of the majority by accumulating capital "through multiplication, and not the division of properties."[175]

Thus, where the *Semanario Artístico* emphasized the benefits and improvements savings brought to the artisan's life and, doubtlessly, the effects of these on social stability and the productivity of the workshop, Gálvez as representative of industrialists (and Alamán, who paraphrased his findings) privileged the effects of banks on the policing of order, the wealth of the nation, and the ultimate transformation and integration of the working classes into capitalist society. At the end of the day, these positions did not contradict each other. While it is true that the savings bank as an institution—the Fondo—became a positive model for artisan articulation and the improvement of their welfare, both industrialists and master-artisans saw in this same institution an instrument capable of finally modernizing the manners of the working classes through the capture and expropriation of the very condition that made the limited freedom of the artisan, or the working poor, possible: their wages.

CONCLUSION

Despite the fact that the Junta de Artesanos and the Dirección e Industria imagined slightly differentiated futures, one protecting what existed (the artisan) and the other imagining a different way of organizing that future (the mechanization and modernization of industry), their respective discourse hinged on the control and suppression of the worker, on the emptying of his interiority and on his transformation into mere procedure, into instrument. The economic imaginaries of independence were only capable of positing a world in which only elites existed as subjects, articulated on top not of a society composed, in its majority, of indigenous communities, poor Indian, mestizo and white artisans, and legions of unpaid soldiers, but of an objectified, productive, and obedient mass. When all was said and done, beyond the colono, there was no positive figuration of work in existence. After the attacks on the figure of the artisan of the late 1820s, which originated in the previous century, and after the institution of the economic imaginaries of independence, marked by what we can only say was an inherent misanthropy, the possibility of the rehabilitation of the actually existing artisan was evacuated, emptied. For Alamán, Antuñano, and the industrialists of the Dirección de Industria, it was necessary to eliminate the artisan and replace him with a wage worker that figured as yet another gear in a machine. The master craftsmen of the Junta de Artesanos, on the other hand, recovered an abstracted figure of the craftsman and recognized that it was necessary to rescue that ideal by transforming the actually existing artisan. This transformation implied the elimination of personal contingency and his total surrender to the labor apparatus. If it did not transform him into a cog in the machine, it did interlock his life into the greater cog of workshop productivity in a way similar to Antuñano's. In both cases, the actually existing worker represented a danger precisely because of the possibility of his free movement. In other words, industrialists lashed out at the artisan for being attached to repressive customs, but they did not do this, in Mexico at least, to celebrate his liberation in all social senses, his transformation into an autonomous, individual, liberal subject. They did it, instead, to try to create a worker that could be subjected to the new forms of modern industry. Eric Van Young's summation about Alamán can also be applied to most industrialists: they wanted modernization, without modernity. The master craftsmen, on the other hand, wanted to re-impose the restrictions of yesteryear and activate the customary morality of the past in order to eliminate or restrain what little freedom—of movement, of employment—had been achieved.

The world of the artisan lost the little influence and hold it had over politics after the 1850s and, faced with the onslaught of new technologies, the free market, the concomitant loss of the guild as horizon, the imbrication of state and owners of the means of production, embraced new collective forms and imaginaries that focused their energies on workers' welfare and the symbolic realm. The political languages of associationism, mutualism, and socialism soon became active and gave symbolic coherence to new articulations of class solidarity and mutualist ethics and programs, which formed the base of many an artisan society and association of the second half of the nineteenth-century. Yet, having lost its foothold in the locations and processes of production, these artisan organizations lacked the capacity to defend or stake out a space for the particularity of their form of labor.[176]

Alamán and Antuñano's dreams of industrialization and perpetual development also went largely unrealized until the latter part of the 1860s. It was around this date when the tide of the "second industrial revolution," which spurred a rapidly expanding Atlantic economy, buoyed foreign trade in Mexico, re-activated the exploitation and exportation of natural resources and increased the flows of capital, entrepreneurship, and technology. The formal subsumption of labor into the capitalist mode of production expanded rapidly around then, and the wage-earning population tripled between 1861 and 1895.[177] As Edward J. Beatty has written, "newfound political stability under the governments of Benito Júarez (1867–72), Sebastián Lerdo de Tejada (1872–76), and Porfirio Díaz (beginning in 1876) established favorable conditions through a combination of personalistic and institutional initiatives in which long-standing interest in material progress could gain real traction."[178]

Very much like we have seen in this chapter, the elites in the second half of the century were as misanthropic as their predecessors and as dismissive of the nation's human resources. Beatty writes that until the first decade of the twentieth century, elites insisted on a "vision of Mexico in the North Atlantic mirror, one that equated mechanized technologies with European accomplishments, cultures, and peoples."[179] Of course, a corollary to the economic, technological, and industrial modernization of the last quarter of the century was the creation of the conditions of possibility for new figures and collective articulations of the working class. These new forms of collectivity were stronger than the artisan associations of the past and emerged hand-in-hand with a new generation of workers' newspapers that, in the words of Illades, functioned as a "laboratory in which [the working class] built its own representation of [its] social life, and where new labor institutions and projects were distilled."[180] The matter of the customs and manners of the working classes continued to be regular objects of inquiry in these papers. Yet, often we find that the manners to be extirpated were precisely the individualist mores proposed in the early part of the century. As the editors of *El Socialista* wrote in their first issue on July 9, 1871, "it is necessary to come together, to discipline ourselves, to throw out bad habits and retrograde ideas from among us and give ourselves the embrace of brothers so as to work together, not for the particular good of an individual, but for the good of all."[181] As Illades writes: "If the law atomized workers by individualizing them, the workers' press [of the last decades of the nineteenth-century] helped to shape their identity and reconstitute them as a collectivity."[182] These new collectivities, in turn and with time, re-entered the political arena and, through the following decades, struggled and succeeded in expanding the rights of workers and, thus, played a foundational role in the transformation of the economic imaginaries of Mexico in the twentieth century.

CHAPTER 3

The Vagrant

Vagrancy, Police, and the Opacity of the Social

Political economy, therefore, does not recognize the unoccupied worker, the workman, insofar as he happens to be outside this labor-relationship. The cheat-thief, swindler, beggar, and unemployed man; the starving, wretched and criminal working-man—these are *figures* who do not exist for *political economy*, but only for other eyes, those of the doctor, the judge, the grave-digger, and bum-bailiff, etc.; such figures are specters outside the domain of political economy.

Karl Marx, *Economic & Philosophic Manuscripts of 1844*

During the first half of the nineteenth century, the vagrant haunted all figuration of labor in Mexico. An able-bodied man of productive age, the vagrant preferred *not* to toil the fields or engage in honest employment despite economic downturns and elite belief of a national scarcity of labor. Most often of indigenous extraction or mestizo, the vagrant would rather loaf and loiter than respond to the economic imperatives and republican duties on which the new nation attempted to found itself. The vagrant was not yet, or necessarily, a criminal, but it was only a matter of time until he crossed the law, seeing as all honest living called for a trade, office, or occupation. This inevitability generated great anxiety among the Creole elites, whose concern for the industriousness of the polity had as much to do with the populating and activation of the territory, as seen in the previous chapters, as with the regulation, normativization, and demarcation of the newly independent citizenry's productive life, which both structured and threatened Mexico's developmentally necessary economic and political stability.

This interest in the productive life of the people, in its customs, manners, and mores, was pivotal. It had been and would continue to be widely debated. Yet, not too long into post-independence life, it became obvious that it was not only a matter of putting the populace to work. It was a question, even more importantly, of instilling a "spirit of enterprise," a work ethic that, with time, would give way to what Giorgio Agamben has called a form-of-life, "a life that, in its sequence, makes itself that very form, coincides with it."[1] Creole elites and *letrados* of all stripes sought an inculcation of a productive mentality that would banish the vices that, in their opinion, interrupted the aggrandizement promised by the land's proverbial wealth.[2]

As historian Timo H. Schaefer has written, post-independence legal culture based itself on the values of labor and domesticity, and "drew a line—firm in principle but indistinct in reality—between virtuous workers, to whom it gave rights and protections, and profligate idlers," whom it expelled and marginalized.[3] A writer of the time insisted on the importance and urgency of drawing and affirming said line on 1824 in the pages of *El Sol.* The author warned that, while it was already too late to make the first independent generation industrious, for they had been raised under Spanish, illiberal tutelage, "if the evil is not hacked at the root, even if the rotten branches have been cut," the ill of unproductivity would also spread to subsequent post-independence generations.[4] "It is better to prevent or avoid than to punish," he noted and insisted that "idleness is the origin of many evils: *multam malitian docui otiositas*."[5] He was so sure of this principle that he went on to offer a small amount of money, which the editors of *El Sol* doubled, to set up a call for papers for a contest which would select the best reader-submitted analyses of "the causes of the idleness, laziness and consequent vices of our plebs; the legal, governmental and economic means of containing and correcting them in those already-vicious, and of preserving from them those who are not," as well as an explanation of "the idle, lazy and poorly entertained . . . that if they are not already given to thievery, it is only a matter of time that they do so to satisfy their vices and maintain a semblance of the exterior decency that conceals them."[6] The contest itself did not amount to much, and its only submission would be a loosely relevant proposal for a system of charitable associations and public safety, written by Benito José Guerra and then Bourbonist, and future conservative monarchist, Francisco Sánchez de Tagle years earlier but unpublished until then, which barely touched the convener's call.[7] Yet, both the call for papers and Guerra and Sánchez de Tagle's submissions attested to the renewed elite concern with the idleness of the populace, of the "plebe," with the belief that, as Charles Hale has written, "until the Mexican people were employed in productive industry, the country would remain economically impoverished and politically chaotic."[8]

In this new mission, the administrative imagination of the Bourbon ideologies of governance were useful. Viceregal anti-vagrancy discourse and policy soon became essential elements to the economic imaginaries of independence. Vagrants had been pursued in Mexican territory since at least the sixteenth century. But, like elsewhere, it was only in the second half of the eighteenth century, when the rising tide of political and economic modernity saw the moral outrage vagrancy generated in the past collide and coalesce with the emergent capitalist economic imperatives so as to beget repressive policy.[9] Convinced as they were about the lack of hands and the underpopulation that interrupted Mexico's economic futures in the aftermath of independence, the vagrant quickly became *the* urban figure which Creole statesmen could not risk to ignore.

Nineteenth-century elites engaged with anti-vagrancy, as discourse and policy, as a matter of "police." In the politico-administrative thought of the eighteenth century, which still held in the 1820s, police (*policía)* organized social life by linking "citizenship in an organized polity" with "personal comportment and private life."[10] From the sixteenth century onward, police had "implied the subordination of individual desires and interests to those of the community, a subordination guaranteed by ordinances and laws."[11] According to Bernard E. Harcourt, what began to be called the "public economy" in the eighteenth century fell strictly within this domain. Harcourt has drawn attention to how the earliest "public economists," including, for example, the young Adam Smith, believed that it was proper police that "ensured the abundant provision of necessary foods and commodities."[12] That is, police implied the administration of subsistence and markets so as to guarantee the economic well-being of the nation and, consequently, the liberty of its polity.[13] Even after the emergence of *political economy*, with its insistence in the separation of spheres, the imbrication of the economic and (what we now refer to as) police remained, with the penal sphere serving as the outer limit to the market's "natural order."[14] Karl Marx noted this in the fragment of the *Economic and Philosophical Manuscripts of 1844* quoted in the epigraph at the beginning of this chapter, where he addressed the incapacity of political economic discourses to give an account of those willingly or unwillingly excluded from the labor relation. This is the reason why, while playing a key role in the economic imaginaries of the period, the vagrant had no explicit part in properly economic discourse.[15]

Anti-vagrancy legislation, as known to Mexican lawmakers of the first half of the nineteenth-century, built primarily upon three Spanish statutes decreed between 1745 and 1820. First, the *Real Orden* of April 20, 1745, established the foundations for the modern approach to anti-vagrancy and secured the state's foothold into the privacy of its subjects. Secondly, the Decree of May 7, 1775, better known as the *Ordenanza de Levas* (Impressment Ordinance), and was widely recognized as one of the more thorough and celebrated legislative achievements of its time.[16] Lastly, the 1820 *Decreto XXVIII* of the Cortes de Madrid attempted to reform anti-vagrancy procedures in a liberal key, but was only successful in putting the previous two back into circulation in 1821 Mexico. Of these three, it was the *Real Orden* and the *Ordenanza de Leva* which determined Mexican policy throughout the nineteenth century. Whereas the *Real Orden* typified and, as a result, constructed the figure of the vagrant, abstracting and jettisoning his social circumstance, the *Ordenanza* provided the preferred and most convenient avenue for the reinsertion of the wayward citizen: the *leva* (impressment or forced recruitment into the army).[17] These measures, as Lucio Ernesto Maldonado Ojeda notes, moved beyond "the old emphatic notion of errant vagrancy, characteristic of certain social groups since the Middle Ages (pilgrims, crusaders, gypsies, etc.), to focus on the new forms of work and social leisure that urban development brought with it experienced by the main cities of the Metropolis and those of its American colonies during the eighteenth-century."[18]

The *Real Órden* of 1745 did not offer a *concept* of vagrancy per se, despite being the clearest and most modern Hispanic description of the vagrant to date. It did create, however, an extensive typology which would go on to survive it and arrive almost unchanged at the desks of the legislators of the First Federal Republic. The typology, as Silvia Arrom has noted, was particularly gendered, and, unlike ancient legislation, marked vagrancy as a male problem, jettisoning the unemployed and idle woman to other spheres.[19] The scheme, as I mentioned earlier, abstracted the vagrant from his circumstance and listed sixteen types of vagrant behaviors and practices, distributed along two axes: unemployment and deviance.[20] Whereas the first took the manners, comportments, and habits of the unemployed as symptoms of moral dissolution; the second sorted through the deviant tendencies of the openly immoral.[21] Both axes were built on the implicit understanding of an economy of abundance in which idleness was, invariably, purposeful and, thus, spoke of moral fault.[22]Likewise, Arrom believes that the *Real Órden*'s censure of even aristocratic idleness, of the "free or voluptuous life" (la vida libre o voluptuosa), attested to its early internalization of Enlightened economists and jurists' contempt of leisure.[23] The decree's vagrant typology comprised a wide social spectrum and an ample field of application which was not reduced to public and social life, but extended well into private and domestic spheres.[24] The law indiscriminately denounced disengagement with work, adultery, gambling, and occupations considered socially unproductive.[25] All of these, in one manner or the other, had ill effects on the "felicidad" of the nation. Put differently, insofar as the happiness of the nation depended on all aspects of private and public comportment, it encompassed life itself and, as a result, required its policing. By the end of the eighteenth century, as Ana Hontanilla writes, "[i]f religious discourse had [already] criminalized the supposed lewd immorality of the vagabond, the economic discourse criminalized the unproductiveness of the unemployed and the itinerant."[26]

While the 1745 *Real Orden* made visible—or rather, produced—with great consequence for independent Mexico, the features of the vagrant, it was the 1775 *Ordenanza de Levas* which gave definite form, in the Mexican case, to the ensuing disciplinary sentence.[27] The 1775 *Ordenanza* codified the most influential approach to battling vagrancy in both Spain and Mexico and gave it legislative shape.[28] It summarized and condensed all previous anti-vagrancy legislation in the name of efficiency, "so as to reduce them to a single and constant rule of police, free of the inconveniences and abuses that its execution had suffered until now."[29] The condensation was imperative, the *Ordenanza* stated, because despite the excess of decrees, determinations and royal orders issued in different ages, none had led to the "healthy effects that were desired, because the procedures were not simplified."[30] After the *Ordenanza*, and well into Mexico's independent life, the *leva* or impressment into the army became the customary disciplinary action against vagrancy.[31] Through forced recruitment, municipal governments often expelled behaviors considered anti-social and immoral—namely, failure to satisfy the expectation of industriousness—in the contexts in which they arose.[32] Like in independent Mexico, the *Ordenanza* presented the forced recruitment of vagrants as a mercy done to gainful peasants and artisans, for it exempted them of their duty to serve in the common enterprise of the protection of the nation, and allowed them to dedicate themselves more fully to their labors.[33] If the vagrant was not capable of serving in the army, the *Ordenanza* recommended they either be destined to the Armada, or secluded in a hospice or a house of mercy (casas de misericordia).[34] Whatever their destiny, it was paramount "that neither the character nor the damages that idleness brings with it no longer subsist in the Kingdom, detrimental as they are to the universal industry of the people, on which the common happiness largely depends."[35]

This police logic and the implicit program within anti-vagrancy legislation of what was called in a different context the correction of customs (corrección de costumbres) were easily translocated to its Mexican application and soon became a touchstone in the economic imaginaries of independence.[36] As we will see, after separation from Spain, Mexican legislators engaged in a process to modify vagrant typologies so that they were more clearly delimited to the circumstance of the sustained economic and social crisis of the early independent period and to the likeness of the groups of the urban proletariat that caused anxiety to well-to-do elites.[37] For all the discomfort the vagrant generated, the figure also represented an opportunity. Many Mexican *letrados*, following in the steps of Spanish political economists, like the Count of Campomanes and Jovellanos, viewed the vagrant as a diamond in the rough, a "potential resource that, if properly tapped, could provide labor to increase productions," as Arrom notes.[38] Thus, in the aftermath of its founding, Mexico declared war on the vagrant and launched into a series of projects, institutions, and debates meant to capture the figure so as to transform it, if possible, into an industrious citizen. Like Marx's epigraph suggests, this war did not take place in economic pamphlets, treatises, or reports, but in legislative chambers, municipal assemblies, newspapers, and on the city streets. In this chapter, through an engagement with its policy, practice, and discourse, we will see how, anti-vagrancy functioned as a conceptual resolution to what the elite saw as the problem of development in a post-war economy plagued by the scarcity of free labor as well as by pre-capitalistic habits. Transformed into policy, anti-vagrancy generated the legal devices necessary for the forced transformation of men into workers; for the sculpting, out of the idle masses, of a standing reserve of labor. Yet, as we will also see, at the center of anti-vagrancy beat a hermeneutical question about the possibility of dispelling the opacity of the social so as to properly identify the actual boundaries of labor's opposites; it was a question destined to undermine elite dreams of a republic of labor and its concomitant police state.

A REPUBLICAN ANTI-VAGRANCY: THE VAGRANCY LAW OF 1828, POLICE, AND THE SCENE OF DISCERNMENT (1821–30)

In an 1821 report given at the Consulate of Veracruz after Mexican independence, José María Quirós, secretary of the body's governing board, interrupted his long treatise on possible avenues of economic development to argue that, on the road to aggrandizement, it was necessary to reduce the number of vagrants that roamed urban centers through the activation of their self-interest (interés propio) and "love of work" (amor al trabajo). Quirós held that it was the newfound state's duty to "effectively adopt the measures that are most conducive to both, so as to avoid that, due to their inapplication, they become useless to society, but to also provide them with all possible resources so that, *even if they do not want to*, they enrich themselves and can contribute sufficiently to the relief of the state's needs."[39] In the same spirit but in the pages of his *Abispa de Chilpancingo* (The Chilpancingo Wasp, 1821–1823), Carlos María Bustamante summoned the image of the Athenian Areopagus as a model for the proper government of the new state. The Areopagus, he wrote, once had the power to punish idleness and "ask every citizen about the way in which they satisfy their needs. Begging and abandonment, in those who have no other patrimony than their labor [brazos], should be punished by public authority."[40] Neither Quirós nor Bustamante were unique. In their off-hand remarks, they voiced a general, elite consensus about the imperious necessity of anti-vagrancy; this consensus would gain strength during the 1820s, as it responded to a postwar economic context characterized by a dispersion and rearticulation of the territory's industries and wealth, the disarticulation of the central state's fiscal power, a massive displacement of the population, and an intensifying decapitalization of the economy.

Quirós's and Bustamante's call for the policing of the citizen's industry—anti-vagrancy—built on the still-active Bourbon ideologies of governance which inherited Hispanic regalism's dream of a police state capable of molding the character and aspirations of its subjects. Traditionally, these ideologies have been subsumed into the grand narrative of the "Bourbon Reforms."[41] According to this narrative, the second half of the Spanish eighteenth century was marked by the attempt of enlightened reformers, under the reign of Charles III (1759–88), to limit the power of the church, create institutions of learning, reactivate the productive capacities of both the metropolis and its overseas viceroyalties, strengthen the military, and reconsolidate imperial power over the American colonies through the sidelining of local Creole authorities, among other things. Ultimately, the ambition was the restitution and reconstitution of the monarchy's economic, political, and military prestige. This endeavor, the narrative goes, backfired and stimulated an already evolving Creole political subjectivity which, together with the discontent caused by metropolitan meddling and disenfranchisement, triggered calls for autonomy, independence, and, eventually, revolt. For Jorge Cañizares Esguerra, though, the narrative of the Bourbon Reforms is inexact, but "offers a satisfying account of 'the 'Enlightenment' that furthermore links 'reforms' to the undoing of the Spanish Empire."[42] Cañizares Esguerra and many other historians and critics distance themselves from this account so as to shed light on a less cohesive yet more nuanced interpretation of Bourbon initiatives and ideologies. As Gabriel Paquette has shown, Bourbon governance is but one of these key components. For Paquette, Bourbon governance was the result of the marriage between the regalism of eighteenth-century Spanish political economy and the political language of *felicidad pública*, or public happiness.[43] Against the polycentric and corporative structure of the Habsurg Empire, Spanish regalism sought the expansion of royal executive intervention in all spheres of society and a diminishment of the autonomy of privileged corporations so as to direct and modernize the Spanish Empire from above.[44] Paquette holds that regalists believed that "[g]overnment action could mold the character and shape the aspirations of the Crown's subjects."[45] In other words, its core principle "was the state's pre-eminence and supremacy in relation to the Church, albeit accompanied by the state's protection and support of the Church and its attendant institutions."[46] This extension and enlargement of sovereign rule was phrased in, and justified through, the political languages of patriotism, Visigothic precedent, and foreign ideas.[47] More importantly, as Paquette notes, it was in the language of *felicidad publica* and scientific administration in pursuit of this goal where Bourbon reformers found a discursive device capable of justifying the state's police—that is, its intervention into the economy, into its subject's lives, and the infringement on ecclesiastical wealth and property.[48] Public happiness, in this usage, was ubiquitous in late eighteenth-century political discourse.[49] For Paquette, "[t]he increase of public happiness in Spain became, like 'improvement' in contemporary Georgian Britain, a 'new criterion' for responsible administration and a mission toward which government might legitimately expand its powers."[50] The result was an ideology of governance predicated on the creation of a police state that was capable of guaranteeing social order, political prestige, and a productive economy.

These principles were foundational in the economic imaginaries of independence. Despite the fact that the 1824 Constitution furnished the new nation with a republican framework and institutions and made of its population a body of citizens, the main tenets of Bourbon governance maintained their hold on the logics and discourses of police at the local level, the level in which most anti-vagrancy legislation and practice took place, limiting in practice the very freedoms celebrated in the new magna carta. According to Eric Van Young, conservative stalwart Lucas Alamán believed this disconnect to be essential to nineteenth-century Mexican politics. For Alamán, the municipal council was "a bulwark of rational political authority and a link with the foundational institutions of Iberian heritage."[51] As Lucío Maldonado Ojeda has written, if there was a salient characteristic of anti-vagrancy throughout the nineteenth century, it was the sheer unconstitutionality of all its iterations.[52] This did not mean that anti-vagrancy remained unlegislated. In fact, the years between 1825 and 1828 would see a veritable attempt at, in a sense, nationalizing anti-vagrancy. As we will see in what follows, at stake in these legislative debates were the guiding principles of the police state vis-à-vis the labor of the citizenry. On one side, there were those that were sure that a punitive police, according to Bourbon logic, was necessary for the subsumption and subjection of an idle populace into the new imperatives of economic development. On the other, there stood some that believed that the separation of civic and moral life was necessary if republican guarantees were to hold. For these, the state should approach the question of industry in a rehabilitative key, offering the tools for the transformation of the idle into productive workers. These debates led, most importantly, to the 1828 Vagrant's Law, the only federal legislation that managed to pass through both chambers of Congress until 1853 and set the ground for anti-vagrancy's Mexican fate.

TOWARD A REPUBLICAN ANTI-VAGRANCY LAW

On the spring of the year of 1828, almost three years after it was originally conceived, Congress managed to pass a comprehensive anti-vagrancy law that, according to president Guadalupe Victoria, would lead to an improvement of public morality that benefited republican life.[53] The legislation's cornerstone was the formation of the *Tribunal de vagos* or Vagrants' Tribunal, a special institution meant to combat the capital's growing scourge of vagrants, layabouts, idlers, loafers, and sloths. While charged with policing the populace's industriousness, the Vagrants' Tribunal was never supposed to be at the forefront of this task. In theory, other social institutions—the household, the school, the church, and the workshop—functioned as the first line of defense against idleness. The Tribunal, instead, served as a sort of rearguard, a device meant to operate only at the extreme conjuncture when a national subject was proven to be irresponsible of his own liberty, careless of his most basic property—his labor—and, as a result, an obstacle to the nation's prospects. Most legislators agreed that the Tribunal was the State's last resort to make a citizen productive. What they did not agree on, as we will see, was whether the Tribunal was a punitive or a rehabilitative institution.

When the proposal for the Tribunal was first brought into discussion in the Chamber of Deputies on February 23, 1826, two years prior to its final passing, this question revealed a rift within what amounted to a consensus, despite the stringent partisan spirit of the times, with regard to the propriety of anti-vagrancy policy and the creation of a Tribunal as an institution dedicated to this sole purpose. Article 14 of the bill, which catalyzed the debate, adopted preexisting viceregal policy and stipulated only one sentence for those processed as vagrants: "the penalty of 8 years of service in the armed forces whether in the permanent army or in the national navy."[54] As mentioned in the introduction to this chapter, the *leva* or *impressment* into the army had been stipulated as anti-vagrancy's main sentence by the *Ordenanza de Levas* of 1775. Impressment "describes coercive recruitment performed by police or press gangs."[55] For historian Peter M. Beattie, "military impressment made army enlisted service a semicoercive labor system and a protopenal institution."[56] Impressment entailed the expulsion of the socially burdensome vagrant from within the city, and the coerced-soldier's dispossession of the rights and duties given by the republic he was pressed into protecting. Previous articles had been criticized over questions of relevance, redundancy, and language, but these objections had never held back the question of the establishment of the Tribunal itself, which, for deputy Lorenzo de Zavala, one of its proponents, was the measure's main contribution. Article 14, however, generated enough political and ideological disagreement to bring the measure's progress to a grinding halt. After a pair of procedural comments by two of his colleagues, deputy Manuel Posada of Puebla objected to the project because of what he considered the reactionary and punitive aspect of the Tribunal, represented by its embrace of the *leva*.

For Posada, as it was first presented, the bill simply countered the subject's vagrancy with a punishment that, for him, was as ill-conceived as it was misdirected.[57] The *leva* targeted vagrancy's effect and not its cause. Moreover, eight years of military service was an exaggeration, and did nothing to rehabilitate man to his proper, natural industriousness. That is, Posada objected to a conception of the Tribunal as a punitive institution. For the deputy, the "ley de vagos," as the project was called, drew too heavily on viceregal policies and on Bourbon precedent. As a result, the law retained the despotic frame in which these policies had originally been crafted. This despotic disposition, he noted, was antithetical, first, to the republic as a political entity, and, secondly, to the country and the times. He argued that there were other facts to consider when crafting a truly republican "ley de vagos:" the character of Mexicans, the historical conjuncture, and the possible existence of unknown albeit successful models drawn from "civilized" countries. For Posada, it was only through these considerations, through a careful reflection on what anti-vagrancy was expected to do in Mexico and in the nineteenth century, that appropriate measures to "radically cure" the ill could be conceived.

Despite Posada's insistence on the despotic dispositions of the bill, it is important to acknowledge that the new institution took its distance from viceregal policy and had been conceived by Zavala and company as a profoundly republican apparatus. Zavala was one of the most ardent supporters of a populist expansion of the political and of the enfranchisement of the poor during the 1820s, and the procedural innovations within the Vagrants' Law bill must be acknowledged as a meaningful attempt to transform the police apparatus of the new republic. According to the bill, the Tribunal put the vagrant's sentence not at the hands of a judge or any single authority, but of honorable citizens and peers. It likewise gave the right of rejoinder to the accused, and, in this sense, procedurally if not conceptually, it displaced the despotic nature of arbitrary verdicts, and opened a space which, by its very existence, acknowledged the possibility of the misidentification of the vagrant. These procedural innovations were very much an early iteration of what James Sanders has called American republican modernity. Embedded in the proposed procedures was an attempt to acknowledge popular concerns and to assert a form of republican universalism—the idea, in Sanders's words, "that all people, in spite of differences of class, race, or nationality, shared a basic human fraternity and enjoyed rights and citizenship."[58] That said, the fact that the innovation was only procedural, as does its inaugural disinterest in qualifying a long-lasting *leva* as the sole punishment for vagrancy, attests to the centrality of the consensus vis-à-vis the righteousness of anti-vagrancy policy, even among progressive figures like Zavala, whose political base was most directly affected by these measures.[59]

Posada's objections were largely ignored, but his colleague from Puebla, Senator Juan Nepomuceno Rosains raised a similar protest and returned to the first of the legislation's articles. Like Posada, Rosains referenced preexisting viceregal laws which dealt with the vagrant, but not with the goal of critiquing them. Rather, he insisted that they offered more precise and timely sentences than the eight years of military service.[60] This new law, he continued, did not attempt to innovate nor did it present the development of noteworthy measures to "radically cure the ill." To build on the existing legislation, Rosains, like Posada, believed it was necessary to acknowledge the materiality of Mexico's conjuncture. Vagrancy had three root causes for Rosains; the lack of education and employment opportunities, and the fact that a large portion of the population was underemployed and did not earn enough to even guarantee their livelihood. In that sense, for Rosains, vagrancy was the not a problem in and of itself, but a symptom of the social and economic circumstance of the present. If the legislation did not attempt to deal directly with these matters, it was best to move for its dismissal and to allow for the existing judges and institutions to deal with vagrants as they had until that point. Other deputies held Posada's and Rosains' line.

Zavala relented, but only to admit he was willing to shorten the convicted vagrant's time in the army.[61] Seeing an opening, Valentín Gómez Farías, deputy from Jalisco, took the opportunity to build on Posada's and Rosains' suggestions and propose that the bill should consider integrating recent colonization projects. He held that bringing anti-vagrancy and colonization together would lead to the rehabilitative horizon to which the senators from Puebla gestured, and benefit both the vagrant and society. Gómez Farías had not only been one of Ortíz de Ayala's early supporters in the 1822 Congress, he had also been the architect of the General Colonization Law of that year, which despite being indefinitely postponed, had been influential. He imagined the deployment of the vagrant's coerced labor within the new settlements much like Ortiz de Ayala did, as a type of forced apprenticeship with the potential of making productive wage-earning citizen out of the idle. Gómez Farías's suggestion echoed in the Chamber and garnered more than enough support for the vagrants' law bill to be withdrawn so as to provide time to study the possibility of integrating anti-vagrancy and colonization. The immediate embrace of the deputy's proposal is telling, and speaks to the imaginative pull of colonization, the idealization of the colono, and to the concomitant conceptualization of the colono's settlement as an engine not only of profit and labor, but also of example. The retraction of the anti-vagrancy bill represented a victory for Posada and Rosains. But the victory was minute if one considers that, by simply catering to the objectors, the original proponents of the bill would still achieve their aim: the legislative furthering of the state's police.

When the *ley de vagos*'s bill was brought up for discussion again, on March 29, its drafters had not only added colonization as part of the sentence, but also a clause that considered placement in a correctional facility as an option. Article 14 now read: "Those who are declared *vagos* by the court will be sent: — 1. to the armed forces. — 2. to the navy. — 3. to colonization. — 4 to houses of correction."[62] These modifications aside, Rosains' objections did not acquiesce. He observed that the numeration of each possible sentence could have the effect of insinuating a hierarchy instead of a range of possibilities which would be determined in a case-by-case scenario. For this reason, the article could be read as stating that all vagrants would be drafted into military service until its ranks were full, only to then be sent to the navy, and so forth. Precision was necessary, he insisted, and the bill's sponsors agreed, voting to eliminate the numeration. Another senator, noting a previously ongoing debate about the quality of the citizenry eligible for the army's draft, put forth the question of whether vagrants belonged in the military in the first place. Forced inscription qualified the armed forces negatively, as punishment and sentence, and not as duty.

Zavala retorted and, unlike the previous month, went on to defend the *leva* as rehabilitative tool. He reprised arguments the Chamber had heard before the previous month, when three other deputies, including Gómez Farías, expounded the benefits of the impressment of vagrants in a discussion regarding a report by the Minister of War. The deputies, like Zavala, had insisted that the first to be impressed (aplicarse á las armas) should always be vagrants and criminals, not only because it was a benefit bestowed upon them, but also upon society at large, "freeing her from useless men, who are very close to being criminals; and of the damage that she would suffer from it because of the deprivation of useful arms in other branches of industry."[63] For these deputies, the impressment of vagrants was a necessary and conditional evil particular to a historical conjuncture of economic depression, underpopulation, and social crisis. Impressment followed a vicarious logic in that, in their telling, the pursuit of vagrants benefited society as a whole in that their forced recruitment—understood as unfree labor—was useful in that it spared from military service productive men already engaged in agriculture, the arts, or other industries. Zavala's arguments succeeded and held.[64] Thus, by the adjournment of the 1826 Senate and even though the biggest modifications to the bill had been the inclusion of colonization and houses of correction as potential destinations for prosecuted vagrants, Posada's and Rosains' objections led to a general reframing of the discourse around anti-vagrancy, which now privileged a rehabilitative logic and discourse. Their qualms about the bill, though, revolving as they did on questioning the ends of anti-vagrancy and the real nature of the vagrant, foreshadowed the debates that would consume the next thirty years of anti-vagrancy policy, as we will see later in the chapter. In terms of the bill, the adoption of rehabilitative language was a minor change but one which would become relevant in the following decades. Unfortunately, support for the measure notwithstanding, the Chamber of Deputies dallied and did not pick it up again until 1828. In the meantime, pre-existing viceregal practice continued to dictate the *leva* as the primary vehicle for battling vagrancy, laying to naught the legislative shift of anti-vagrancy's ends.

ANTI-VAGRANCY RAIDS AND THE SCENE OF DISCERNMENT

Unaddressed in these first debates, however, was the question of the scene of discernment on which all anti-vagrancy depended; the precise conceptual and spatio-temporal instance in which the lived activity of subjects came into the purview of authorities which determine, classify, and engage it through schemas of abstract labor. These scenes were quintessential for anti-vagrancy, as it depended on the transparency of the social, on the capacity to verify and fabricate a warranted assertion about the truth of a subject's character, about the nature of his industriousness, and, as a result, discern (or rather, produce) the vagrant.[65] It was precisely the question of vagrancy's transparency which, on March 1827, brought the Chamber of Deputies' inaction to a head. A federal raid against vagrants in Mexico City had gone wrong earlier that month and had mistakenly rounded up many an honest working man, along with the idle. According to a witness who identified himself only as "J.R. y S.," under the guise of anti-vagrancy, public and individual liberties had been trampled "in a way that, in the empire of despotism, would have been carried out with similar scandal and panache."[66] Gangs of men employed by neighborhood lieutenants, he reported, roamed city streets at all hours and, on a whim, detained any man with the pretext of checking their occupational status. Before detainees had the chance to provide proof of employment, these men illegally apprehended them and transported them to their headquarters. There, the detainees would waste away, for a day or two, even if they proved that they were indeed honestly employed. In these encounters, there was never any consideration for the detainees' employment, for the fact that a workday had unnecessarily been wasted. Nobody involved, he surmised, ever claimed responsibility if the lost wages put the detainees' families in peril. In a similar vein, a deputy from Mexico insisted that the victims had been the working poor, not vagrants, who had vanished as soon as it began.[67] The botched raid, then, had devolved into a "persecution of good men, honest citizens and miserable artisans, who are those who have the need to roam the streets . . . with no other qualification than their poor and humble clothes."[68] The witness asked, indignant: "And this is what is called an anti-vagrancy raid [recolección de vagos]? And is there a man in this republic that sees and tolerates it?"[69] The deputy reiterated the sentiment and reported that his constituency was full of terror at the sight of the mischief and arbitrariness that had been and continued to be committed in the name of a republican and free government. These sentiments echoed, in turn, in both Chambers of Congress, where their members openly condemned the *leva*'s procedures, and insisted that changes to anti-vagrancy legislation were necessary.[70]

Many legislators opposed taking this indignation seriously. They argued that any interruption to anti-vagrancy raids would be more detrimental than its opposite. Yet, another influential group of representatives insisted that raids should be suspended for the near future, because the fact that anti-vagrancy agents could mistake a vagrant for a productive citizen was extremely concerning. The possibility of the opacity of the social created a problem within anti-vagrancy because it pointed toward the possibility of vagrancy's fugitivity. They moved on this and a resolution to this respect passed the Senate.

None of the public outcry placed the blame on anti-vagrancy practice itself. Even the most critical accounts focused on the procedures through which anti-vagrancy was deployed and on the scene of discernment itself. All would have agreed that, in principle, vagrancy hacked at the foundation of the republic. They insisted, after all, that the real vagrants had vanished or escaped. What worried them was the reality that misinformed anti-vagrancy procedures were damaging the very public happiness in the name of which it was carried out. Their claims, then, were driven by an implicit demand for a more thorough, a more nuanced anti-vagrancy practice; a practice capable of matching vagrancy's tenacity while at the same time remaining true to the republican form of government dictated by the constitution and, thus, avoiding the impingement on individual liberties seen in the past. They demanded a *republican* tactic to win the battle against vagrancy. In this, of course, they never considered the possibility that the question of anti-vagrancy, having been formulated within the horizon of Bourbon regalism, could only be answered according to its despotic frame of reference.

Whether the critics of the 1827 raids knew it or not, the Vagrants Tribunal proposed by the 1826 legislation was, in effect, the answer to part of their demands. This was the case even before the senators from Puebla, Rosains and Posada, brought up the qualms that led to the reformulation of its ends as rehabilitative in 1826. Regardless of their condemnations of its original punitive sentences and the despotic disposition which framed it, the truth of the matter was that Lorenzo de Zavala and other writers of the original anti-vagrancy bill had carefully conceived of the institution's *procedures* as thoroughly republican, as we said. Granted, the appeal process, affirmed by Zavala and his co-writers, was not entirely new. The 1775 *Ordenanza de Levas* had put the sentencing of vagrancy at the hands of justices, responsible for the processing, hearing, and punishing of the accused, but it had also granted the latter a right of appeal that depended on an extensive process of proof. Yet, the *Ordenanza* had also determined that, because *levas* could not wait, the sentencing of vagrancy could be expedited and executed despite the potential for appeal and recourse. In other words, the quintessential *leva* legislation of the viceregal period created a weak process of appeals that ran parallel to the raid and the military draft and, thus, put the suspect at the mercy of the anti-vagrancy agent, much like it happened in 1827. In contrast, Zavala's original bill, as well as the version that became law in 1828, sought to create a safeguard for the rights of the accused by strengthening the process and putting the sentence at the hands of a neutral tribunal composed of a primary chairman (alcalde primero) and two aldermen (regidores adjuntos), of whom one would rotate monthly. If there existed prima facie evidence, the accused would be kept imprisoned throughout the tribunal's deliberation.[71] For the sake of efficiency, the tribunal would meet twice a week and was responsible of gathering eye-witness evidence and character references within four days of the original denunciation. The session in which these were to be discussed and deliberated upon was open to the public, public decency permitting. A guilty verdict required a minimum of two votes from the members of the Tribunal, and until these came, the accused's rights would be protected. The verdict, moreover, would require the sentence to be made public, so that any interested party could be informed of the final destination and duration of the accused's sentence. Finally, the accused had the right to appeal the Tribunal's deliberation, and the members of the jury would hear this appeal within four additional days.

To summarize, while the 1826 bill for the Vagrants' Law sought to continue the pursuit of the vagrant with the goal of banishing him through the *leva* for the benefit of public happiness, this decision was put in the hands of neutral officials and peers, who impartially judged the accused so as to come to a more exact sentence. In this way, the bill's proposed process foreshadowed and preemptively satisfied the demands that emerged in 1827 and appeased the anxiety generated by the widespread mistrust of the government's anti-vagrancy operations. In this sense, if viceregal anti-vagrancy contained an anti-deliberative vein built on a presumption of social transparency, Zavala's *ley de vagos* opened a space for public opinion and deliberation and, thus, acknowledged the limits of this transparency. This acknowledgment allowed for republican politics within anti-vagrancy legislation in that, in theory, it undermined any pretense of a privileged access to the sort of moralist truth which lay behind the scene of discernment of prior legislation. The addition of the 1826 reconceptualization of the institution's ends as therapeutic to Zavala's procedural innovations technically resulted in an institution that transcended the subtractive anti-vagrancy practice of yore, replacing it with a summative police mechanism that, in theory, reoriented the wayward subject into proper republican and industrious citizenship while respecting his rights and individual liberties.

After the 1827 raids, anti-vagrancy legislation and its reform received new life. On March 3, 1828, the president signed the Senate's 1826 bill, which had passed quickly through the Chamber of Deputies in the preceding weeks, into law. Its *bando* (broadside) was widely published a week later through Mexico City newspapers. The Vagrants' Tribunal had been born. Yet, legislators' best intentions notwithstanding, the very practical question of the procedure for anti-vagrancy agents and their raids fell largely outside of the reach of the law's twenty-one articles. While the law broke down the definition of vagrancy and went to great lengths to guarantee due process and to explain the workings of the Tribunals, it had done nothing to address, in practice, the question of the scene of discernment. Even though, as we have seen, the law short-circuited the conclusiveness of prima facie evidence by cracking open its verdict to deliberation, it could not do without the presumption of transparency necessary to the scene of discernment. This presumption marked the limit of republican anti-vagrancy; it emphasized the disconnect between the elite's belief in the existence of the vagrant as an intentionally idle subject and the necessity to pursue him, which presumed the transparency of the social and "rational" legislative policy, which acknowledged vagrancy's opacity.

A week after the law passed, yet another botched raid took place and shone a light on anti-vagrancy's unremitting shortcomings. Details of the March 10, 1828 raid, the first under the new law, are not clear, but it seems that, in his eagerness to put the new law into practice, the Governor of the Federal District of Mexico City, José María Tornel, did not heed the Ayuntamiento's concerns with regards to its capacity to fulfill the requirements stipulated by the law.[72] The previous Saturday, March 8, the Ayuntamiento had informed Tornel that, first, they were understaffed, and, secondly, that an anti-vagrancy raid would probably yield more people than they could fit in their municipal jail and that these, who were suspects waiting for trial and not felons, would have to be put in the same space as the "true" criminals. The situation would not only be inappropriate, but also unsustainable. The governor, however, dismissed these points and insisted that the apprehension of vagrants was of high priority and should not be overencumbered or slowed down with the excuse of a lack of a budget. If funds were lacking, Tornel argued, they should suspend their investment in ornamental works and hire the necessary staff. What was important, for Tornel, was to wage the war against vagrancy now that a process existed to appropriately and legally do so. Aware of the limitations of the law, Tornel held that, with time, they would figure out the details and improve the legislation, because no law is complete when it has just been passed. Bucking to the pressure, the Ayuntamiento agreed to put three hundred men on the operation.

As expected, things did not go according to plan. On March 16, the Sunday after the raid, Tornel wrote a brief note to the editors of the *Correo de la Federación Mexicana* in which he claimed that his office was not responsible for the disorder caused by the raid.[73] To prove it, he attached a series of letters in which a secondary chairman (*alcalde segundo*), the city attorney (*síndico*), a deputy, and the superior sergeant of the police (*cabo superior*) repeated his orders as originally given. All noted Tornel's insistence that rights should be protected and "that unknown individuals who, because of their dress and decency, have the presumption of innocence in their favor, should not be apprehended."[74] According to them, Tornel had emphasized that the raid was only supposed to apprehend those who seemed suspect, whether because of their dress or the place where they were caught. If things went wrong, said the city attorney, it must have been at the level of the Ayuntamiento. To blame were the subalterns and auxiliaries who were deployed, whom the city attorney believed had certainly flown off the handle.[75] The problem, for Tornel and company, was not the anti-vagrancy order itself, but, again, its implementation. That is, they held that the problem remained the actual scene of discernment, for which they were not responsible.

The responsible party—the Ayuntamiento—argued however that the problem preceded implementation. For the Ayuntamiento, as expressed by one of its aldermen, despite the careful consideration that lawmakers had given to the procedures of the Tribunal and the forms to penalize or rehabilitate the vagrant, the actual definition of the category remained vague. Regardless of the alderman, the law's sixth article had indeed offered a specific vagrant typology. Legislators had come to it after extended debate when it was first brought up in 1826. In the session in which they discussed it, they made sure to modernize the legislation by dealing only with vagrants understood as "those who live without earning their subsistence by lawful and honest means," and not with the expansive moral catalog of the past.[76] They also considered, debated, and rejected attempts by many legislators to mark as vagrants those who were *socially* unproductive, underemployed, or who were seasonal agricultural laborers *momentarily* unemployed. In the end, the 1828 law broke down the vagrant to four categories:

> First. Those who without trade or profit, property or income, live without knowing that their subsistence comes to them by lawful and honest means. Second. The person who, having some patrimony or emolument or being the son of a family (hijo de familia), is not known for any other job other than that of gambling houses, bad company [. . .] and does not demonstrate any interest to find gainful employment in his sphere. Third. The person who is vigorous, healthy, and robust, or injured but able, yet sustains himself by

> asking for alms. Fourth. The son of a family who is not of use at home or in town, and is only known to scandalize his parents with little reverence or obedience, and with the exercise of bad habits, without propensity or application to their assigned career.[77]

That is, unlike eighteenth-century legislation, the law defined vagrancy mainly as idleness and as economic unproductivity. This was yet another of the law's innovations. By jettisoning the wide catalog of moral faults that viceregal legislation had considered as extensions of vagrancy, as well as by excluding underemployment, the law's writers attempted to insert a separation between the public and moral life of men, and to further limit the category of vagrancy to the economic life of the polity. According to the legislation, what remained within the reach of police, within its jurisdiction, was the positive space of a vagrant's agency—that space in which the subject intentionally and explicitly embraced vagrancy and idleness, rejecting the productivist imperative. In this, anti-vagrancy was grounded on the belief that the vagrant decision, the active and intentional negation of work, was the act that threatened the social contract and, thus, betrayed the duties of subjects. Yet, in spite of the apparent specificity of these categories, the truth of the matter was that they said very little of the actually existing urban populace. They also removed the alleged vagrant from the social relationships and networks that interlinked subjects, and with which anti-vagrancy agents had to deal with on the ground. Historian Richard Warren tells of how a frustrated alderman explained that, of his three auxiliaries responsible for pursuing vagrants, one owned a wine shop and the other a café and he could not expect them to denounce "those who contributed to their subsistence."[78]

Indeed, after its inauguration, the Vagrants Tribunal's carefully engineered procedures resulted in a reduction in the number of the city's vagrants. But the reduction did not derive from the Tribunal's capture and rehabilitation of the city's idle masses. Against the hope of legislators and moralists, ninety percent of those apprehended in raids were able to prove that they were indeed not vagrants. The Tribunal became, then, an instance through which citizens cleared their name from the accusation of vagrancy. The defense of most rested on their industriousness, which they managed to prove, time and time again. Warren writes that, in his frustrated appeal, the alderman noted that "many of those arrested claimed to be skilled artisans suffering from an economic slump and not sloth."[79] Historian Timo Schaefer notes that "[t]hroughout the country, men or the families of men," who were captured as *vagos* and forced into the army during the 1820s and after, "authored petitions and collected testimonial evidence attesting to their *hombría de bien*, or good character."[80] Studying hundreds of these petitions, Shaefer shows how most described the alleged vagrants "as hard-working rather than idle, sober rather than drunk, and altruistic rather than selfish," and "deplored not just the loss of freedom but also the moral injury effected by recruitment."[81] That is, despite the fact that the law's authors had insisted that the underemployed or the seasonal laborer should not be pursued, when it came down to the scene of discernment, anti-vagrancy raids were only capable of producing such subjects. Whereas the vagrant seemed to be transparent and omnipresent to legislators, the figure proved to be opaque and inaccessible to those deployed to transform anti-vagrancy policy into practice. Schaefer concludes that the petitions that proved alleged vagrants' honest occupations "gave dramatic depth to the idea that society was constituted through the practice of masculine labor."[82] These petitions, moreover, also belied the economic imaginaries of elites. Taking them into account, it becomes possible to hold that the dreamed republic of labor was already real, albeit not within an economy of abundance in which work opportunities were plentiful, but in a context of scarcity, plagued by post-war economic depression.

In the long run, the Vagrants' Tribunal seemed to have backfired. Its low rate of results stymied the initial zest of the institution and, after a couple of months, the regularity of the Tribunal's meetings, which were supposed to be weekly, began to decrease.[83] Despite this initial failure, different versions of the institution spread through the nation's cities. Over and over, in Mexico City and elsewhere, it stumbled upon the same obstacle: the contradiction between the perception of widespread idleness, the reality of the masses' work habits and the economic situation. To be sure, this disconnect was antithetical to the elite's economic imaginaries and, as we will now see, in the following decades, the blame for anti-vagrancy's failures would not fall on the practice itself, but on the republican constraints attempted by the legislators of the first post-independent decade.

AFTER ACORDADA: ANTI-VAGRANCY'S EXPANSION AND THE POLICE STATE

The year the Tribunal was founded, 1828, ended in turmoil. An insurgency launched as a reaction to the electoral victory of moderate Manuel Gómez Pedraza effectively annulled the presidential election results and led to rioting and the looting of the Parián, the city's principal market and a symbol of the wealthy Spanish and Creole merchant classes. Independence hero and populist leader Vicente Guerrero, who had lost in the ballot box against Gómez Pedraza, assumed the presidency to popular acclaim, yet was ousted the following year by a Thermidorian reaction led by Anastasio Bustamante. Bustamante's rise marked the beginning of a decade of elites forming anti-popular coalitions—an interrupted decade, surely, if we take into account Valentín Gómez Farías's 1833–34 radical administration, yet a decade nonetheless. As Richard A. Warren has written, "[t]he leaders of the movement that unseated Vicente Guerrero developed a critique of Mexico's political system based on the premise that instability, crime, and fiscal uncertainty were all linked to radical politics."[84] Moderate sectors of the 1820s, chastened by fear of popular revolt, "joined more conservative elements in creating new political structures based on the assumption that the popular political mobilizations of the previous two decades had been an obstacle to both order and progress."[85] This new political articulation of the *hombres de bien* or "decent men," eventually culminated in a new constitutional document called *Las Siete Leyes* or Seven Laws in 1836, which effectively ended the Federal Republic founded in 1824.

The reaction to 1828, the rise of the *hombres de bien*, and the move to centralism brought about a strengthening of anti-vagrancy discourse and policy, which concluded the republican push of the 1826–1828 debates and the 1828 law, and rehabilitated many of anti-vagrancy's viceregal elements. This recovery of Bourbon anti-vagrancy politics came hand in hand with a new emphasis on economic matters and forms of governance in which the echoes of Bourbon police resounded. The political activity of Mexico's first independent decade, the 1820s, had prioritized political and constitutional affairs, and its economic agenda had been guided by a somewhat passive federal state content with, or immobilized by, an outward-looking economic policy, which mostly imagined Mexico as organized around regional export-based industries such as commercial agriculture and a recuperated mining sector. This changed starting with the Bustamante government (1830–32) and continuing with the *hombre de bien*-led Centralist Republic (1835–46), both of which placed a renewed emphasis on the state of the economy and the fiscal crises at the national and provincial levels. These economic directives were buttressed by innovative protectionist measures, the rise of the Banco de Avío, the industrial development bank—seen in the previous chapter—that was deployed as a tool to jump-start modernization, the creation of specific policy to sustain an internal market, and a general move to transform the centralized state into a Bourbon-like active economic agent capable of reshaping the labor of the polity and securing the economic independence of Mexico. Chapter 2 focused on this period and its characteristic push toward the industrialization of manufacture and the replacement of artisan labor within the new modern factory. The sections that follow, however, focus on the retrenchment of popular liberties in the name of security, property, and a well-functioning economy that made anti-vagrancy of paramount importance for the fulfillment of the territory's economic promise.

THE 1834 MEMORANDUM, THE VAGRANTS' CENSUS, AND VICEREGAL RETURNS

The shift in anti-vagrancy did not happen suddenly, despite the consensus over the deficits of the 1828 law. Calls for tougher anti-vagrancy measures and police began soon after the revolt of Acordada, and the fears of class warfare inspired by the sacking of the Parián market muted, for at least a decade, republican demurrals over free labor and individual rights. Despite its deficiencies and lack of results, the 1828 law was to remain in place, not because it was considered good legislation, but because many believed it would be more effective to reform it through smaller measures than to abolish it and begin from scratch. August 8, 1834 saw the publication and circulation of one such measure, a memorandum (una circular) by Minister of Relations Francisco María Lombardo, which began the indirect recuperation of viceregal precedent.[86] The 1834 memorandum expanded, in the Federal District, the reach of post-independence anti-vagrancy policy through a series of articles that established a legal instrument capable of materializing the social transparency once thought necessary by Quirós and Bustamante to combat idleness and vagrancy: a vagrants' census.[87]

The memorandum's preamble, signed by President Antonio López de Santa Anna, affirmed that the executive understood that the abundance of vagrants in Mexico City was the result not of a lack of legislation, but a lack of compliance. To tackle the malfeasance, the document called not for a re-writing of the 1828 Law, but for a re-purposing of a regular pre-election census, originally meant to identify valid voters and issue the relevant ballots. Transformed into an anti-vagrancy tool, the census would not only produce the legally prescribed updated voter roll, but also an accurate roster of the city's vagrants. This cataloging would be carried out on a block-by-block basis by an honest and industrious neighbor who would be hired as agent (Article 1).[88] Being local, the agent would be able to produce, in a matter of two weeks, an account of each person residing in the assigned area. Listed would be their name, their parents, their age, their nature or origin ["naturaleza u origen"], their neighborhood, their marital status, their profession and, finally, their work address. If a citizen self-identified as a merchant, they were to specify their merchandise and where they carried out their business. If they identified as intermediaries of any sort, they would have to prove their trade by sharing their records. Both had to be ready to produce documents at the behest of their neighborhood's agent, so that the legality and certainty of their occupation was proved (Article 9).[89] The agents would also list any businesses, workshops, and factories established in their blocks and gather a list of its workers. This would also apply to manor houses, which were to provide the agent with lists of any servants and peons they hired (Article 2).[90] Moreover, the agent would record, privately, any local brothels, casinos and "houses of scandal" (Article 5).[91] This data would, then, be turned in to the area's superiors (señores regidores comisionados de cuartel)." By September 1, these men should, in turn, through cross-reference, be able to ascertain the city's real vagrants (Article 3 and 4).[92]

Read in the context of the haphazard raids of the past, the vagrants' census theoretically eliminated the contingency of anti-vagrancy raids by displacing the scene of discernment. No longer would the vagrant have to be caught in the nebulous act of not being employed. He would not have to be trusted, either. By producing lists of citizens that could be cross-referenced with the lists of employment reported by businesses, workshops, factories, and manors, the census produced an accurate and exact account of the industry of the territory—the desired transparent image of the social—and removed the burden of taking the vagrant at his word, while leaving in place the safeguards provided by the 1828 law for a fair trial. Lombardo, the Minister of Relations, said as much later in the month, when he explained, in reference to the August 8 memorandum, that its purpose had been to counteract the ease with which, when tried in the Tribunal, vagrants were able to prove their supposed employment and, thus, be absolved.[93] The transparency the memorandum tried to establish was to be implemented actively. From that day on, it stipulated that employers were to be held responsible for the behavior of their workers (Article 14).[94] It also mandated that, starting immediately, artisans had to be able to produce documents which proved their good behavior in order to be hired at any workshop, while servants—whether they be domestics, coachmen, lackeys, "or any other denomination"—had to carry, at all times, a document that listed their duties, salary, and current and previous employers (Article 14).

These innovations did not alter the 1828 law directly. The 1834 memorandum's major deviation from 1828 rested in its definition of the vagrant. Reversing the work carried out by the legislators of the previous decade, they insisted the Tribunal would "keep in mind" (tener presente) viceregal precedent, key among them the *Real Orden* of 1745, when judging potential vagrants or the evidence these submitted to prove their industry.[95] As mentioned in the introduction to this chapter, the *Real Órden* of 1745 mapped a typology of the vagrant—the clearest and most detailed in Hispanic law—along an axis of unemployment and another of deviance.[96] While the reference did not entail an official adoption of the *Real Orden* (this would happen later, as we will see), it did reactivate its open-ended definition and worked toward undoing the 1826–28 attempts to mark clear lines between the public sphere and the private sphere, and between underemployment and unemployment. When coupled with the vagrants' census and the active surveillance of working classes implied in Article 14, the 1834 memorandum effectively stipulated a police state according to the logics of Bourbon governance. While the decree did not actually criminalize the working classes of Mexico City, it did insert them into a scopic regime similar to Bustamante's Areopagus, a fantasy grounded on the state's total surveillance of the citizenry's industry.

Despite its attempt at a radical expansion of policing, the 1834 decree affirmed the 1828 law's therapeutic project. As we know by now, the latter's sentencing had indicated that vagrants were to be either enlisted in the army or navy, where they were to go in the name of an industrious citizen; sent to a colony, where they would labor and, eventually, become independent workers; or to a house of correction, where they were supposed to learn a craft. The new decree omitted the mention of colonization—seeing as it was circumscribed to Mexico City— and simply stated that, now, all vagrants were to be either sent to a correction house, where they would immediately learn a trade, or to the army. Even those destined to the armed forces, though, were to go to the correction house and be educated into an occupation or skill, while they waited for their military assignment and transportation.[97] The following article developed the latter idea, but it did so not by referencing the work of the twenties, but by turning to viceregal dispositions— the "Royal order of November 16, 1767, repeated in 785 and 786, and communicated to all the courts in an order dated September 11, 1788."[98] These royal decrees allowed it to stipulate that, even if the vagrant satisfied the length and terms of their enlistment (terms meant to protect the integrity of the rights of the citizen), they would not be relieved from their duty unless they proved that, during their time in the army, they had indeed learned a skill or trade that would allow them to live honestly and decently. After their discharge, the reformed vagrants had to specify where they planned to settle down, so that the relevant authority could stay vigilant and avoid the reason for their pursuit to be repeated.

Abandoning the vicarious logic of the 1828 *leva* sentences, the 1834 memorandum insinuated that the only acceptable end to anti-vagrancy was either the complete rehabilitation of the vagrant into gainful worker, or perpetual service in the armed forces. For its drafters, then, the lack of proper, full-time and honest employment justified a close to complete disenfranchisement that no longer needed to be explained or rationalized. The affront of vagrancy threatened society and, as such, proper police entailed its complete elimination. This starker approach to sentencing, and the effective reestablishment of a strengthened Vagrants Tribunal, were the 1834 memorandum's legacies, after the vagrants' census came to naught in the succeeding year. In this way, the document brought to the surface what appeared to be a consensus amongst the elites about the need to recuperate *some* of anti-vagrancy's viceregal aspects, and inaugurated a process that would continue through the decade until it solidified into law in 1845.

THE DARKENING HORIZON OF ANTI-VAGRANCY, 1836–1842

Between January and February 1836, the *Mosquito's* editors published an extended piece which, among other things, called not simply for a "consideration" of viceregal law, as did the 1834 memorandum, but for its explicit adoption.[99] Interestingly, its author, "Argos," did not quote directly from the *Real Orden* or the *Ordenanza de Levas*. Instead, he copied long passages of what he presented as current and still active Spanish law, collected in former royal scribe and member of the Spanish Royal Council (*Consejo real*), José Marcos Gutiérrez's *Práctica Criminal en España (*1804*).* In other words, by turning to Gutiérrez's tome, originally published in 1804, he hoped to instruct the reading masses ("the public, which for the most part is not made of lettered men, nor are books available to all") so that they themselves could identify who qualified as a vagrant and the measures put in place, in Spain, to successfully combat them.[100] Knowledge of proper and active anti-vagrancy law could inspire Mexican lawmakers to strengthen local legislation and, so, put an end to urban criminality by nipping it in the bud, the vagrant.[101] Throughout the text, Argos added footnotes to emphasize the deficiencies of Mexican vis-à-vis Spanish law. For example, he pointed out that in Mexico there were no active agents dedicated solely to anti-vagrancy, whereas there were three per locality in Spain.[102] In the most telling of these glosses, published on February 16, 1836, Argos went beyond noting legislative differences and rehashed a common argument regarding the leniency that local officials showed vagrants. When this point had come up in the past, others attributed it to human sentiment or an agent's familiarity with the vagrant. Let us remember the frustrated alderman's account, mentioned earlier, of how one of his officials responsible for pursuing vagrants owned a wine shop and was unwilling to pursue his potential clientele. Argos, on the other hand, believed the failure of anti-vagrancy practice had less to do with customs than with political ideas. Local officials believed, he wrote, "[t]hat everyone is free to work or not," but they were mistaken, for "legal freedom is of another order and it cannot exist if it harms society, as it is effectively done by the idle, lazy and poorly entertained, from whose ranks all the criminals and evildoers come out."[103] Insofar as vagrancy was understood as a choice, an individual's decision to not work, it threatened the well-being of the republic and justified the state's intrusion and policing. While not innovative in and of itself, this splitting of freedom and the subsequent exaltation of "legal liberty" would go on to justify anti-vagrancy's viceregal turn in the darkening horizon of the period between Texan Secession (1834) and the US-Mexico War (1846).

Two articles from April and July 1842 are telling in this regard. Between the two, they shed light on the available moral positions vis-à-vis vagrancy in the darkening horizon of the period. In both, the question of legal liberty is implied as they come up with exclusionary arguments for anti-vagrancy. As we will see, gone was the spirit of the mid-1820s legislators who had tried to abolish such logics through the modernization of anti-vagrancy and the insistence on individual rights. With the return of the modes of Bourbon governance already detailed, the matter of the habits and customs of the working classes came, once more, into view.

On April 1842, the editors of *El Conciliador*, the official paper of Veracruz's administration, called for an active campaign against not only vagrancy, but laziness ("holgazanería").[104] Laziness, argued the author, was a contagious disease in the body politic. Its mere existence was dangerous because it was visible, because it put the lie to the strict relationship between survival and labor through the exemplification of a life outside the work imperative. The mere sight of poor people who, without industry or work, are fed and clothed could lead others to believe that "it is a very pleasant thing to do nothing, and they choose the idle life," and once laziness became habit, it was too late, for it did not matter how miserable the circumstances, a vagrant always took a liking to his way of life.[105] In order to truly tackle this ill, the author wrote, authorities had to extirpate it at its root. His suggestion was to engage poor children at an early age. That is, to put them to work far from the bad examples of their parents, and so avoid the development of bad habits, "because having spent childhood and youth in idleness, it will be extremely difficult to achieve a suitable application of them; and neither the vigilance of the government nor the zeal of the magistrates, can later cut the root of the evil."[106] All others already lost to the habit of laziness would have to be rigorously punished and forced to become useful. If, even when forced, the bad habit of idleness was not let go, "it is better to let the idle die than to keep them in idleness."[107] Where in 1834, the memorandum had been stark in its reduction of anti-vagrancy's ends to industrious rehabilitation or perpetual service in the armed forces, for *El Conciliador*, the matter was clearer: industry or death.

El Siglo Diez y Nueve did not necessarily echo calls for the death of vagrants the following July, but it did insist on drawing a line between two groups within the nation's population; those whose rights had to be defended and upheld, and those who had to be forcefully transformed. *El Siglo*'s editors wrote, "man, we repeat, is never vile or despicable because of his occupation. As long as he has an employment useful to the state, whatever it may be, he must be welcomed among his good sons. Wanting to survive without working, this is what degrades him, and he constitutes him a vile being."[108] These "vile beings," held the editors, were not part of the people ("el pueblo"), made up of artisans, farmers, merchants, employees, and soldiers, but of the "populacho," that body which grouped the vicious, the informal, the dissipated and unemployed, "with whom no considerations should be had, if not to correct their excesses."[109] Labor, for the editors, was not simply a vehicle through which to guarantee the means of survival, but a matter of self-improvement. A habit of consistent work allowed the individual to improve physically *and* morally, and furthered their intellectual capacities, which in turn led to a development of the private customs and, subsequently, public virtues. He who was continually employed and kept busy was less exposed to vices than the underemployed individual who worked only three or four days per week and wasted the rest away, misspending the money he should invest in his children's education. That is, labor was doubly productive in that it produced both economic and moral value, and these values trickled down to the family and, in turn, to the nation. The same, unfortunately, applied to laziness. Laziness or idleness, insofar as they were morally degenerative and economically unproductive, imperiled both the well-being of an individual's family and the economic stability of the nation. Such potential damage reduced an individual into the category of the vile and separated him from the people whose rights had to be considered and taken care of. The editors wrote: "vices and idleness make private fortunes decline, and this decline produces later that of the nation."[110]

Conflating the moral and the political, the private and the public, the editors of both papers embraced the despotic disposition contained within anti-vagrancy and held that idleness, insofar as it was a private decision, justified full disenfranchisement. This intensification of the vagrant's vilification underwrote the viceregal turn and took full legislative shape in the 1845 Ley de Vagos. Unlike previous legislation, which persecuted the unemployed, underemployed, and idle so as to transform these into productive bodies, this new law expanded the capaciousness of vagrancy and strengthened the process to visibilize and prosecute it. As we will see, the law aimed at the transformation of the idle into the productive, but also to the complete refashioning of what was, until then, a legitimate striated panorama of labor composed of a variety of temporal and spatial arrangements of work—forms of partial, seasonal, or mobile employment—and their concomitant forms of life.

THE 1845 *LEY DE VAGOS*, THE FLATTENING OF LABOR, AND ANTI-VAGRANCY'S DESPOTIC DISPOSITION

In 1845, the Governor of (the former state, now Department of) Mexico signed new state-wide anti-vagrancy legislation that attempted to reform the deliberative apparatus of the 1828 law, while remaining largely faithful to the viceregal returns of the 1834 memorandum.[111] Like the latter, the law adopted an expansive definition of the vagrant. Unlike it, though, it did not simply refer to the viceregal catalog, but listed the categories and adapted them to present circumstance. The policy defined vagrants according to twenty-one categories. The first three of these came from the 1828 law—the unemployed, the "hijo de familia" who wasted his fortune in idleness, and the healthy beggar. The rest were wide-ranging. It included the pensioned soldier who still begged for alms, the disrespectful son, the drunk, the employed person who did not work the whole day, the laborer who without reason only worked half the week, the domestic abuser, the traveling entertainer and salesman, and the gambler. That is, it penalized not only the unemployed, but also the partially employed, underemployed, the seasonal laborer, the migrant, and the immoral, effectively establishing what we could call a threshold of industriousness and morality which sought to define the proper limits of what could be considered an employed and productive citizen. Moreover, the law ordered, as expected, for the vagrant's persecution by each and every instance of police, and multiplied the Vagrants' Tribunal, stipulating the creation of new instances in every county capital (cabecera de Partido) in the state.

The 1834 census proposal was absent in the legislation, but the new law still moved to undermine the vagrant's word through other means. The multiplication of Tribunals would be accompanied by the inclusion, in each trial, of an instance in which the prosecution could present three official witnesses. The presiding officer of the Tribunal could also gather three additional ones for the prosecution. Before, it had only been the defense that presented character witnesses. Drawn from the most decent of the accused's neighbors, the prosecution's deponents would report what they might have heard regarding the accused. Furthermore, the law stipulated that the Tribunal would produce, in a periodic manner, lists of those qualified as vagrants, to be published and posted in public areas and county capitals and disseminated in newspapers. The brunt of the law, then, focused its energies on strengthening the Tribunal and increasing its power to prosecute. The inclusion of honorable neighbors and the publicizing of the guilty would allow for an increased transparency at the local level, through permanent and horizontal surveillance and the expansion of public knowledge vis-à-vis declared vagrants; this transparency, in turn and theory, would democratize and simplify the scene of discernment and, thus, close the procedural loopholes that had undermined anti-vagrancy since the 1828 law. In other words, through the reporting of processed vagrants in the papers and the inclusion of character witnesses drawn from polite society, witnesses not necessarily known by the accused, the law effectively transformed every member of said social sphere, which coincided with the elite, lettered minority that made up the political nation, into a potential anti-vagrancy agent, an instrument of the police state they so desired.

In terms of the law's proposed sentences, the leva was brought back as the vagrant's first destination. This was not surprising considering the country was intent on replenishing its armed forces, still reeling as they were from Texan secession and multiple foiled expansionist expeditions by Texan settlers. The rest of potential sentences, though, took up the spirit of the 1834 memorandum, for which the only acceptable absolution took place through gainful employment. The 1845 law tried to make this commitment to labor as the sole path to rehabilitation fit within the industrializing push of the 1840s, studied in the previous chapter. So, the possible sentences offered by the legislation approached social productivity in a strictly economic sense. After forced recruitment, the law offered, as potential rehabilitative destinations, the new industrial factory, the rural work camp, "obrajes," and, for minors, artisan workshops. What all of these had in common, according to the law, was their capacity to guarantee a worker's occupation while keeping them "secure" (asegurados). In other words, the proper transformation of the vagrant—and of work in general, now that once-legitimate forms of industry were criminalized—could best take place in the disciplinary space of the factory floor, the labor camp, and so on: spaces where the individual's labor was inserted into a hierarchical structure of power that could properly direct it, while creating surplus value in one way or another.

What we see in this aspect of the legislation, then, is the fantasy of a police state empowered to eliminate all forms of non-work and irregular employment so as to subsume its practitioners into generative spaces which begot non-qualified, exchangeable and flattened labor. Collaborating in this fantasy, as we have seen, was polite society now deployed as unofficial policing body—the very same society to which the potential owners of these factories and labor camps belonged. As can be gleaned from this, the 1845 law's innovations were promising for supporters of anti-vagrancy. Coupled with the contemporaneous displacement of artisan labor pushed on by a rising class of industrialists, also belonging to said police society, the law would have resulted in both the elimination of idleness and the modernization of labor as social relation in Mexico. It would have also materialized the police state dreamed of by the Mexican political nation, a police state in which the lives of poor folk could be legally captured and reformed according to the imperatives of modern (bourgeois, capitalist) morality.

A few weeks after the law's publication, *El Siglo Diez y Nueve* was the first to balk in the name, for the first time since the 1820s, of individual liberties.[112] The *Siglo* did not come to the defense of the idle, but their argumentation echoed the experience of the hundreds of victims of botched anti-vagrancy raids who insisted on their innocence and, thus, of the incapacity of police to properly pierce through the opacity of the social and discern an individual's industriousness. Let us remember, as was mentioned before, that by the 1830s it became commonplace to criticize the 1828 anti-vagrancy law as a measure that was too lenient and too easily fooled by real vagrants. The increasing expansion and redefinition of the categories of vagrancy had been meant to give teeth to the legislation and to close the many loopholes that allowed for miscreants' escape. This same and constant redefinition was telling in and of itself, for it spoke about elites' certainty, despite their incapacity to ascertain any evidence, of the existence of a vagrant and idle population. The 1845 law had further expanded the definition, to include partial employment among other forms, so as to close down any remaining technicality that allowed a vagrant to claim honest occupation. In this manner, the law's drafters must have been sure that they finally gave a proper description of the actually existing vagrant. For the *Siglo*, however, in their pursuit of the actually existing vagrant, the 1845 law had overreached and overstepped. On the one hand, the editors attacked the new categories of vagrancy as being too capacious, too open-ended. Like the witness of the

1828 raids quoted earlier in this chapter, the editors held that, by throwing such a wide net, the law allowed for despotic and criminal acts. Any police agent could easily apprehend the most honorable of men, under the pretense of vagrancy, and arrest him for up to a period of nine days, while the process detailed in the law ran its course. On the other, these same categories implied a worrisome expansion of the reach of police well beyond the public realm and into the spheres where it did not belong. After reviewing the list, the editors concluded:

> Of course, it is known that all of these men can be qualified in any which way, but they are not *vagos*: a very industrious man may not respect his parents or may mistreat his wife, and yet he is far from being *vago*. It is obvious to all that only the Inquisition could have authorized such investigations. Between the domains of legislation and those of morality there is a border that cannot be crossed: morality descends into the most intimate bosoms of conscience; but laws cannot cross a residence's treshold. Whoever disrespects or disobeys his parents is a pervert who lacks one of the holiest precepts of morality and religion; but no one has the right to inquire whether he commits this offense . . . We repeat it: the legislator who crosses the a household's front door, reestablishes the Inquisition, directly attacks individual freedom: he disturbs the social order: he upsets the foundations of public morality . . . this law threatens everywhere the sacred rights of independence, security and personal freedom. We believe that the departmental assembly of Mexico did not have the powers to pass it: that if it did, it has used them in an inconsiderate and dangerous way; and finally, that the same assembly, or the authority to whom it corresponds, will of course proceed to prevent it from having its dire effects.[113]

As this fragment shows, the *Siglo* effectively questioned anti-vagrancy's despotic disposition. For the editors, any time anti-vagrancy went beyond the limited purview of the 1828 law, which had constrained its pursuit to a somewhat strict and economic (and unsatisfactory, for elites) understanding of idleness and unproductivity, it erased the boundaries between the realm of the law and the realm of morality. A productive and well-employed man could very well be immoral, but that was of no concern to the State, they held. To breach, in its inquiry, into the domestic sphere was to reestablish the Spanish Empire's most infamous of institutions, the Inquisition. That is, to pursue anti-vagrancy according to the 1845 law was to revive the cursed institution at the heart of a republican state. Of course, the paper's editors were not against anti-vagrancy itself, and when they took up the matter again by October of that year, they insisted on this fact.[114] They argued that anti-vagrancy raids might produce some results were the category limited to "true and simple vagrancy" (la verdadera y simple vagancia), yet the excessive crimes detailed by the law had, ironically, overwhelmed the tribunals the law had multiplied in the name of efficiency.

The *Siglo's* editors remained caught in the quandary of anti-vagrancy; the simple fact that even the most elemental conception of vagrancy was not as transparent and easily pursued as the editors and the elites believed it to be, and that, in practice, whatever republican modification its procedures were submitted to would be rendered ineffective insofar as anti-vagrancy was always already a despotic mechanism. Some already acknowledged this fact and shrugged it off, as done by a reader of *El Monitor Constitucional*. In a response to *El Siglo*'s original criticism of the law, the editors of *El Monitor* published a letter, written under the pseudonym "El enemigo de los vagos" (The Vagrants' Enemy), which reprimanded the other paper's editors for their general position vis-à-vis the law, and argued that the fact that anti-vagrancy had returned to the legislative agenda was a matter to be celebrated, "insofar the *vagos* not only live on the sweat of others, but with their bad example, many become the same as them."[115] The writer dismissed the brunt of the *Siglo*'s accusation by simply acknowledging that whatever despotic vestige was present in the legislation was not to blame on the specific legislators, but on the tradition from which they drew it, the *Real Orden* of 1745. He held that the 1845 law simply attempted to put some order to the question of vagrancy, which had been abandoned for too long and, thus, left up to individual authorities' arbitrary judgment. The law's formalization, even if it reproduced viceregal dispositions, was ultimately a good thing. Ignoring the rewriting and redefinition of vagrancy in the law, the writer argued that the only innovation in the measure was the inclusion of honorable neighbors in the Tribunal, and, for him, this in fact further cemented the law's good effect, because it brought in neighbors of good standing.

Telling in this exchange is, first of all, the fact that *El Siglo XIX* and *El Monitor Constitucional* and its readers were not representative of the most conservative voices in the political panorama of the 1840s. In a rough generalization, we could say that whereas the former represented moderate liberals, some of whom supported the centralist administrations of the 1830s and 1840s, the latter spoke for a wider spectrum of anti-centralist, liberal positions. That is, between the two publications, they represented a large part, if not the majority, of the political class in Mexico, and surely most *hombres de bien*. Secondly, and perhaps most importantly, *El Monitor*'s avowed indifference to the despotic disposition of anti-vagrancy was noteworthy because it attests to the fact that most members of the *hombres de bien* understood, in the 1840s at the very least, the quandaries of anti-vagrancy and were willing to look beyond them insofar as these were a means to an honorable end. The fact that these laws mostly targeted the same urban, uneducated masses, whether unemployed or underemployed, on whom they blamed in large part the state of the nation, helped. That is, the utility of anti-vagrancy transcended its politics. Any capitulation within the basic terms of anti-vagrancy would have implied surrendering the police power to engage and intervene in the life, customs, and manners of the people; to give up on nation-building as was understood by the political class, as the necessary and forced transformation of the Mexican masses. So, the reader of *El Monitor* concluded his letter insisting that the law was not perfect and, like all laws, would require subsequent modifications and amendments, based on experience, but in the meantime, it could only have a good effect.

These results were not to come. Surprisingly, the law never specified the Tribunal's rules and procedures, despite its promises to do so, and, as a result, the institution never convened. Throughout the following months, legislators issued multiple clarifications until, eventually, they prohibited asking for more explanations and ordered the measure's implementation. Their effort was for naught. Soon after, in 1846, the United States invaded Mexico and the need for soldiers led to the suspension of any and all judicial instance that interrupted the forced recruitment of men, Vagrancy Tribunals among them. Mexico would emerge from the war in 1848 a drastically different country, both territorially and politically. Yet, *El Siglo*'s demurral in the name of individual liberties and its editors' insistence on the despotic disposition of police would, between 1848 and 1851, begin to gain ground and with time become a critical frame from which to appraise anti-vagrancy policy. The 1845 law would also return, of course, and, albeit criticisms, its main innovations would hold.

THE CIRCUMSCRIPTION OF ANTI-VAGRANCY (1848–1849)

If, in 1845, *El Siglo*'s concern vis-à-vis the despotic dispositions of anti-vagrancy could be shrugged off through a mere acknowledgment that any surviving illiberal aspect of police measures were not to be blamed on the legislative intentions of politicians, this position seems to have lost its appeal in the aftermath of the war with the United States.[116] With the exception of a piece of anti-vagrancy legislation passed in Mexico City in July 1848, which reinstated a reduced Vagrants' Tribunal and reaffirmed and recirculated the 1845 Law, the years between 1849 and 1852 saw, instead, a renewed legislative and cultural attempt to restrict the definition of the vagrant to what was strictly its public iteration.[117] The first hint of this turn came not from legislative chambers, but from a *proyecto de ley* written by a commission within the Ministerio de Justicia in 1849.[118]

The brunt of the Ministerio de Justicia's proposal lay in the abolition of the Tribunals, which it considered cumbersome and ineffective, and their replacement with magistrates (*jueces menores*). The proposal would come to be called the "proyecto de jueces menores," who would be on duty every business day of the year and who, within seventy-two hours, would resolve each case, giving the vagrant a chance to appeal and present his witnesses. Their innovations went beyond this, though. In its definition of the vagrant, the proposal did away with the unwieldy inventory inherited from viceregal legislation and its resurgence in the previous years—let us remember that the 1845 law listed twenty-one categories. With these expansive definitions, it also jettisoned those categories that were not strictly related to economic productivity, to labor, and considered as vagrants only the unemployed (Art. 105) and the individual who "having an honest trade, does not habitually exercise it, but wanders [vaga] most or considerable part of the days" (Art.111).[119] Surely, the distance it took from the tradition did not entail a complete break with the 1845 law. If it dissented from the latter, it was in its re-establishment of a separation between the explicitly private sphere and the public, and therefore economic sphere. In fact, in its narrowed-down definition, it allowed for the carrying over, from the aforementioned legislation, of the legal attempt to flatten the panorama of labor. That is, it insisted on the pursuit of both the idle and the insufficiently productive and so reaffirmed that threshold of industriosity which dictated not only that a citizen must work but that they must do so consistently and constantly.

The proposal also took its distance from the other instances seen so far in this chapter in its sentencing. Completely eliminating impressment into the army, the commission proposed only to subject the vagrant to labor in order to rehabilitate him as laborer. On the one hand, it would condemn the unemployed vagrant to service in public works for a period lasting between six months to two years. On the other, it sent underemployed vagrants to a prison workhouse, where they would work on the trade of their knowledge. If the underemployed vagrant so desired, he could avoid the punishment through the payment of a fine. Unlike past anti-vagrancy instances, even if processed, in neither case would the vagrant forfeit their rights, and, thus, would always receive a wage. The vagrant sent to public works would earn a fourth of what a "free worker" earned and the one sent to the prison workhouse would earn half a wage, the remainder to be appropriated by municipal funds.

These slight but meaningful changes to anti-vagrancy were neither a complete reversal of the viceregal retrenchment that began in 1830s, nor did they gesture toward a return to the attempt at crafting a republican anti-vagrancy of the 1820s. The new *proyecto de ley* did push back at the impingement of moral categories that resulted from the conservative reaction and social anxiety of the previous decade, but it did not dismiss the effects this moralism had had on the public conception, among the elites, of what entailed productive employment. That is, the establishment of a threshold of industriousness, in 1845, which allowed for the disavowal of any form of partial or seasonal employment and, ipso facto, flattened the categories of labor so as to produce only one recognizable form of employment, could only have been developed through the elimination of the separation of spheres and the intrusion of police into the private and moral life of the citizen. After all, the dismissal of other work arrangements had been grounded on the fact that these did not employ the totality of the individual's time and, thus, did not fully exploit their potential, leaving inordinate amount of idle time unexploited and, thus, at the risk of vagrancy. If, in 1849, the new proyecto de ley sought to reestablish that separation, it did not seek to return its borders to where it had previously stood. Instead, it adopted the condemnation of the vagaries of underemployment, which in itself impinged on what had once considered the private. At the same time, by going ahead and eliminating the more explicitly moral categories of vagrancy, it came to a definition that strictly circumscribed anti-vagrancy to a policing of (waged) labor as a social relation. In the same spirit, its sentencing limited anti-vagrancy's role to the restitution of that relation. Its drafters' insistence on the continued wage of the sentenced vagrant attested to its rehabilitative aims and cemented the commission's endeavor to eliminate anti-vagrancy's despotic disposition without entirely doing away with its potential to intervene in the life of the people.

El Siglo's reaction to the *proyecto de ley* did not wait. Its tone was markedly different from their prolonged criticisms of the 1845 law.[120] The editors asked for clarifications, lamented certain ambiguous points, yet its arguments were largely adulatory. The proposal, after all, could be said to have responded to their demands of the past—it clearly stuck to the separation of spheres, leaving morality out of the provision, and targeted specifically the idle and underemployed. This, of course, did not stop them from offering potential suggestions. Only one of these is relevant for our argument here. After applauding the precision in the definition of vagrancy, they lamented that the drafters of the project had felt it necessary to differentiate between the unemployed and the underemployed vagrant's prescribed sentences.

They strongly believed that "[t]he very nature of the crime defines the penalty, so that it is not possible to make a mistake in its choice."[121] The decision to chastise unemployed vagrants with public works was misguided, they held, because "forced to perform the most disgusting tasks publicly, in daylight and most times almost naked, [the accused] lose even the last remnants of modesty and of morality, and indulge in the most disgusting cynicism. And will it still be believed that by such means the correction of those sentenced to this sentence can be achieved?"[122] That is, even if the commission guaranteed a wage for those condemned to public works and, thus, preserved a modicum of the individual's dignity, the public nature of the sentence would debase him to a point that would make rehabilitation impossible.

To contextualize their position, the *Siglo* brought in what they held was the social nature of the vagrant. They argued that a quick glance at the situation of the "circle of families of the needy class, to which vagrants commonly belong," would reveal that one of vagrancy's true roots was the "misery, abandonment and lack education of parents," which "makes the childhood and youth of the children spend in idleness, or in the performance of household chores."[123] At home, boys were assigned fewer labors than girls, and, thus, they often came of age without having acquired discipline or learning a lucrative trade. The editors asked, then, "Shall we therefore say that those unfortunates are not guilty? No way; we will say yes, of course [they are], but half of the blame for the crime for which [they] are persecuted is not theirs."[124] Poverty, and not necessarily the willful decision of sovereign individuals, was the intergenerational agent of vagrancy. In this, *El Siglo* was not calling for police's intervention within the domestic sphere, like the Veracruz paper *El Conciliador* had in 1842, as we saw earlier in this chapter. In that instance, the editors of the Veracruz paper had written that, emulating bad examples, children discovered the pleasure of "not doing anything" early on and *chose* the idle life. For them, idleness was a decision, then, driven by individual choice, and, thus, the solution, for the editors, had been to call for governmental intrusion into the lives of poor children so as to short-circuit this decision through child labor, hacking at the roots before they took hold. In contrast, *El Siglo* simply sought to acknowledge that if vagrancy was related to poverty, it had to be considered a social and not an individual problem. As a result, condemning the vagrant to public works did nothing to treat the illness. The only option, for *El Siglo*, was for the State to offer the discipline and education impossible in the impoverished household of the have-nots. Luckily, the *proyecto de ley* already offered an answer, they said. What the editors called for was that the unemployed vagrant be pressed, like the underemployed, into the prison workhouse instead of public works, where they would not simply serve their penance but also learn a trade that could guarantee their livelihood in the future. If the commitment to rehabilitation was true, it had to be available for all vagrants.

By disavowing governmental intrusion into the private lives of individuals, *El Siglo* limited the state's sphere of engagement, restricting its activity to either indirect, preemptive public policy or remedial action. Thus, it gestured toward a deviation from the foundation of moralistic voluntarism—and Bourbon regalism, tout-court —on which anti-vagrancy rested and moved to what we could call a sociological understanding of vagrancy. While this was a development, as we will see in the next section, the move did not represent a total break with the moralism and exemplarism of the traditions of anti-vagrancy nor did it imply a questioning of the necessity of police. After all, for the editors, the vagrancy of the underemployed, which they considered worse than that of the unemployed because this was indeed a decision *not to labor more*, was not only punishable but to be abhorred. The editors' goal was not to obstruct the pursuit of the vagrant by attempting to furnish the unemployed vagrant with a materialist alibi, or to hinder police access to the private. From their perspective, they were in fact simplifying the problem of anti-vagrancy and, in tandem, moving toward a thoroughly modern position—to appear in the pages of the paper in 1851.

For *El Siglo*, a police state was still called for if a government was to guarantee the security of people and their interests. So, despite their reservations, on August 1849, they insisted that a thorough, preemptive approach to pursuing anti-vagrancy was still lacking, urged the authorities to develop a constant surveillance of urban spaces and public roads, and suggested the development of a civil registry which gave an account of everybody coming in and out of the city, and those found in restaurants, etcetera. The editors acknowledged that "all of this, at first glance, seems difficult, and it is believed that it restricts the will of citizens, but it does not."[125] Through such a registry, they wrote,

> it would be known, as it should be known, what is the profession of each person, the means they have to live and even the hours they employ on their job. This, say what you want, is a positive guarantee, because when a man knows that the authorities watch over his actions, he makes sure that they are good, and if he does not have employment, for fear of punishment, he will look for an occupation, and he will become fond of it later when he begins to acknowledge the advantages that he derives from it. The man who works, the man who makes a regular living without risking his life, does not

> embark on the detestable and dangerous path of crime; but when administrations neglect their duties on this point, *vagos* multiply, and here is the germ of all evils.[126]

Put simply, *El Siglo* was suggesting their own version of the 1834 vagrants' census. The registry worked, mainly, as a police device capable of producing an accurate account of the industry of the people—down to the hour—, to be used in the pursuit of vagrants. But it functioned also as deterrent. Like in Carlos María de Bustamante's dreamed-of Athenean Areopagus, each citizen, knowing himself to be under police surveillance would willingly or unwillingly find employment so as to avoid the consequences. Once embedded in labor as a social relation, the individual would steer clear from deviance. Were the interpellation to fail, then, the anti-vagrancy apparatus would step in, not to punish him for the breach, but to reform him. Police, for the editors, was a generative practice.

El Siglo's police state has to be taken as a distillation of the anti-vagrancy efforts we have seen so far in this Chapter, as an an attempt to transcend the missteps of the previous decades. In fact, the 1849 *proyecto de ley*'s narrowing down of vagrancy and its origins was but a step toward the elaboration of a more perfect police. For the editors, the viceregal disposition within anti-vagrancy had produced a muddled account of the social through their disavowal of the borders between the legal and the moral. As a result, these encumbered the deployment of police power by bringing into its jurisdiction the innermost sanctum of citizens, inaccessible and off limits as it was and should be. In a sense, then, for *El Siglo*—and this was true for all post-independence engagement with the matter—the problem of anti-vagrancy was ultimately hermeneutical. For anti-vagrancy to work functionally, legally, discursively, and politically proper categories were necessary. Only with the correct hermeneutical schema would the dissipation of the opacity of the social and the discernment of the true vagrant be possible.

The Ministerio de Justicia's "proyecto de ley de jueces menores," which had opened the door to *El Siglo Diez y Nueve*'s reflections, would continue making the legislative rounds for the next four years, until it was finally signed into law in 1853. Through the intervening years, it gained adherents and, because it was seen as a major shift in the matter of anti-vagrancy—it had effectively called for the circumscription of anti-vagrancy to the policing of (waged) labor as a social relation, as we have seen—it consistently opened the door for the sort of debate and reflection that led to a clearer conception of the police state dreamed of by elites and, more importantly, to the splitting of vagrancy.

POLICE AND VAGRANCY'S SPLIT (1849–1853)

By 1851, *El Siglo* would offer a potential hermeneutical schema for the dissipation of the opacity of the social. This schema would be contained in what historian Lucío Ernesto Maldonado Ojeda calls the "new conception of vagrancy," one fully crisscrossed by the sociological and the economic.[127] Vagrancy would not be developed or thought beyond this "new conception" in the first half of the nineteenth-century in Mexico.[128] Soon after, though, a whiplash of historical contingency would erase the work.

El Siglo's argument began with the presumption that, *avec* the "wise and prudent Jovellanos," the true wealth of a nation consisted on its capacity to achieve full employment. If this was the case, the editors held that good government entailed a state's willingness to invest all of its administrative energies in both guaranteeing the availability of work for all of its citizenry and policing and apprehending all who neglect this imperative.[129] Truism affirmed, the editors went on to offer a historical survey of anti-vagrancy legislation in Spain and in Mexico, paying particular attention to the Royal Order of 1745 and, then, the Law of 1828. Their intention was to call for proper legislation and implementation—the Comisión's *proyecto de ley* of *jueces menores* was still far from becoming law. The editors then switched gears and offered what would become the new conception of vagrancy through a paraphrasis of an "escritor de nuestros días," who they did not name but was Spanish economist and jurist Manuel Colmeiro y Penido (1818–94).[130] Because the fragment is relevant, I quote it *in extentio:*

> Idleness can be voluntary or forced on individuals; accidental or habitual; simple or qualified. Voluntary idleness implies a vice, a true development of customs, that an administration is obliged to correct for the wellbeing of the vicious, for the safety of all and to avoid a bad example. Forced vagrancy is a particular misfortune, the daughter of ignorance, either a form of improvisation or the result of certain general causes impossible to counteract by a single man. This genre of innocent idleness, or lack of work, must be remedied by the influence of public charity if the help of private charity were not enough. Accidental idleness, although voluntary, is not the vice itself, but its announcements; it is the seed, not the fruit. Because they are still mild disorders and usually private, they are the result of domestic conduct and fall within the sphere of morality, which itself falls under the rule of administration. However, political authorities can fight this indirectly, inspiring the love of work in the people through education, and encouraging perseverance with the encouragement of reward. Usual, voluntary vagrancy involves a state of war with society, a man who lives in opposition to the general interest, and

> is his constant enemy. In simple idleness, there is a danger of disturbing public order; in qualified idleness, or when its accompanied by aggravating circumstances, public order is in fact disturbed. The first is fought through preventative means, within the limits of administrative power; the second is a common crime, which must be repressed and punished by the competent judicial authority. It follows, then, from all the above, that the authorities are always the ones that directly or indirectly have to prevent vagrancy, and avoid the evils that it causes society; [the authorities have to] put into practice all repressive means, seek the education of the people, which we will not tire of calling for; develop the industry; agriculture should preferably be protected; undertake public works of public utility; see to it that charity is not blind or indirect, and, only then, will vagrancy be reduced; with these small efforts, the administration will be able to contain and destroy it.[131]

El Siglo, through Colmeiro y Penido's definition, split the heart of vagrancy into two. On the one hand, vagrancy was still what it had been in the viceroyalty, voluntary vagrancy, a willful choice or intentional infraction by an autonomous individual, moved by his passions rather than his true interests, an active deformation of customs and habits. It was the state police's responsibility to repress, punish, and correct it, in the name of the individual, general well-being, and exemplarity. This here vagrancy—what before, in 1849, they simply had referred to as the idleness of the underemployed—was the true target of anti-vagrancy because it was a declaration of war on society and the general interest. On the other hand, forced or naive vagrancy was not a vice in itself but a symptom, an effect and not a cause; it was idleness *in potentia*. Forced idleness was the consequences of particular conjunctures which were impossible for an individual to work through by himself. The naive vagrant was, thus, an accidental vagrant. Yet, *El Siglo*, through the Spanish jurist, was not arguing that naive vagrancy was completely deprived of a will, but that its will was dramatically shaped, formed, and determined by the context itself. The naive, vagrant intention was born from the wider circumstance and not from within the individual. In this sense, this form of vagrancy did not necessarily disturb society insofar as it was the product of a society that was in itself disturbed—riled by war or by a lack of work, etcetera. Put differently, for *El Siglo* and Colmeiro y Penido, forced vagrancy was an opaque vagrancy, one which would always escape the ends of anti-vagrancy and prove its mechanisms misguided because the apparent ill was not in the body of the vagrant but everywhere else. The immediate effects of this form of innocent vagrancy were moral and were, therefore, outside the reach of legal or penal persecution. In any case, its effects had to be targeted indirectly, through what the jurist called *administration*: the procurement of popular education, industrial development, investment in agriculture, the initiation of public works projects, and a utilitarian bent to charitable practices.

Colmeiro y Penido's understanding of administration, implicit in *El Siglo* but undiscussed in their excerpt, was closely related to, yet distinct from the eighteenth-century conception of police. For the Spanish jurist, administration represented a wholly modern and scientific approach. Administration, wrote Colmeiro y Penido, was the confluence of political right, civil jurisprudence, public economy and statistics: "The first [political rights] points out its sources, the second [civil jurisprudence] draws its limits, the third [public economy] communicates its principles and the last [statistics] suggests data and news."[132] That is, administrative rule, for Colmeiro y Penido, deployed political and civil law, according to the principles of the public economy, using statistical data when available, to engage with the social. If Bernard A. Harcourt has argued that, even after the emergence of political economy and its separation of the spheres, the imbrication of the economic and the police remained active, with the penal sphere serving as the outer limit of the economic, Colmeiro y Penido's administration positioned itself somewhere in between the economic and the penal, pointing at the more administrative aspects of police as the organization of social life.[133] As such, between 1851–1852, Colmeiro y Penido's use of administration and its utility to Mexican lettered elites augured the development of a new form of governance beyond police which overcame Bourbon ideologies of governance. Taking it as a point of departure, *El Siglo* split vagrancy so as to offer a modern, yes, but more importantly, *administrative* account of the problem, one which took into consideration not only the question of police and the general well-being of society, but the confluence of political rights, civil jurisprudence, public economy, and statistics.

Positions similar to *El Siglo*'s vis-à-vis vagrancy echoed during the same period in juridical circles, state commissions, and municipal assemblies, as historian Lucío Ernesto Maldonado Ojeda has shown. A few, moving beyond economic and political contingencies and their effects on the polity, foreshadowed the scientism of the latter part of the nineteenth-century, when they brought to bear "the climate and the natural inclination of man to pleasure, "as extraneous factors that led to forms of naive vagrancy.[134] In *El Siglo* and in these other interventions, the splitting of vagrancy, the acknowledgment of a form of opaque vagrancy, inaccessible to anti-vagrancy's scene of discernment—a scene that was now to be defined *administratively*— effected a foreclosure of vagrancy as a heuristic device and of police as the state's claim to subsume the private life and manners of the citizen.

Even if *El Siglo* still called for the persecution of voluntary vagrancy, their opening of the category to history, to context, liquidated its potential. After all, as many historians have shown, the majority of cases that passed through the Vagrants' Tribunal were, unsurprisingly in light of the economic and political panorama of post-independence Mexico, cases of forced vagrancy. Most "vagrants" consistently managed to prove their industriousness by bringing in witnesses that attested to the fact that their present situation—their current bout of unemployment, their displacement from a place of work, their not-working every day of the week—was different from their general situation of honest employment. Of course, as we have seen, elites were blind to these qualifications and would consistently complain that the witnesses must be false, that the system was broken, etcetera. Yet, despite the many deliberative innovations to, or despotic transformations of, anti-vagrancy, the results yielded continued this trend. Ultimately, the recognition of a form of opaque vagrancy, one which was not what it seemed because it did not entirely emerge from a willful and individual decision, ignored the fact that even the most intentional forms of vagrancies were equally opaque, equally subject to contextual contingencies.

Another logical corollary of vagrancy's split was that if the state was to insist in its pursuit of vagrants that had now been granted an interiority and a history, it had to assume new duties. As Maldonado Ojeda recounts, Luis Rivera Melo, a lawyer in the Cabildo de México would develop a similar argument with regards to anti-vagrancy and propose to the former body that it should draft two petitions to Congress with regards to it. One would request the suppression of forced impressment into the army as a potential sentence. The other would insist on "the obligation that society has to provide work for those who, with a desire to work, cannot find what to do and the injustice with which a penalty is imposed on those who do not work when their vagrancy is innocent."[135] Even if it came to naught, Rivera Melo here glimpsed at anti-vagrancy's logical ends: if the state called for the full employment of the population, it had to be able to guarantee the very possibility of employment. Anti-vagrancy without the right of work was a non sequitur.

This new conception of vagrancy and its corollaries did not and could not hold within the economic imaginaries of independence. In the pursuit of economic aggrandizement, of the subsumption of the territory and the population into the state and its capitalist horizons, police as a tool of restraint and vertical intervention, as the mechanism which made possible, in the words of Gareth Williams, "the direct governmentality of the sovereign qua sovereign," was indispensable.[136] Thus, these developments in anti-vagrancy were swept away by the same historical conjuncture that *El Siglo* tried to take into consideration. For a moment, though, it seemed as if they had succeeded. 1852 and 1853 saw these arguments seep into local legislative debates to the point that, on January 1853, the 1849 proposal of jueces menores that simplified vagrancy, and which led to *El Siglo*'s extrapolations, became law in the Federal District of Mexico City. Yet, months later, in August 1853, President Santa Anna signed the first nationwide anti-vagrancy law since 1828. The law adopted the magistrates (jueces menores) proposed by the previous legislation and abolished the Vagrants' Tribunal. To simplify and standardize anti-vagrancy, which *El Siglo* and many others had called for, it derogated all local legislation on the matter. Yet, it went ahead to define vagrancy following the expansive viceregal model, while declaring, as potential sentences, forced impressment into the army, colonization, and, lastly, any rehabilitative measure of choice to the magistrate. Santa Anna's law marked a new beginning in anti-vagrancy and, like a forced reset, set the ground for a general re-staging, in the second half of the nineteenth century and in a radically different atmosphere, of the arguments we have seen throughout this Chapter.[137]

CONCLUSION

For Lucío Maldonado Ojeda, the questions of vagrancy and anti-vagrancy "corresponded" more to the instability of post-independent Mexico rather than the modern and capitalist state of the latter part of the century—a state which had largely pacified the territory, suppressed armed struggle, and began a process of rapid industrialization.[138] For the historian, the ratification of the 1871 Penal Code in Mexico City, which formalized and settled a definition of vagrancy, and its subsequent adoption by most cities and states, effectively put an end to anti-vagrancy's embattled history of republican reform and viceregal returns, studied in the preceding pages. Said penal code, wrought under a liberal administration, began a process through which the police and policing as a mode of governance were professionalized and institutionalized; a process which sought to transform the police, in the words of Pablo Piccato, into "an instrument of the state rather than an extension of barrio life."[139] The excision of the police from "barrio life" entailed a deepening of the borders between the private and the public, a de-personalization of policing which, in theory, necessarily abandoned the moral horizon considered inseparable from the question of anti-vagrancy.

Much like the 1828 law, the 1871 penal code's definition of vagrancy abandoned viceregal moral catalogs and excluded the matter of underemployment, so as to focus only on the economic question of unemployment. Its Article 854 reduced the definition of the vagrant to the simple circumstance of idleness; a vagrant was "he who, lacking the means and income, does not exercise any honest industry, art or trade to survive, without having a legitimate impediment."[140] Processed as such, the accused vagrant would be given a period of ten days, wherein he was to show proof of having acquired honest employment. If he failed to do so, and was unable to post bail, he would be arrested and imprisoned until he either paid the fine, or proved to have learned a trade.[141] Despite many succeeding amendments, the Penal Code would only be replaced after almost sixty years in 1929.

The 1871 penal code's anti-vagrancy articles remained caught in the quandaries studied in this chapter. Like all its preceding iterations, this latest revision was incapable of acknowledging and engaging with the material and historical realities of unemployment. For all its attempts at offering a rational and liberal punitive code, the adoption of the matter of vagrancy was the adoption of the irrationality that beat at its conceptual center as well as of the despotic disposition which underwrote all anti-vagrancy action. Thus, regardless of Maldonado Ojeda's conclusive statement, it is important to emphasize that anti-vagrancy's correspondence to the postcolonial moment—to the economic imaginaries of independence, in fact—did not entail its inoperativity within the context of late nineteenth-century Mexico. In fact, I would hold that the formalization and institutionalization of anti-vagrancy effectively confirmed that anti-vagrancy had always been a by-product of the capitalist horizon inaugurated in the eighteenth century, and not necessarily of the forms of Bourbon governance which had determined its procedural identity. The rising tide of capitalist imperatives, after all, had been the common denominator that drove both Bourbon reforms as well as the subsumption of a subject's productive life into the jurisdiction of governance and police. With the intensification of the modernizing zeal during the last quarter of the nineteenth century, the battle against idleness continued to be a central concern. If vagrancy as a heuristic category that allowed for the policing of the productive life of subjects seemed to reach its twilight, it was not because such policing had been foreclosed but because it was beginning to be transformed according to increasingly biopolitical forms of governance that would reach maturity toward the middle of the twentieth century, and which would entail a parcelization of life's constituent pieces, each of which was to be assigned to a different jurisdiction and institution for policing. Like colonization, vagrancy was ultimately an ideologeme: one which sustained the fantasy of both the complete subsumption of life into the productive horizons of capitalism as well as of the possibility of full social transparency—the capacity to aptly distinguish between the thousands of productive and idle instances which make up the everyday existence of the population. And yet, unlike colonization, interrupted by material reality only on the rare occasions in which its policies were implemented, anti-vagrancy had to consistently and effectively withstand and persevere through its impossibility every day and everywhere.

Conclusion

The colono stands in the middle of a vast field, in front of an impressive homestead and acres of budding crops far to the North of the territory. His harvest, like usual, will be plentiful, and the returns will fund and fuel the further improvement of his instruments, the education of his offspring, and his investments in modern industries and commerce across the national territory. Almost a hundred and ninety *leguas* or eight hundred kilometers to the south, a former artisan skillfully operates a machine, powered by hydraulics, surrounded by his wife and children, all employed in the same factory floor, located in an industrial village, miles from the city. The urban center's streets are clean and empty, with the exception of carriages crossing back and forth, of industrious servants going about their tasks, in and out of orderly stores, without a moment's delay. Two nights before, an anti-vagrancy raid was carried out, and it yielded the few remaining loafers in the most disreputable of city blocks. These men, quickly but justly tried by a court dedicated to this sole purpose, now cross shamefully through a plaza, marching behind a soldier, knowing that their idleness has led to their banishment. These vagrants form a perfect line, moving in step. Some are destined to be impressed into the army, others to labor at a colono's settlement. Both sentences will attempt to improve their ways, to give them an opportunity to be reformed and join the ranks of the productive. That colonia, that factory, that city, all are the loci where Mexican aggrandizement is produced, where the providential wealth of the land meets the enlightened industry of the polity, where incredible riches are reaped, where Mexico's place is secured among the enlightened nations of the world.

It is a dream, of course. Let us say that a shout in the distance breaks through it. After all, "[t]here are an extraordinary number of street-cries in Mexico [City]," wrote Frances Calderón de la Barca during her sojourn in the country between 1839 and 1842, "which begin at dawn and continue till night, performed by hundreds of discordant voices, impossible to understand at first."[1] The noise attests to the real urban milieu, and not the fantasy of the economic imaginaries. There is the *carbonero* selling coal; there is the grease-man, lard; the butcher, his salted beef; the cook who yells back from the door of the house where she works, asking if anybody has the specific ingredient necessary to prepare a houseguest's wished meal; an indigenous woman, a *cambista*, sings out a request for a barter, she offers *tejocotes* for peppers; a *voceador* yells the news of the day for the newspaper that employed him this week, and his headlines are hyperbolic but carry a kernel of truth and that is enough; soon after, an ambulatory salesman peddles needles and pins and shirt-buttons and tapes and cotton balls and mirrors. He is the most popular of all, and is quickly surrounded by the cook, who jumps out from her perch at the door, and a dozen other housekeepers. His thunder is stolen by a "sharp note of interrogation," the woman who sells *gorditas* has appeared and her steaming product flies off her basket in the hands of, yes, those housekeepers, but also of dozens of servants that are already carrying out errands through the streets, and artisans on their ways to and from their workshops.[2] The beggars appear later, and so do the harassing leperos, and the false invalids, and, annoyingly, they mix with the noon-time vendors of more foodstuffs and candies and products. The streets are alive with commerce and so are the stores that line them, the reputable outlets housed in the Parián market, and, infamously, in alleyways and dead-end streets, the *pulquería*s of pitched canvas tents, held up by poles and ropes, that dispense their fermented maguey sap.[3] Everywhere men and women are working, laboring, keeping the pulse of the city, the country going.

The lettered men studied in this book see all of this, they live through it, partake, and yet they find it disagreeable. Or, at the very least, not up to the standards of the country they imagined they would one day lead. They ignore or misunderstand most of it, just like they ignored or misunderstood reports of the slave-owning colonos up North, whose lands were made productive under the whip; of the French migrants who attempted to settle the Tehuantepec Isthmus but died in the process; of the causes of indigenous discontent in Yucatán and elsewhere; of the reality of the underemployment of the artisans that crafted the stuff of the everyday. Instead, to explain, interpret, and think through the infinite set of facts, acts, and actions that make up the world which they inhabit they turn, like all of us, to a series of inherited and limited schemas.

In this book, we have studied the significant role played by three figures that are quintessential to understanding the economic imaginaries of the period. Notwithstanding the turbulent circumstances of the three decades surveyed, these figures—the colono, the artisan, and the vagrant—were deployed rhetorically and politically in a consistent manner because they allowed for satisfactory and convincing solutions to the very material problem of nation-building—or national economy-building, to be more precise—to the anxiety-inducing elite quandary of what today we would call underdevelopment. These figures, thus, allowed for narratives that attempted to articulate a harmonious story of the economic future and development of the nation in the aftermath of independence; a story whose plot ultimately belonged to the genres of primitive accumulation. In each and every deployment, though, these figures faltered in the face of material circumstance, and their proponents were often at odds to explain or rationalize these failures as circumstantial, structural, or the result of the cultural obstinacy of Mexico's population. As we have seen, Mexican elites believed that the universal, classically liberal conception of man as laboring animal, as moved by interests and a desire to develop his own property, became inoperative when deployed in the territory. That is, what political economy sold as a universal truth of man—labor, property, self-interestedness—Mexican elites believed, excluded their compatriots; if Man naturally worked, Mexican man did not.

Was Mexican exceptionality the result of the Mexican citizen's customary existence, history, or an effect of the landscape? This question flustered post-independence elites, but did not daunt them. What kept them looking forward—optimistically in the first decade, less so in those that followed—was the certainty of the proverbial wealth of the land they occupied. This belief, as we have covered, was an effect of the eighteenth-century mining boom which had put the Mexican heartland at the center of a global silver economy, and which had generously benefited most elite families with diversified holdings. Whether the lettered men studied in his book had experienced this golden age firsthand, or benefited from its legacy, they did not doubt its potential. After all, Alexander Von Humboldt's surveys of the territory in 1803 and 1804 had confirmed the land's potential, and had predicted that all that was necessary was an enlightened administration capable of making it productive.

In the aftermath of independence, colonization projects were the cornerstone in most plans that sought to make Humboldt's predictions a reality, as explored in Chapter 1. As an operation, colonization guaranteed the effective occupation of the land, the foundation of industrious utopian enclaves, at first spatially and socially differentiated from the rest of the nation—and, thus, freed from its historical obstacles— but which, eventually, would expand and transform the entirety of the national territory from within. The *colono*, an enlightened, entrepreneurial, sovereign individual, productive and undistracted, stood at the center of these plans, and whether he was an immigrant or an enterprising veteran, he offered a model of the future Mexican citizen. The figure's gravitational pull distorted the economic imagination, and was so strong that, beyond the *colono*, there existed no positive figuration of labor in the economic imaginaries of Creole elites between 1821 and 1852. For all the celebration of the wealth that the territory promised and the moral power of free labor, when faced with the sheer material impossibility of the creation of a coherent national economy and market, the lettered men who broached the question of the new nation's economic fortunes could not conceive of an economy driven by the industry of its current population. Everywhere they looked within their urban milieus, elites interested in economic matters only saw a growing number of idle bodies.

Even men like Mariano Otero (1817–1850), who attempted to develop proto-materialist and proto-sociological analyses of the national situation, were incapable of moving beyond this cultural impasse. Otero had criticized the shallow analysis of his peers and, in his 1842 *Ensayo sobre el verdadero estado de la cuestión social y política que se agita en la república Mexicana*, set out to show that "in the moral world, just like in the physical world, everything is linked, everything has its cause and its end."[4] To understand what was really happening in the country, he argued that it was necessary to look at property relations. The organization of private property was "the generating principle, [the] fact that modifi[es] and comprehend[s] all of the other factors and from which all social phenomena that appear to be isolated emerge."[5] Precisely because, since independence, all those that had set out to understand the "constitution" of Mexican society had ignored these, they had been incapable of recognizing that said society "had its own physiognomy, and that it was not at all like the European societies with which we are always comparing ourselves only because we have borrowed their social organization's names without in any way having its constituent parts."[6] Unfortunately, Otero's critical and methodological approach, his "arid examination of the constitution of society considered under purely material relations," did not lead him to consider the multiple aggravating factors and economic conditions that impaired the possibility of full employment.[7] Instead, like the other representatives of the economic imaginaries we have studied in this book, Otero culturalized material problems that were political in nature, and attributed their root causes to, mostly, the unshakeable weight of colonial history and its inherence in the everyday life of the people, in their customs and work habits. Even after all his careful analysis, Otero looked at the artisan and echoed the arguments we have seen by other members of an anxious elite, seeing only an underdeveloped and stupefied worker, whose labor was insufficient for a modern economy.[8] For men like Otero and Estevan de Antuñano, the industrialist we studied in Chapter 2, the embeddedness of the artisanal workshop, of the craftsman's labor and customs, and the distance between these modes of production and those elites believed proliferated in the modernizing nations of the western world, transformed the laboring artisan not into a figuration of work, but of its opposites, a stand-in for unproductive customs, obsolete technologies, underemployment, and corruption.

Like Antuñano and Lucas Alamán, those who sought to launch the industrialization of Mexico through the modernization of the cotton industry, consistently tried to transform the artisan into a modern wage-worker, to remove the instrument from the artisan's hand and to figuratively insert the man into the machine. Even those that set out to rescue the moral integrity of artisan labor could only produce plans in which the actually existing worker emerged as a problem, as an equation to be constantly policed and disciplined. In this context, anti-vagrancy promised a way through and offered a police procedure capable of pursuing and excising the idle and unproductive elements that held the nation back. And yet, as Chapter 3 showed, despite decades of innovation and application, the result of said policies—and the vagrant himself—remained elusive. The raids that were supposed to capture miscreants mostly supplied men who claimed to be employed and who, given a chance, managed to prove it. Unlike the lettered men who called for anti-vagrancy and the policy-makers who crafted the tools for its implementation, both of whom could clearly draw the line between a productive and an unproductive life, and despite the consistent expansion of the reach of the police, the operatives who were charged with the responsibility of capturing vagrants seemed to be incapable of discerning between work and its opposites, between the moments of downtime needed for the reproduction of life and the moments of idle pleasures that were said to impair such reproduction.

Through this inquiry into the period between 1821 and 1852, *Mexico, Interrupted* has drawn attention to the poverty of the Mexican economic imaginaries. The truth of the matter was that, as has become evident by now, the colono, the artisan and the vagrant were signs taken for wonders, or rather, ideologemes taken for full concepts; partial and vague and, precisely for this reason, so powerful and captivating. The three figures would go on to survive well into the last quarter of the century, and even beyond, as shown in the closing pages of each of the book's chapters. Yet, despite the figures' tenacity, their contexts of enunciation changed and, as Timo Schaeffer has shown, the replacement of labor with property as the quintessential value of liberal discourse during the Porfiriato (1876–1910) carried with it a transformation of the horizon of the economic imagination. It was not that labor as a category lost its symbolic and moral power—in fact, the languages surrounding the imperatives to work remained unchanged—but that work's link to civic morality had been sundered.[9] As a result, once the centrality of labor had been displaced, and so neoclassical republican universals dismissed, the inherent misanthropy that had once surreptitiously characterized the Creole economic imaginaries of the first half the century was finally laid bare, and given right of way.

Notes

INTRODUCTION

1. All translations, unless otherwise specified, are my own. "¿No estais asociados con los tiranos que por espacio de trescientos años han saqueado, devastado y aniquilado a la América, con los déspotas que han tenido a vuestra Nación siempre exausta, siempre exangüe, en la más deplorable escaséz, en la más absoluta miseria?" *El Despertador Americano*, June 3, 1811, 27.
2. "¿Quiénes han estancado la Sal, el Tabaco, el Azogue, la Nieve, el Tequexquite, los Colores, el vino Mescal, la Pólvora, en una palabra los ramos todos de la industria, sin dexar en que trabajar al Criollo honrado, ni con que proporcionarse una mediana subsistencia?" *El Despertador Americano*, June 3, 1811, 28.
3. "Entre tanto, redobla el pobre Criollo su trabajo, riega la tierra con su sudor, y no pocas con su sangre, acorta más y más el alimento a su familia, y no siendo esto bastante, se ve precisado a invocar la muerte, como único fin de su miseria." *El Despertador Americano*, June 3, 1811, 29.
4. "La libertad de romper todas las trabas de la industria, de dar ocupación a nuestros Nacionales para que no se corrompan, como hasta aquí, en una forzosa ociosidad, de surtirnos por nosotros mismos de quanto hemos menester, y no comprarlo todo de séptima u octava mano, de beneficiar nuestras Minas de Azogue, &c, &c, &c, es un libertinaje, una libertad quimérica, un ente de razón, que la estupidez indiana no quiere realizar." *El Despertador Americano*, December 20, 1810, 10.
5. "es ya tiempo de que sus beneméritos habitantes comiencen a á experimentar la diferencia que hay entre el estado de un pueblo que disfruta de su libertad política, y el de aquel que está sujeto á un yugo extrangero." *Gaceta Imperial de México*, October 13, 1821, 47.
6. See Timothy Anna, *The Mexican Empire of Iturbide*, 34. Also, Barbara H. Stein and Stanley J. Stein, *Crisis in the Atlantic Empire*, 641–47

7. Stein and Stein, *Apogee of Empire*, ix.
8. Beatty, "Riqueza, polémica y política," 243–44.
9. The *Gaceta*'s article fits neatly into the repertoire of what James E. Sanders has called "American republican modernity," a "counter mentalité" that celebrated an imagined modernity in which Latin America represented a new standard, structured around the centrality of republican politics. For Sanders, while the repertoire of American republican modernity would gain strength later in the century, it saw earlier iterations throughout the Americas. The *Gaceta* is an early example of it. Sanders, *The Vanguard of the Atlantic World*, 5.
10. Stein and Stein, *Edge of Crisis*, 58, 391.
11. Tutino "The Americas in the Rise of Industrial Capitalism," 32.
12. Salmerón Sanginés, "El mito de la riqueza de México," 139.
13. Jessop and Oosterlynck, "Cultural Political Economy," 1157.
14. Jessop and Oosterlynck, "Cultural Political Economy," 1157.
15. Pani privileges political imaginaries over ideologies or "state projects" for that very reason. "[un] complicado entramado de visiones del mundo; de símbolos y representaciones, de principios, aspiraciones y prejuicios; de experiencias e influencias; de filias y fobias—las reprimidas y las que no lo están tanto—que componen el horizonte intellectual y cultural que comparte un grupo de hombres." Érika Pani, *Para mexicanizar*, 24.
16. Jessop and Oosterlynck, "Cultural Political Economy," 1158. For philosopher Charles Taylor, the difference between, say, a "social imaginary" and a "social theory" would be that, unlike theories, imaginaries are shared between a group of people and articulate images, histories, stories, legends, and explanations of social phenomena, which are not expressed in theoretical terms. The distance between imaginaries and theories varies, and often theories metastasize and infiltrate imaginaries and viceversa. See Taylor, *A Secular Age*, 172–73.
17. Richard Weiner notes that nine editions of Humboldt's work were published between 1810 and 1830. The original edition was first published in French. In total, there were two French editions (Paris, 1811 and 1825), two editions in Spanish (Paris, 1822 and 1827), four in English (London, 1811, 1814, 1822; and New York, 1811) and a German edition (Tubingen, 1809–1811). See Weiner, "La riqueza legendaria de México," 262n4. For Salmerón Sanginés, very few books had such an impact in Mexico as Humboldt's did, and it quickly became widely quoted, commented, expanded on, and debated during the first independent decade, becoming the authoritative account of the territory's geographical and economic facts. That said, he insists this impact began after 1822, when its Spanish edition was distributed in Mexico. See Salmerón Sanginés, "La riqueza legendaria," 141. My own research suggests otherwise. For example, in 1820 advertisements announcing the publication of *Memoria sobre la población* by Fernando Navarro y Noriega assumed its public's familiarity with Humboldt's text, insofart as it notes that Navarro and Noriega's work "rectifies some of Baron Humboldt's inevitable inaccuracies, a detail which makes said Memoria

commendable . . . ." See *Gaceta de México*, November 16, 1820, 1178. The following year, on November 24th, 1821, the *Gaceta Imperial* advertised the sale of the French edition of Humboldt's work. Both facts suggest that the French edition had circulated widely, perhaps in its 1811 printing.

18. Salmerón Sanginés, "El mito de la riqueza legendaria," 140.
19. Covarrubias, "Riqueza, Ilustración y población," 83.
20. Weiner, "La riqueza legendaria de México," 262.
21. Covarrubias, "Riqueza, Ilustración y población," 107. Weiner notes that Humboldt ignored the question of capital, dismissing its role in the generation of wealth. Humboldt believed that capital was ancillary to the exploitation of wealth, but not to its creation. For Humboldt, nature created wealth, and labor simply extracted it. See Weiner, "El declive económico," 74.
22. Salmerón Sanginés, "El mito de la riqueza legendaria," 141.
23. "Los luminosos escritos de V. S. relativos a América, frutos de sus talentos y de sus viajes a esta parte del globo, han sido recibidos generalmente con aquella estimación que reclaman sus interesantes materias y las noticias de que abundan. Ellas hacen formar un cabal concepto de lo que podrá ser México bajo una buena y liberal Constitución, por tener en su seno los elementos todos de la prosperidad, y su lectura no ha contribuido poco a avivar el espíritu de Independencia que germinaba en muchos de sus habitantes, y a despertar a otros del letargo en que los tenía una dominación extraña." Quoted in Ortega y Medina, *Humboldt y Mexico*, 203.
24. Weiner, "El declive económico en México," 73.
25. McCaa, "The Peopling of Nineteenth-Century Mexico," 605.
26. McCaa, "The Peopling of Nineteenth-Century Mexico," 603.
27. McCaa, "The Peopling of Nineteenth-Century Mexico," 608.
28. See Hämäläinen, *The Comanche Empire*.
29. "La naturaleza—se argumenta—ha sido prodiga con el mexicano: le ha dado todos los climas, el trópico y las nieves perpetuas; agricultura y minerales; territorio extenso; largas costas; ríos; cielo azul, limpio siempre. Pero el mexicano es ignorante, perezoso, indisciplinado, prodigo, imprevisor, susceptible, rebelde. ¿Qué puede hacerse en estas condiciones? ¿Qué de extrano tiene que el pais este atrasado, que haya pobreza y aun miseria, a pesar, en medio de tanta riqueza?." Quoted in Salmerón Sanginés, "El mito de la riqueza de México," 76.
30. Cosío Villegas's conclusion was, in Weiner's telling, that "Mexico was economically disfavored by nature," and, thus, needed to build a new national consciousness, a new understanding of its economic potential and its territory, that could ground a revolutionary horizon and policy to be adopted by the Post-Revolutionary State. See Weiner, "Antecedents to Daniel Cosío Villegas's Post-Revolutionary Ideology," 93.
31. Jameson, *The Political Unconscious*, 73.
32. Jameson, *The Political Unconscious*, 88.
33. Jameson, *The Political Unconscious*, 103–4.

34. Van Young, *A Life Together*, 6.
35. Pratt, *Imperial Eyes*, 175.
36. Simon, *The Ideology of Creole Revolution*, 32–33.
37. Simon, *The Ideology of Creole Revolution*, 32.
38. Sánchez, "Entrevista a Yásnaya Elena A. Gil."
39. Hernández, *Mexican American Colonization*, 303.
40. Hernández, *Mexican American Colonization*, 303.
41. Hernández, *Mexican American Colonization*, 303.
42. Joshua Simon terms the ideological disposition of the hemispheric Creole elites as "anti-imperial imperialism." For Simon, the constitutions these men crafted imitated the centralisms (at a regional or national level) of their imperial predecessors and deployed them as a framework for a national expansion that, in theory, differed from the imperial expansion of the past. It was a form of governance that sought to consolidate "control over previous unincorporated populations as means of spreading what they regarded as a uniquely enlightened way of living under political institutions animated by ideals they had discovered in the course of fighting for their freedom." See Simon, *The Ideology of Creole Revolution*, 32–33.
43. Knight, "Mexican Peonage," 55.
44. Knight, "Mexican Peonage," 55.
45. Marx, *Capital*, vol. 1, 873. I engage with Marx not for the purposes of historical context, but as a theoretical or heuristic took with critical utility. As will be seen throughout this book, many of Marx's critiques of the political economies of Adam Smith and David Ricardo can be productively applied to texts from the Mexican context.
46. Marx, *Capital*, vol. 1, 874.
47. Marx, *Capital*, vol. 1, 874.
48. Capitalism did not begin, of course, with independence. The transition from one mode to another (from an "x" to a "y"), even if unarticulated as such, was part of the narrative imagination of the economic imaginaries studied here, as we will see. In practice, however, there was no such transition. As Jason Read has explained, the many elements that later would begin to coalesce to articulate the "capitalist mode of production"—elements that only become intelligible as such retroactively—stemmed from the "margins and 'pores' of the old society and only begin to occupy center stage in terms of their effects, the effects of constituting a new economy and a new mode of production." Read, *The Micro-Politics of Capital*, 24. For Roger Bartra, to better understand the economic and political milieu of Mexico and other such countries, it was necessary to leave behind developmentalist narratives, and understand that the concrete character of a mode of production is "conferred upon it by its historical articulation with other determined modes of production, as well as by its own specificity." Marx suggested as much, according to Bartra, and accounted for the fact that various precapitalist modes of production were transformed,

through the nineteenth-century, into processes of production of capital. That is, the rise and expansion of capitalism in Mexico throughout the nineteenth and first half of the twentieth century entailed the subordination of other modes of production which, now subordinated, survived and acquired a double character (their own, and that of their subordination to capital). This also meant that dominant modes of production contained within their own internal structures mechanisms that make possible said articulations. Bartra, *Agrarian Structure and Political Power in Mexico*, 7–8.

49. I use "form of life" rather than way of life to differentiate the phenomenon described from that of a "lifestyle." Whereas the common use of the latter implies a personal choice or decision, in using form of life I am echoing the work of Giorgio Agamben. As I explain in Chapter 3, Agamben defines the concept as a "a life that, in its sequence, makes itself that very form, coincides with it." See Agamben, *The Highest Poverty*, 99. More so than a personal choice, a form of life implies the inseparability of a life from the ways, acts, and processes of living. Another useful elucidation of the concept is offered by Rahel Jaeggi, who uses it to refer "to forms of human coexistence shaped by culture," manifested and materialized "in fashion, architecture, legal systems, and forms of family organization, in what Robert Musil called 'the durable stuff of buildings, laws, regulations, and historical traditions' that constitutes our lives." See Rahel Jaeggi, *Critique of Forms of Life*, 3.

50. The Reaction or the Thermidorian Convention was the reactionary coup d'etat that culminated the most radical phase of the French Revolution. The new Thermidorian regime came to power on the 9 of Thermidor of Year 2 (July 27, 1794) with the imprisonment of the Jacobin leaders, Maximilien Robespierre, Louis Antoine de Saint-Just, and their eventual execution. I use the term here in a descriptive manner to refer to the period that goes from Anastasio Bustamante's *pronunciamiento* of the Plan de Jalapa on December 4, 1829 until the fall of the Centralist Republic of Mexico in 1846. With the exception of the short-lived liberal government of Valentín Gómez de Farías between April 1833 and April 1834, the period came to be characterized by the active curtailment of the civic liberties achieved in the first post-independent years, the attack on popular mobilization and politics, and the strengthening of police and disciplinary instances at the municipal level. In the eyes of their proponents, these measures sought to "restore" order and good government across the territory. "Thermidor" has been used as a descriptive concept often. To name one example, Leon Trotsky spoke of Joseph Stalin's rise as the emergence of a "Soviet Thermidor" (*The Revolution Betrayed*, 86–113). French theorist Alain Badiou has engaged with the "essence" of Thermidorian reactions and argued that these imply the imposition of illegibility on a previous egalitarian horizon, its progressive depolitization and its pathologizing reduction at the hands of figures that participated in the event itself ("The Courage of Oscurantism"). For a sustained account of Badiou's use, see Corcoran, "Thermidorian."

51. The field of nineteenth-century Latin American cultural studies in English is slowly moving beyond strictly literary sources. Joshua Lund's work on Luis Alva and Ignacio Manuel Altamirano in *The Mestizo State* offers a model on how to develop critically rich readings and insights from available archival materials that have critical and historical force. Ana Sabau's recent book *Riot and Rebellion in Mexico: The Making of a Race War Paradigm*, published while I was already revising this one, offers an ambitious (and stirring) model for the study of the long nineteenth-century. Starting from the late eighteenth-century, Sabau traces the development of the race-based narrative of race war through a series of flashpoints, which are not simply limited to New Spain/Mexico but expand to include Haiti and its effect on the Creole political imagination. The situation is different, and heartening, if we look beyond cultural studies. Scholars working in cultural and intellectual history, and adjacent subfields, consistently produce rigorous, critical accounts of the period. This book builds on much of this work. To keep it brief and strictly tied to Mexican studies, the work of contemporary historians, working in Spanish and in English, such as Alfredo Ávila, Silvia Arrom, Edward Beatty, José Enrique Covarrubias, Sonia Pérez Toledo, Rafael Rojas, John Tutino, and Richard Weiner, and of critics such as Elías José Palti, to name a few, is frankly inspirational. If nineteenth-century cultural studies is to have a future in the US academy, it will have to consistently and continuously engage with the work of these scholars.

CHAPTER 1

Epigraph. "Y sabían que tarde o temprano el territorio de su santuario iba a ser reclamado por la República insaciable que quién sabe en qué momento decidió que tenía que gobernar cada milímetro cuadrado del territorio inmenso en que estaba asentada, como si hubiera necesitado los altos impenetrables de la Sierra Madre—no los necesitaba: siguen vacíos." Enrigue, *Ahora me rindo y eso es todo*, 59.

1. González Navarro, *La colonización en México*, 140.
2. Nemser, "Biopolitics in Latin America," 4.
3. *El Siglo Diez y Nueve*, April 7, 1844, 391.
4. Nancy, *Noli me tangere*, 15–16.
5. "Esta palabra viene del sustantivo colonia, que significa cierta porción de gentes enviadas de orden de algún principel . . . a establecerse en otro país recién conquistado o descubierto." *El Monitor Constitucional*, October 7, 1845, 3.
6. "Población o término de tierra que se ha poblado de gente extrangera, trahida de la Ciudad Capital, o de otra parte. Los Romanos llamaban tambien assí a las que se poblaban de nuevo de sus antiguos moradores." *Diccionario de Autoridades*, v.2, "colonización."
7. "[El Sr. Paz] observó que la voz *colonización* no es propia del proyecto, y así

convendría substituirle la de *población*, que es verdaderamente de lo que se trata." *El Sol*, August 2, 1824, 193.

8. "Cuando los puntos del globo de que tenemos noticia fueron mejor conocidos por las descripciones de los viajeros, muchas familias abandonaron su patria para ir a procurarse a otro suelo mas rico, cómoda y segura subsistencia." *El Monitor Constitucional*, October 7, 1845, 3.
9. Sánchez, "Una ciudadanía experimental," 10.
10. Sánchez, "Una ciudadanía experimental," 3.
11. Lund, The *Mestizo State*, 2–3.
12. Hernández, *Mexican American Colonization*, 27.
13. González Navarro, like other important historians from his generation, came of historiographical age within historian Daniel Cosío Villegas's *Seminario de Historia Moderna* and the institutions Cosío Villegas founded, such as *El Colegio de México*. González Navarro's work was influenced by Cosío Villegas's own positions, forged in the 1940s, a period which, according to Charles A. Hale, saw the transition in public policy from an agrarian approach to a privileging of urban industrialization. This transition went hand-in-hand with an intellectual renewal among those concerned with history and culture that revolved around a commitment to national self-critique. Cosío Villegas's work, and many of his followers, including González Navarro, would be marked by a certain "disillusionment at the drift of the country after 1940," when the Post-Revolution entered its "developmentalist" phase and "reverted to the priorities and many of the characteristics of the regime of Porfirio Díaz." This developmentalist turn (and Porfirian return) evinced that the nation's political leadership had failed to be faithful to the "meaning" of the revolution itself: "political democracy, economic and social justice, and the defense of national as against foreign interests." This disappointment with the present launched Cosío Villegas and, later, his colleagues, to a revision of nineteenth-century Mexican history which placed the period of the Restored Republic (1867–76)—the presidencies of Benito Juárez, Sebastián Lerdo de Tejada, and José María Iglesias—at its center, as the high point of Mexican political history. Hale writes, "The Restored Republic is for Cosío the beginning of Mexico's 'modern history,' for it marked the first real attempt to govern the nation constitutionally." See Hale, "Liberal Impulse," 482–83. As Laura Angélica Moya López and Margarita Olvera Serrano have written, "For Cosío Villegas, if there were three fundamental races in México, the solution [to the social and economic problems faced by the nation] were to be found in their fusion," racial and educational. See Moya and Olvera Serrano, "La sociología mexicana de Daniel Cosío Villegas," 132. These same ideological commitments mark González Navarro's work on colonization.
14. Hernández, *Mexican American Colonization*, 28n8.
15. Lund, *The Mestizo State*, xv.

16. "la abundancia que rasga su seno para comunicar sus preciosidades sin medida," and the "industria que va á dar entretenimiento á multitud de brazos que por trescientos años permanecieron inermes y sin acción." *Gaceta Imperial*, October 6, 1821, 21.
17. "Este país dichoso va á formar la esperanza del europeo discreto y laborioso." *Gaceta Imperial*, October 6, 1821, 21.
18. *Gaceta Imperial*, October 6, 1821, 19.
19. *Gaceta Imperial*, October 6, 1821, 19.
20. "aquella fuerza que regla los sucesos del mundo conforme conviene á sus inescrutables disposiciones" and la sublime empresa de la independencia del reino." *Gaceta Imperial*, October 6, 1821, 19.
21. *Gaceta Imperial*, October 6, 1821, 20.
22. *Gaceta Imperial*, October 6, 1821, 21.
23. Reinert, *Translating Empire*, 27.
24. Reinert, *Translating Empire*, 27.
25. Reinert, *Translating Empire*, 24.
26. Reinert, *Translating Empire*, 25.
27. Reinert, *Translating Empire*, 25.
28. Reinert, *Translating Empire*, 25.
29. Reinert, *Translating Empire*, 28.
30. Reinert, *Translating Empire*, 27.
31. *Gaceta Imperial*, October 6, 1821, 19.
32. *Gaceta Imperial*, October 6, 1821, 19.
33. "Al resonar en aquel continente la noticia de que la religion, la union y la libertad dulcemente hermanadas con la paz, la abundancia y la moderacion son las columnas del Imperio, volverán sus ojos y desearán con ansias trasladarse a él para vivir como hombres libres, y dejar de ser presa de la garra terrible del despiadado despotismo." *Gaceta Imperial*, October 6, 1821, 21.
34. Foucault, *Security, Territory, Population*, 286.
35. Foucault, *Security, Territory, Population*, 286.
36. Anna, *The Mexican Empire of Iturbide*, 25.
37. See Rafael Rojas, "El México de Iturbide. Indicios de un imaginario imperial," 48; and Anna, *Mexican Empire*, 40. At this point in time, the institutions which the Junta Provisional Gubernativa upheld were still the viceroyalty's. To avoid a vacuum, the Junta had reinstated the Spanish Constitution of 1812 immediately after independence, and decreed that viceregal governing structures and officials were to be retained and considered legitimate.
38. Foucault, *The Birth of Biopolitics*, 5.
39. Foucault, *The Birth of Biopolitics*, 5.
40. *Proyectistas* were analysts and administrators who, after considering a nation's available "scientific" and "statistical "data, diagnosed the state's present political, social, and economic situation so as to identify and theorize avenues—and policies— for future national development. Put broadly, *proyectistas* sought to

optimize a state's fiscal apparatus, as well as to identify areas where the state could intervene in order to increase production. For more on *proyectismo* and proyectistas, see Stein and Stein's *Edge of Crisis*, 480 n16; *Silver, Trade, and War*, 267; and *Apogee of Empire*, 30.

41. Quoted in in Kelly and Hatcher, "Tadeo Ortiz de Ayala," 77.
42. See Covarrubias, "Riqueza, Ilustración y población," 83.
43. Poovey, "Between Political Arithmetic and Political Economy," 62.
44. Poovey, "Between Political Arithmetic and Political Economy," 63.
45. "con la idea de regenerar y dar un impulso a todos los ramos de este opulento y vasto Imperio" Ortiz de Ayala, *Resumen de la estadística*, 3.
46. "el hombre puede escoger con el termómetro en la mano, el terreno más análogo a sus especulaciones y constitución, rodeado de atractivos lisongeros e inocentes." Ortiz de Ayala, *Resumen de la estadística*, 15.
47. Covarrubias, "Riqueza, Ilustración y población," 115.
48. Ortiz de Ayala, *Resumen de la estadística*, 27–31.
49. "civilizar y dar ocupación a una multitud miserable, que al paso que es la polilla del Estado, puede exponer la tranquilidad pública, porque los vicios propios de la ociosidad e indigencia minan los estados." Ortiz de Ayala, *Resumen de la estadística*, 89.
50. Ortíz de Ayala, *México considerado*, 86.
51. Hale, *Mexican Liberalism in the Age of Mora*, 151. It might be productive to differentiate between physiocracy and liberalism for purposes of clarification. Emerging in eighteenth-century France, physiocracy preceded liberalism *a la* Adam Smith in offering a coherent economic theory, and in arguing for the liberalization of goods and grain laws. The liberalization of such laws would limit the state's inefficient and arbitrary administration of the economy, and give way for the "natural" rule of the market. Physiocrats, in fact, coined "laissez-faire" as an expression. In terms of economic philosophy, physiocrats believed that all value was generated through agriculture and produced by the land. Everything else, including industry and commerce, was secondary to that fact. For physiocrats, a nation proved and expressed its political independence—and self-sufficiency—through the level of its exportation of surplus grain and foodstuffs. As Yves Charbit has said, physiocracy was a philosophically justified program or doctrine of economic development based on the modernization of French agriculture. This program had, as its goal, the strengthening or restitution of an absolutist monarchical state's power. That is, by liberalizing grain laws and allowing the natural rule of the market, the French economy would grow exponentially and, in turn, so would the wealth of the nation and the economic power of the absolutist monarchical state. Charbit, "The Political Failure of an Economic Theory: Physiocracy," 878. Liberalism *a la* Adam Smith, on the other hand, privileged the market's invisible hand as a self-regulating institution, as well as its capacity to underwrite the collective concert of self-interested individuals. If for physiocrats, the productive force of the land was

at the heart of the wealth of the nation, for classical liberals, true wealth lay in the competitive and progressive division of labor.

52. "una pequeña parte del territorio Imperial, con una mediana población apática y sin emulación." Ortiz de Ayala, *Resumen de la estadística*, 64.
53. Ortiz de Ayala, *Resumen de la estadística*, 54.
54. "La verdadera riqueza del Imperio Mexicano no se funda, pues exclusivamente en la explotación metálica, que influye poco en la prosperidad real de una Nación; se funda en los productos de la tierra, que es la base de la opulencia segura." Ortiz de Ayala, *Resumen de la estadística*, 65.
55. Tutino, *Mexican Heartland*, 173.
56. Tutino, *Mexican Heartland*, 173.
57. Tutino, *Mexican Heartland*, 191.
58. Tutino summarizes it well when he writes that for the Mexican elites, "[c]rops consumed by families had no value." See *Mexican Heartland*, 191.
59. The Colonization Committee was composed of Juan Antonio Rivas, Rafael Leandro de Echenique, José Ignacio Esteva, Melchor Muzquiz and, joining by April 1822, Juan Bautista Arizpe and Marcial Zebadúa. On May 31, 1822, Ambrosio Martínez Vea, Valentín Gomez Farias, Jose Ignacio Muguiro, José Antonio Gutiérrez de Lara, Refugio de la Garza, and Antonio Elozúa become part of the commission. Lorenzo Zavala joins later in the year.
60. *Actas del congreso constituyente mexicano*, 21–22.
61. Among Ortiz de Ayala's supporters was Manuel Mier y Terán, to whom he would dedicate his 1832 volume. Mier y Terán represented Chiapas in the Constituent Congress and would later lead an expedition that sought to inspect the border between Texas and the United States, and give an account of the situation. From that point on, he was adamant in his belief that Texas was slipping from Mexican hands. For a great account of Mier y Terán's life and context, see Ávila, *Camino de Padilla*.
62. The *Program* served as the Comisión de Relaciones Exteriores' report of their work to date as well as the preamble to the first colonization bill they produced. A Creole lawyer, Azcárate y Lezama (1767–1831) occupied a series of official posts in the Mexico City Ayuntamiento during the first three decades of the nineteenth-century. He was one of the signatories of the 1821 Act of Independence, a member of the Provisional Governmental Junta, a foundational member of the Sociedad Económico-mexicana de Amigos del País, and a close-associate of Iturbide. Through the marriage of daughter Juliana, he was 1832–1833 president Manuel Gómez Pedraza's father-in-law. The *Program* is the key text of his brief bibliography. For more, see Vázquez Semadeni, "Azcárate y Lezama."
63. "tan fértil, de temperamento tan benigno, tan rica en metales y en producciones naturales, que cuando se lee la descripción de que ella hacen los geógrafos, al paso que se cree hablan del Paraíso." Azcárate y Lezama, "Programa," 12. Azcárate y Lezama considered various historical surveys of Texas and decided

in favor of Humboldt's calculation of the region's extension—174,966,750 acres—and subtracted the territories occupied by "pueblos, misiones, presidios, ríos, montes y lagunas," coming up to a total acreage of 58,322,250, to be populated and exploited through the colonization policy. Flattened by the desire of aggrandizement, the fact of the harshness of certain climates and the lack of arable land went unregarded.

64. Azcárate y Lezama, *Un programa*, 12
65. "espaciosas haciendas, muchas de las que son mayores que la misma España, y en el territorio de otras caben la España y la Francia." Azcárate y Lezama, *Un programa*, 17.
66. "el arrendatario teme entregarse a su cultivo y beneficio porque no se las quiten después de mejoradas; el resultado es que ni el señor ni él sacan toda la utilidad de que son suceptibles, y el Estado se priva de muchos derechos justos, que de otra suerte percibiría." Azcárate y Lezama, *Un programa*, 17.
67. "El hombre quiere y aprecia lo que le cuesta mucho trabajo para prepararle después comodidad y descanso; se deleita en la obra de sus manos y no apetece más que disfrutarla." Azcárate y Lezama, *Un programa*, 20.
68. Azcárate y Lezama, *Un programa*, 19.
69. "Véase cómo una sola Provincia puede rendir más de lo que producía la Nueva España toda en las inermes manos de su antiguos dueños que la tiranizaban." Azcárate y Lezama, *Un programa*, 18.
70. Moses Austin died on June 10, 1821, and Stephen F. Austin began to act on his claim close to a year later, after informing the governor of Texas at San Antonio de Bexar. Wary of the shifting political landscape, he traveled to Mexico City to validate his father's grant that same year and spent months in the process, only to have it voided by the new colonization law. For more, see Hernández, *Mexican American Colonization*, 54–55.
71. Later in life Azcárate y Lezama reported having had an interview with Joel R. Poinsett, the American representative in Mexico, in which the latter informed him of the US government's interest in Texas and Austin's forays. See Vázquez Semadeni, "Azcárate y Lezama," 27.
72. "los interesados sean los que a su placer tomen las tierras y elijan los lugares, ni tampoco señalen y pueblen los puertos, sin que haya concurrencia de mexicanos y fuerza armada que los defienda." Azcárate y Lezama, *Un programa*, 13.
73. "a su antojo sin orden ni dar aviso a las autoridades; que si no todas, la mayor parte no trae pasaporte, ni otro documento que manifieste su buena conducta y proceder; de lo que es de inferir sean las más corrompidas que no caben, ni son toleradas en un país tan libre." Azcárate y Lezama, *Un programa*, 71–72
74. "Es imposible que un Gobierno que vive bajo la más exacta policía ignore las negociaciones de los particulares." Azcárate y Lezama, *Un programa*, 11.
75. "el particular interesado en algún negocio es el que mejor calcula sobre su interés y sus observaciones presentan al Estado un modelo en lo adaptable de lo que debe ejecutar." Azcárate y Lezama, *Un programa*, 11.

76. Azcárate y Lezama, *Un programa*, 11.
77. See Caro Baroja, "Las 'nuevas poblaciones' de Sierra Morena y Andalucía: un experimento sociológico en tiempos de Carlos III," and Alcázar Molina, *Las colonias alemanas de la Sierra Morena.*
78. See Azcárate, *Un programa*, 14–16.
79. As Jennifer M. Spear has written, Spain did not assert sovereignty over the Californian territory it claimed until the 1700s, when both Russia and the British expressed interest. Only then did it launch its missionization program, as part of what has been called imperial power colonialism, colonization projects driven by the effort to fend off imperial rivals. Spear, "Beyond the Native/Settler Divide," 428–29.
80. In *Chino: Anti-Chinese Racism in Mexico, 1880–1940*, Jason Oliver Chang addresses Juan Azcárate y Lezama as representative of Creole racial logics, built on Indian hatred, beliefs of African docility, and Asian erasure. Chang, *Chino*, 37–38. While Chang is, in general, correct, I believe his oversight of Azcárate y Lezama's Chinese inclusion misses an opportunity to think about China's place in post-independence Creole imaginaries. As we have seen, Azcárate y Lezama's account of China did not consider the actual presence of Chinese or Asian-descendent subjects on the territory, but it contemplated the possibility of an acceptable future Mexican-Californian citizen of Chinese extraction. That is, in the *Program*, the anti-Chinese discourse that Chang traces in the second half of the nineteenth-century—that is, in the period of what Lund calls the "mestizo state," is not yet fully operative and, as a result, is an example of the proleptic racialization of the economic and political discourses of the post-independence era. This is not to say that the representation of Chinese settlers did not participate in an orientalist register. It did, and Azcárate y Lezama's claims about Chinese overpopulation and the prevalence of infanticide as a demographic check reproduced what had, by the eighteenth century, become an Enlightenment trope. See Kow, *China in Early Enlightenment Political Thought* and Aravamudan, *Enlightenment Orientalism: Resisting the Rise of the Novel.*
81. "Aquel vastísimo Imperio logra de una población mayor que lo que puede sostener; por eso es permitido a los padres matar a los hijos pequeñitos cuando sus posibilidades no alcanzan a mantenerlos." Azcárate y Lezama, *Un programa*, 38.
82. ". . . extraídos después a los mercados de la Asia activará en el comercio de un modo extraordinario y útil a nuestro suelo." Azcárate y Lezama, *Un Programa*, 39.
83. Azcárate y Lezama, *Un programa*, 64.
84. "todos los extranjeros que a los tres meses de presentados en las Provincias no se hayan ocupado en algún ejercicio o industria conocida, serán desterrados de ellas, o se aplicarán a las armas." Azcárate y Lezama, *Un programa*, 66.
85. "por condición[,] no puedan separarse de la Provincia que elijan durante los seis años de la franquisia de los derechos." Azcárate y Lezama, *Un programa*, 20.
86. Congost and Luna, *Agrarian Change and Imperfect Property*, 12–13.

87. Congost and Luna, *Agrarian Change and Imperfect Property*, 21.
88. See Congost and Luna, *Agrarian Change and Imperfect Property*, 18. Congost and Luna note that, while in principle, the owner of dominium directum could confiscate the land if rent was not rendered, in practice, "eviction was often difficult to carry out, in part because it was heavily dependent on the value of any improvement made by the tenant and [their] capacity for negotiation." See Congost and Luna, *Agrarian Change and Imperfect Property*, 22. In fact, when reformers attempted to replace emphyteutic contracts with absolute property rights, emphyteutic tenants often rejected the offer. As Congost and Luna write, "[w]hy re-purchase a property of which [tenants] were, in effect, full owners, with quasi-perfect property rights?." See Congost and Luna, *Agrarian Change and Imperfect Property*, 20.
89. Corredera, "Labouring Horizons," 281.
90. Corredera, "Labouring Horizons," 281.
91. Luna, "Property Dominum," 93.The colono had a long, disparate history in the Hispanic Empire. While it is true that the United States stood as the model of successful population increase, it is also true that the Mexican colono drew its semantic steam from the Hispanic archive.
92. "pues no sabemos que leyes o condiciones impondrán a los irlandeses y canarios a quienes les den tierras." *Actas del Congreso Constituyente*, 23.
93. "pues necesariamente algo han de tributar a los contratantes; y síguese por último que de este nada tocará al fondo del imperio benefactor." *Actas del Congreso Constituyente*, 23. The fear that colonos might be exploited by greedy landowners would survive the current debate. See, for example, a July 1826 exchange between two senators in the Provincial Congress of Veracruz, when that assembly debated a new regional colonization law, developed in consultation with Ortiz de Ayala. Like the 1822 detractors and against another congressman who argued that men were free to contract their labor to others, congressman Manuel María Carvajal questioned the relationship between empresario and colono. Because the former would have invested their capital on the latter's transplantation to Mexico, "el empresario no se contentará solamente con reembolsar su dinero, sino que también especulará para sacar las ganancias posibles, y de este modo serán los colonos una especie de esclavos suyos" (3044). Thus, he held, the migrant, once the promise of industry, would meet a similar fate to that suffered by the Indians under the Spanish Empire, exploited in tlapisqueras and obrages (3045). See *El Oriente*, September 28, 1826, and September 30, 1826.
94. "en la miseria, como sucede a los desgraciados indígenas, que por lo general no pasan de jornaleros, trabajando siempre para otros por un mezquino sueldo que no les basta para subsistir." *Actas del Congreso Constituyente*, 24.
95. *Actas del congreso constituyente*, 23.
96. According to Gómez Farías, it had been implicit that the colonos would be governed by agents designated by the Empire. He also noted that the authors had commited to include Mexicans in the colonies and, in fact, were planning

on privileging soldiers, for whom they would cover the instruments of their trade. Finally, he held that the contract with the applicants stipulated that they had to labor and cultivate the land as well as sell two-thirds of it in the form of private lots. It made sense that they would gain economically in the process, he concluded, for they would risk and invest heavily on the enterprise. See *Actas del Congreso Constituyente*, 21–23.

97. Composed of a select number of members from the Constituent Congress, the National Instituent Junta (Junta Nacional Instituyente) had been given four tasks that the Emperor believed were necessary for the survival of the Empire—the convocation of a new, improved Constituent Congress, the drafting of a constitution, the solution of the treasury crisis, and the adoption of a general law of colonization. Ultimately, the Instituent Junta proved incapable of living up to its charge and it dissolved itself soon before the Empire itself fell apart. For more on the Junta Nacional Instituyente's work as it pertained to the economic imaginaries of the period, and its justification for the executive powers, see Gutiérrez Negrón, "Instituent Fictions."
98. Colonization work in the Instituent Junta was sheperded by Lorenzo de Zavala of Yucatán, Refugio de la Garza of Coahuila and Texas, José Antonio Gutiérrez de Lara of Nuevo Santander, Carlos Espinosa de los Monteros of Sonora y Sinaloa, and Salvador Porras of Durango. For a summary account of the law's procedural development, see Benson, "Territorial Integrity in Mexican Politics," 279–81."
99. "en lo posible a que las propiedades estén igualmente repartidas." de la Maza, *Código de Colonizacion*, 173.
100. Texas was the sole region where the slave population continued to grow well into the 1830s. See Torget, *Seeds of Empire*, 144.
101. "todos los hijos de los esclavos que después de la publicación de esta ley, viniesen al imperio, y naciendo en él, lleguen a la edad de catorce años." *Actas del Congreso Constituyente*, vol. III, 20.
102. "De esta manera," they argued, "ha creído [el Comité] conciliar su derecho de propiedad que cualesquiera que sean sus títulos, lo han hecho respetable las leyes de los pasados gobiernos y una costumbre inmemoria." *Actas del Congreso Constituyente*, vol. III, 20.
103. "la esclavitud transformada en derecho, y en derecho de propiedad." *Actas del Congreso Constituyente*, vol. III, 58.
104. For this impassionate speech against the measure, see Mr. Godoy's participation on *Actas del Congreso Constituyente*, vol. III, 57–58. The alternative colonization proposal that abolished slavery was presented by Valentín Gómez Farías. *Actas del Congreso Constituyente*, vol. III, 46–52. The prohibition of slavery is treated in Article 41. Gómez Farías let the matter lapse, however, and became the champion of the Committee's lenient position thereafter, probably because he believed the colonization of the territory was urgent.

105. By 1824, Zavala secured a valuable land grant between Nagadoches, the Sabine River, and the sea, where he planned to introduce five hundred Mexican and foreign families as colonos. See Hale, *Mexican Liberalism*, 202
106. "que por último resultado traen la revolución," but to give the nation "leyes buenas." *Actas del congreso constituyente*, vol. III, 61.
107. "de lo contrario no podrían venir, porque los colonos carecían de brazos para sus labores, supuestos que no los hay en las provincias colonizables, ni los apaches y demás gentiles se habían de prestar al servicio de jornaleros." *Actas del Congreso Constituyente*, vol. III, 65–66.
108. Vicente Guerrero abolished slavery by decree on 1829, but the illegality of enslavement did not become part of a constitution until the 1843 Bases orgánicas. See Olveda Legaspi, "La abolición de la esclavitud en México, 1810–1917" for a concise account of the abolition of slavery and its legislation throughout the nineteenth-century.
109. "muchos hombres industriosos con un capital considerable en esclavatura, habituados a aquel género de especulaciones." *Actas del congreso constituyente*, vol. III, 16.
110. Tutino, *Mexican Heartland*, 185.
111. The Tehuantepec Isthmus would continue to capture the imagination of speculators and prospectors well into the 1830s, further spurred in the following years by Ortiz de Ayala's subsequent surveys of the areas between October 1824 and August 1825, reported on in the press.
112. "falta de propiedad y ocupación, es muy poco productiva, y una gran parte por iguales causas enteramente abyecta." Ortiz de Ayala, *Bases*, 2.
113. The government could either cede the revenue generated by a regional saltworks operation, or allow for the importation of then-banned Guatemalan tobacco so as to tax it and provide those earnings, or, finally, ask the Church to donate its silver luxuries. Ortiz de Ayala, *Bases*, 17.
114. Fowler, *Forceful Negotiations*, viii.
115. For Timo H. Schaefer, the creation of armed forces "whose members were not bound by the rules of the ordinary legal order" would consistently undermine the law through the nineteenth century. *Liberalism as Utopia*, 206.
116. See Fowler, *Forceful Negotiations*.
117. "hombres de bien, pero sin fortuna, ni más arbitrios que los que les suministra su ejército." Ortiz de Ayala, *Bases*, 2.
118. "el noble y primitivo arte de la agricultura." Ortiz de Ayala, *Bases*, 3.
119. "padres de familia laboriosos, y ciudadanos industriosos y útiles á la sociedad." Ortiz de Ayala, *Bases*, 3.
120. "[l]a idea que ofrece una colonia es la de la infancia de una sociedad; habitantes sencillos, sin más necesidades que las naturales." *Proyecto de ley sobre colonización, presentado a la deliberaicón del Honorable Congreso del estado de Veracruz* 1.

121. Williams, *The Mexican Exception*, 12.
122. Williams, *The Mexican Exception*, 11.
123. " . . . por la protección divina," and so "al horroroso desierto convirtieron en pueblos numerosos y civilizados." *Fénix de la libertad*, October 5, 1833, 2.
124. "[los hombres] ocupados en el campo, las mugeres en su casa cociendo y haciendo primores en los telares." *Fénix de la libertad*, October 5, 1833, 3.
125. *Fénix de la libertad*, October 5, 1833, 3.
126. See General Manuel Mier y Terán's June 30, 1828, letter to President Guadalupe Victoria, quoted in Howren's "Causes and Origins of the April 6, 1830 decree," 395–98. Likewise, in an 1834 survey of the territory, Juan N. Almonte noted that, in the Brazos Department and the Nagocodoches Department, out of a total population of 17,000 souls, at least 2,000 were black men "introduced" by agreement with the local state administrators. Almonte, *Noticia estadística*, 50, 68.
127. Torget, *Seeds of Empire*, 155.
128. "formar parte del territorio mexicano: así, formándolo, brillarán entre sus vecinos en artes, agricultura y comercio, mientras que perteneciendo a la república del Norte, desaparecen totalmente en la multitud de aquella gente sobresaliente y más ilustrada que ellos." *Fénix de la libertad*, October 5, 1833, 3–4.
129. "Oponerse al voto general de los colonos, producirá disgustos: de hostilizarlos a la distancia de 600 leguas de la ciudad general, ¿quién puede calcular la resultas?" *Fénix de la libertad*, October 5, 1833, 3.
130. "es un general en su casa; todos sus dependientes, inclusas las mugeres, manejan con destreza las armas." *Fénix de la libertad*, October 5, 1833, 3.
131. Sierra, *Tadeo Ortiz de Ayala*, 24–25.
132. Two accounts from the same ill-fated expedition can be found in Maison y Dubouchet, *La colonización francesa en Coatzacoalcos*.
133. "defectuoso sistema adoptado por los empresarios para ldistribución de las tierras, y a la elección desacertada de los colonos, que por lo eneral han sido gente poco a propósito para las labores del campo." Alamán, "Memoria de la Secretaria de Estado y del Despacho de Relaciones Interiores y Exteriores Del Año 1832," 360.
134. Andrew J. Torget writes that: "At least on paper, the new Texas government promised to be the most protective slave regime in North America." *Seeds of Empire*, 171.
135. "[l]a colonia de Tejas se ha perdido, no porque se puso colonia en aquel territorio; sino porque lo abandonó el gobierno, sin cuidarse de los continuos avisos del difunto general Terán." *El Cosmopolita*, November 10, 1841, 4. In other words, Texas's loss was to be blamed, primarily, on a central government in Mexico City which acted like "the metropolis of the rest of the republic" and treated its states as its "colonias tributarias," fanning discontent. See also *El Cosmopolita*, August 28, 1839.
136. *El Siglo Diez y Nueve* wrote: "Estamos palpando lo que nos ha sucedido con Tejas, cuya colonización habría producido considerables ventajas a la metrópoli,

si se hubiera meditado con más detenimiento la ley; pero nos ha ofrecido resultados funestos por la imprevisión con que se procedió, y esta lección debe servirnos ahora para evitar un arrepentimiento nútil y tardío." See *El Siglo Diez y Nueve*, October 21, 1841, 4.

137. Bustamante, *Gabinete Mexicano*, 15–18.
138. Bustamante, *Gabinete Mexicano*, 14.
139. " . . . [q]ue todo negro transfugado de cualquier potencia que aquí se presentase, por el solo hecho de poner sus peis en este suelo, como en un suelo sagrado, quedase libre." Bustamante, *Gabinete*, 14.
140. Bustamante wrote: "...siendo digno de notarse, que entre los individuos que han hecho personalmente la guerra, son muy pocos los verdaderamente colonos cultivadores que se han encontrado." See Bustamante, *Gabinete*, 20.
141. Colonization matters had been housed in the Ministry of the Interior since the 1824 Constitution, a ministry whose reach and powers will be studied in Chapter 2.
142. Tutino, *The Mexican Heartland*, 187.
143. Tutino, *The Mexican Heartland*, 176–77.
144. Tutino, *The Mexican Heartland*, 180–83.
145. In 1837, the Centralist Republic faced its first challenge when a French fleet initiated a months-long blockade of the Veracruz port, the nation's main trading post, which in turn led to the French Pastry War (1838–39) in November. These conflicts drained the national treasury further and pushed the centralist government to turn to *agiotistas*, exploitative money lenders who were the only option left for an administration that had promised to respect the sanctity of individual and Church property. See Fowler, *Mexico in the Age of Proposals*, 25.
146. The 1840s were a whirlwind that culminated with the overthrow of the centralist administration (July 1840), the return of Santa Anna to power (1841–44), the dismissal of the 1836 Constitution and the approval of yet another provisional governing document, the October 1841 *Bases de Tacubaya*. The Bases granted Santa Anna dictatorial powers and convened a new Constituent Congress with the expectation that it affirmed Santa Anna's status quo. When this Congress moved in the opposite direction, it was shut down (December 1842), replaced with a *Junta de Notables* with constitutive powers that would go on to write and pass the *Bases Orgánicas* (June 1843). This was Mexico's third official constitution, a centralist document which moderated the excesses of 1836 and gave some representation to states. Resistance to it, however, led to popular and political revolts which overthrew Santa Anna (December 1844) and intensified the conflict between parties. In the midst of these struggles, the United States invaded Mexico (April 1846), but the presence of its troops did not quell internal strife.
147. The Government of the Second Federal Republic, worried about the invading forces, invited their once-opponent Antonio López de Santa Anna to return so as to lead the national armies. While Santa Anna waged war, Vice President Gómez Farías acted as the executive (December 1846–March 1847). Gómez

Farías picked up where he had left off in the 1830s and expropriated Church property in the name of gathering resources for the war. Unsurprisingly, this catalyzed a pro-Church reaction and, eventually, pushed Santa Anna to undo the vice-president's decrees. In exchange, Santa Anna exacted a hefty donation of much needed funds from ecclesiastical ranks.

148. "conociendo el campo en que tiene que trabajar, obre con actividad e inteligencia, y pueda dar al Gobierno las luces y dictámenes del estudio, la experiencia y la versación." de la Maza, *Código de Colonizacion y Terrenos Baldíos*, 363.
149. Burden, "Reform before La Reforma," 287.
150. For more on Lafragua's emphasis on colonization and his rationale as to why it had not been accomplished, see Burden, "Reform before La Reforma."
151. Burden writes that, "[t]o that end, the agency was charged with professionalizing the notion of development by employing trained surveyors, geographers, engineers, agronomists, cartographers, and statisticians to study, process and compile information on colonizable lands and to devise plans of development." See "Reform Before La Reforma," 287.
152. Additionally, the Dirección would be responsible for serving as the mediator between the colonias' "juntas de industria fabril o agrícola" and any instance of government, whether at the district, state, or national level; the collection of economic data; the promotion of the modernization of agriculture and industry; the granting of patents; the organization of public exhibitions in Mexico City of each colonia's agricultural or industrial products; and, finally, the creation of technical schools that would jump-start the creative energies of the citizenry.
153. This was no surprise, seeing as Lafragua had basically repurposed Alamán's *Dirección de Industria*, discussed in Chapter 2.
154. *El Monitor Republicano*, May 19, 1847.
155. "las simpatías que debe atraer, bastardeándole y haciéndole servir a sus intereses especiales." *El Monitor Republicano*, December 18, 1846, 3.
156. "Esto es abuso, es monstruoso." *El Monitor Republicano*, December 18, 1846, 3. The author insisted that, behind its name, the Dirección de colonización was still the Dirección de industria, but that having acknowledged that after the fall of centralist government "su hora fatal había llegado," it had found in colonization a lifeline. Put simply, the article argued that, after their failed transformation of Mexico into a nation of manufacturing, these characters—who the author claimed were widely despised—were now trying to take over agriculture so as to redirect it toward their industrialist designs. The takeover had only been possible because Garay and Gálvez exploited the fact that Congress was not in session, overstepped their mandate of writing the institution's charter and granted themselves with powers that could only come from elected officials.
157. Gálvez's response, published on December 27 in *El Monitor*, explained the inner workings of the defunct Dirección de Industria, so as to differentiate it from the current enterprise, celebrated the necessity of colonization—"el primer

pensamiento de los ilustrados mexicanos independientes"— and, finally, the righteousness of the *Dirección*. For him, the institution's critiques suffered of a "ceguedad inaudita," a "delirio lamentable." He believed it undoubtable that "[l]os representantes de los Estados de la federación mexicana sólo sabrán escuchar la voz pura del patriotismo, y esa voz pide la ampliación, no las restricciones de las franquicias a los nuevos pobladores." That is, Gálvez was sure that once the Dirección de colonización began its labors, the states would soon fall in line. See *El Monitor Constitucional*, December 27, 1847, 2–4.

158. The anonymous author's critique held that any of the landowners of the Sociedad de Agricultura were more deserving of those roles. He also developed his opposition to the Dirección's "arbitrary powers," which he feared would soon be "mas soberana que el mismo congreso nacional."

159. "un gran castillo de viento encubriendo un nuevo abismo abierto contra los derechos y agonizantes fortunas particulares de todo mexicano; una especulación mas de alguno que busca hacerse célebre." *El Monitor Republicano*, May 19, 1847, 1.

160. "de este centro de la nación, bien desguarnecido por cierto, una parte de sus riquezas y población, para transformarlas en otras de precaria y apuntalada existencia, allá en los confines de la república." *El Monitor Republicano*, May 19, 1847, 1.

161. "poblarlos a fuerza de gracias y sacrificios del gobierno o de las riquezas existentes, que es lo mismo, demás de ser contrario a todo principio de buena economía, es simplemente trasformar una población o unas riquezas en otras, y siempre con demérito muy considerable de la general de la nación; es dislocarlas perdiendo o consumiendo en la variación y las manos interpuestas, diez, v.g., de las que están en productos corrientes, para ver establecidas, cuando se salve bien, cinco en ramos por lo menos dudosos; y que lejos de crearse en esto un auxiliar a la sociedad, es echarla un censo mas." *El Monitor Republicano*, May 19, 1847, 2.

162. "mira como un progreso el que aparezcan algunas creaciones nuevas en suelos incultos de la República, aunque en cambio perdamos cuatro o seis veces mas de población e industria en los puntos que por antiguos, sin duda, no son . . . parte tan interesante en la nación." *El Monitor Republicano*, May 19, 1847, 3.

163. "un desagüe, una sangría más para nuestra escasa riqueza pública, un nuevo censo sobre nuestros ya improductivos trabajos y propiedades." *El Monitor Republicano*, May 19, 1847, 3.

164. "es indispensable que comencemos por establecer un buen gobierno, a cuya sombra se viva con absoluta confianza y satisfacción, y se prospere; sin esta base no pueden formarse colonias; o serían muy onerosas, o apenas formadas se perderían." *El Monitor Republicano*, May 19, 1847, 3.

165. "que se conserven cien haciendas de adobe pero en productos, y los cien telares añosos que las abastecen" rather than "que se levante un gran obelisco ónico o currigueresco en una colonia cualquiera a la memoria de la dirección

o de Sr. MG; porque esas trnasformacioens de establecimietnos antiguos en modernos, y con la pérdida que es inevitable en la transplantación de la cosa, no puede merecer la aprobación de ningún hombre que calcula y que tenga algo sólido y estable que comprometer en la nación." *El Monitor Republicano*, May 19, 1847, 2–3.

166. Let us remember that it was precisely the possibility of an individual's arbitrary power which had worried some members of that first generation of Mexican legislators in 1823 and had, as a result, spurred them to call for an unmediated relationship between State and colono—an unmediated relationship that materialized two decades later in the Dirección's projects.

167. "¿Cómo podría dejar de adaptarse el régimen de la independencia municipal para las nuevas poblaciones, las de estrangeros my especialmente? La distancia a que por lo común se habrán de fundar, las diversas costumbres, hábitos y necesidades, y otras muchas causas, exigen es independencia local para los negocios que solo toquen a los vecindarios." *Proyectos de colonización*, 9.

168. "Muchas concesiones de terrenos y contratos de colonización se han hecho, ¿y cuántos pueblos nuevos están formados? ¿Cuántos terrenos de los concedidos están labrados o aprovechados después de largos años?." *Proyectos de colonización*, 13.

169. "es preciso abrir con dinero del tesoro una senda ancha para aquellos emigrantes que solo tienen voluntad de dejar su país natal, pero no medios para ejecutarlo." *Proyectos de colonización*, 13.

170. "una vez que se presenten a la vista alguna o algunas colonias florecientes, vendrán a ofrecerse las empresas verdaderas, las empresas de los que teniendo fondos los podrán emplear con provecho capitulando las inmigraciones." *Proyectos de colonización*, 13.

171. "los vagos hechos colonos se convertirían en propietarios laboriosos. Esta conversión sería así un bien para ellos y para la república, que se vería purgada de salteadores." *Proyectos de colonización*, 11–12.

172. "a precaver delitos y purgar el corazón de la República de la carcoma devoradora que lo despedaza." *Proyectos de colonización*, 13.

173. "El reparto de tierras con que se invita a los nuevos pobladores, brindándoselas por concesiones liberales, se asemejaría al sarcasmo, si al mismo tiempo la gente indígena no mereciese, estraña en su propio suelo, las miradas de la consideración del gobierno. La población antigua debe ser atendida, para que se multiplique y prospere; y su prosperidad no puede esperarse, sin medios fáciles y abundandes de alimentarse, que para los habitantes del campo, no son posible sin tierra productiva que labrar." *Proyectos de colonización*, 17–18.

174. It would seem, in fact, that the Dirección had little interest in the Northern territories. The US-Mexico War only came into the report as a source of funds, for the Dirección hoped to absorb the payments to be rendered by the United States, as per the Treaty of Guadalupe Hidalgo, to fund the projects mentioned in the report.

175. "[l]as turbaciones de la sierra han tenido orígen en disputas de terrenos." *Proyectos de colonización*, 17.
176. "choques sangrientos y a las represalías de incendio y devastacion; y lo que al principio fue guerra de venganzas, se va convirtiendo en espantosa rebelión." *Proyectos de colonización*, 15.
177. "el cancer interior se reproducirá con la fuerza de las dolencias mortales." *Proyectos de colonización*, 15–16.
178. " Si las poblaciones de la sierra estaban oprimidas, tiranizadas y vejadas, si aquella sublevación ha nacido de que los indígenas se han querido apoderar de los terrenos de los propietarios blancos, por la necesidad de proveer a las primeras de la vida, o por recobrar aquellos de que estaban priviados por indiscretas e ilegales enagenaciones, o por fallos dados bhjo la influencia de los ricos y propietarios, no puede recurrirse a la violenta represión, sino al remedio por las reparaciones." *Proyectos de colonización*, 16.
179. Kazanjian, *The Brink of Freedom*, 156.
180. Hale, *Mexican Liberalism*, 38.
181. "¿Por qué no se habría proceder así con una clase numerosa, que solo por serlo merece grandes miramientos?." *Proyectos de colonización*, 16.
182. *Proyectos de colonización*, 16.
183. "donde la superabundancia de población, y la de trabajadores es origen de [la] miseria." *Proyectos de colonización*, 16–17.
184. *Proyectos de colonización*, 17.
185. *Proyectos de colonización*, 18.
186. "el mejor proyecto para lograr, sin ofender los derechos de propiedad, la mayor división posible de la agrícola y para proporcionar terrenos a las poblaciones que lo necesiten." *Proyectos de colonización*, 34.
187. *Proyectos de colonización*, 34.
188. "un testimonio de la docilidad con que [La dirección] está dispuesta a adoptar las concepciones que no son suyas" *Proyectos de colonización*, 25.
189. *Proyectos de colonización*, 25.
190. *Proyectos de colonización*, 26.
191. See, in this regard, an article titled "Observaciones sobre colonización" published in *El Siglo Diez y Nueve* on September 11, 1848. Authored by conservative writer José Joaquín Pesado, it argued that most lands identified as "baldíos" were actually private properties and that their colonization were to be considered expropriations. The only way to legally colonize Mexico, in his opinion, was to promote it among landowners, who would carry it out if it was in their interest. The article is anonymous, yet Pesado identifies himself as the author in a November 1849 letter to Lucas Alamán. See Pesado, "Carta a Lucas Alamán remitiéndole un artículo sobre colonización."
192. "La colonización es para [la nación] la única esperanza de progreso social y político, y nos atrevemos a decir que la única condición de su ecsistencia futura." *El Siglo Diez y Nueve*, January 4, 1849, 16.

193. These papers were essential to what Elías José Palti calls the nation's "Rousseauian moment," a context of debate in which "todos los proyectos y programas anteriores se volverían obsoletos." As we have seen, in the preceding decades Mexico had experienced and, in the opinion of some, exhausted most of the constitutional arrangements imaginable: lost a significant portion of its territory, spiraled into debt, and faced two foreign invasions. For the new governing elite, Palti writes, "toda inteligibilidad parecía desmoronarse. Aquellas certidumbres que habían puesto en marcha una revolución ya no lograrían explicar las claves que ordenaban un curso histórico ulterior que parecía no obedecer a ningún designio racional . . .; en fin, la visión liberal del mundo se volvería 'una red llena de agujeros.'" See Palti, *La invención de una legitimidad*, 215.

194. "probado casi matemáticamente su irracionalidad." *El Universal*, December 31, 1848, 1.

195. "esa lista enfática de los derechos del ciudadano, es una superchería, un engaño, una hipocrecía de los llamados liberales, para embaucar y seducir al infeliz pueblo." *El Universal*, December 31, 1848, 1.

196. *La voz de la religión* preceeded *El Universal* as the Dirección's first conservative critics. When they had begun to review the 1848 report and its proposals, its editors had been honest and explained that they might have ignored the report altogether were it not for its attempt to establish religious tolerance. Their criticism—which became a thorough-line of the publication from August 1848 until May 1849—must have been expected by the Dirección, as the report did not hide its contempt for religious intolerance. What the Dirección could not have expected was that conservatives would move beyond that issue to question the totality of the colonizing fantasy. Granted, this move took time to coalesce and responded as much to the Dirección and the subsequent and futile legislative debates as to the increasing excitement of liberal papers' defenses of colonization. *La voz*'s first few attacks were careful and treaded familiar ground, insisting on the centrality of Catholicism to the nation and the disordering effects of a potential Protestant presence. They limited their criticism to the specificities of the Dirección's report, avoiding questioning colonization proper. In broad strokes, its coverage shifted between two positions, either insisting that the Dirección acted as if there were not a multitude of Catholics in Europe who, if offered sanctuary and protection, would happily relocate to Mexico—or arguing that any measure should attend to the needs of the Mexican citizenry before attending to foreign designs.

197. *El Universal*, November 19, 1848.

198. "[asentaban] por principio, lo mismo que es materia de disputa." *El Universal*, December 21, 1848, 1.

199. *El Universal*, December 6, 1848.

200. "[l]a tristísima condición de las clases de nuestra sociedad, es el principio radical del atraso de población." *El Universal*, November 19, 1848, 1.

201. *El Universal*, November 19, 1848, 1.
202. "desgracia ha consistido en que no pudimos, como en el Norte, hacer desaparecer la raza indígena." *El Universal*, January 1, 1849, 1.
203. "no tuvimos modelos europeos para manejar los indios embarrancanados en terrenos insalubres, como los tenemos para imitar costumbres; nuestra desgracia, en suma, ha consistido en que nuestro anteojo político presenta una area de cortísima y ruin estensión." *El Universal*, January 1, 1849, 1.
204. "pueblos, que lejos de considerarse como esclavos, van comprendiendo el principio de su soberanía e independencia por debajo de los sentimientos, de timidez y descofianza, que hacen al indio astuto y sanguinario." *El Universal*, November 19, 1848, 1.
205. "¿Qué aventaja, pues, la sociedad con el comercio de los indios? Cambios de ruines efectos, y el espectáculo de una raza degradada y viciosa." *El Universal*, December 29, 1848, 1.
206. *El Universal*, December 29, 1848, 1.
207. "cualquier sistema de gobierno es indiferente a los indios; y no tienen otro juicio ni otro anhelo que el de no ser gravados con contribuciones y gabelas." *El Universal*, December 29, 1848, 1.
208. *El Universal*, December 29, 1848, 1.
209. *El Universal*, January 1, 1849.
210. *El Universal*, December 19, 1848, 1–2.
211. "las abstracciones del ingeniosos sistema del pobre loco Juan Jacobo" and "[e]l hombre no entró en sociedad, nació en sociedad," *El Universal*, February 5, 1849, 2 and 1, respectively.
212. "el sacrificio mayor y más difícil para el corazón humano, es la obediencia y sumisión voluntaria." *El Universal*, February 10, 1849, 1.
213. If anyone migrated to Mexico under the aegis of colonization policies, the editors assumed it would only be "aquella chusma envuelta con una espantosa miseria y en una triste degradación intelectual, que tanto como en México, abunda en las naciones estranjeras, sin más diferencia que la de carecer de toda religión, en cambio de la cual, posee un caudal mayor de charlatanismo y osadía, que apenas comienzan a remedar ahora nuestros indígenas y nuestros pobres léperos." *El Universal*, December 23, 1848, 1–2.
214. "producirá el desarrollo de los elementos de prosperidad y riqueza que la República encierra; pero toda esa riqueza y prosperidad no será en tal caso, dígase lo que se quiera, para los hijos de la misma, sino para los colonos y las generaciones que de ellos procedan." *El Universal*, February 5, 1849, 3.
215. "usos y costumbres distan mucho de la perfección que podemos y debemos aspirar . . . aumentar la población con beneficio de la población existente; en esplotar los elementos de riqueza que encierra nuestro suelo, con provecho de los dueños de este suelo; en perfeccionar las costumbres, sin esclavizarse a aquellos cuyas costumbres se trata de perfeccionar; en ilustrar, en fin, los entendimientos, sin estraviarlos ni alucinarlos." *El Universal*, February 5, 1849, 3.

216. "Gritar con tono magistral: `¡colonización, colonización!" *El Universal*, December 31, 1848, 1.
217. "Nosotros estupefactos con semejante estrategia, ¿qué podemos hacer sino esclamar: ¡ALGO SE HA DE HACER PARA BLANCA SER!." *El Universal*, December 31, 1848, 2.
218. "uno de nuestros ensueños, y al mismo tiempo la pesadilla de los buenos patriotas." *El Siglo Diez y Nueve*, March 17, 1851, 1.
219. Legrás, *Culture and Revolution*, 121.
220. Legrás, *Culture and Revolution*, 121.
221. Legrás, *Culture and Revolution*, 7, 142
222. See Hernández, *Mexican American Colonization*.

CHAPTER 2

Epigraph. "Los hombres empleados en las fábricas, los comprometidos en los talleres, los que se ocupan en su domicilio, ya bajo la dependencia del patrón o ya libremente, los necesitados de cooperación y los errantes que se empeñan por el tiempo de su voluntad y de un modo inconstante, todos ellos se acercan más o menos al ocio y tienen mayor o menor correctivo en sus desarreglos." Prieto, "Artesanos y obreros V," *Obras*, 227.

1. Pérez Toledo, *Los hijos del trabajo*, 89.
2. Pérez Toledo, *Los hijos del trabajo*, 89.
3. Pérez Toledo, *Los hijos del trabajo*, 101.
4. "Esta distancia está mediada por las costumbres y tradiciones que forman parte de un mundo que obedece a ritmos de cambios más lentos." Pérez Toledo, *Los hijos del trabajo*, 101.
5. Pérez Toledo, *Los hijos del trabajo*, 101.
6. Herrejón Peredo, "Grito de dolores," 197.
7. Van Young, *A Nation Together*, 65.
8. Ávila, *Para la libertad*, 86.
9. In yet another of Guillermo Prieto's articles on the artisan from the century's last decades, he blamed the decadence of artisan labor precisely on their massive participation in the struggle for independence. He argued that whereas "indios" and rural laborers returned, after the war, to their hometowns and prior employment, artisans mostly did not and fell into vice "in their newfound freedom," or became "addicted" to a form of politics which was nothing but restlessness, leisure and political offices. See Prieto, "Artesanos y obreros 2," 218.
10. Aljovín de Losada, "Ciudadano y vecino," 196.
11. "Señor mío, como estoy sujeto a un trabajo tan laborioso y mecánico, que en cuanto no estoy en el lo echo menos, (en la bolsa) no he tenido el tiempo bastante para observarlo todo." JMR, *Lo que interesa a la Patria. Por el artesano y su amigo*, 1.
12. Thompson, *The Making of the English Working Class*, 234.

13. Illades and Sandoval, *Espacio social y representación*, 117.
14. "La aplicación bastarda de los principios económicos y la inconsiderada latitud que se dio al comercio extranjero, agravaron nuestra s necesidades, y es uniforme el grito en todos los puntos de la República que se levanta contra un sistema ruinoso en sus bases y resultados. Para que la nación prospere es preciso repartir sus manos laboriosas en todos los ramos de industria y particularmente que las manufacturas sean protegidas pro prohibiciones sábiamente claculadas." Guerrero, *Manifiesto del ciudadano Vicente Guerrero*, 16.
15. Prieto condemned the "ignorancia, la miseria, el abandono y la prostitución en las clases trabajadoras," which for him resulted from the guild's "interdicción del trabajo, con los títulos de la sangre, el aprendizaje, la esclavitud encadenando el trabajo y la cofradía, la fiscalía clerical dentro del trabajo." See Prieto, "Artesanos obreros I," *Obras*, 227.
16. Postone, *Time, Labor, and Social Domination*, 151.
17. Hale, *Mexican Liberalism*, 280.
18. See Alamán, "Memoria de la Secretaria de Estado y del Despacho de Relaciones Interiores y Exteriores Del Año 1832," 366; "Memoria sobre el Estado de la Agricultura y Industria de la República en el Año de 1845," 308–9.
19. Alamán, "Memoria de la Secretaria de Estado y del Despacho de Relaciones Interiores y Exteriores Del Año 1832," 37; "Memoria sobre el Estado de la Agricultura y Industria de la República en el Año de 1845," 233–34.
20. Alamán, *Memoria de la Secretaria de Estado y del despacho de Relaciones Interiores y Exteriores*, 1830, 29.
21. Alamán, *Memoria de la Secretaria de Estado y del despacho de Relaciones Interiores y Exteriores*, 1830, 5.
22. Alamán, *Memoria de la Secretaria de Estado y del despacho de Relaciones Interiores y Exteriores, 1830*, 29.
23. "y ciertamente que quien puede extraer directamente plata, no se ocupa en hacer otras cosas por cuyo intermedio procrársela." *Memoria de la Secretaria de Estado y del despacho de Relaciones Interiores y Exteriores*, 1830, 29.
24. Alamán would make a similar point in his 1832 *Memoria*. See Alamán, "Memoria de la Secretaria de Estado y del Despacho de Relaciones Interiores y Exteriores Del Año 1832," 363.
25. "Un pueblo debe tener a la mira no depender de otros para nada de lo que es indispensable para subsistir, y por tanto, las providencias legislativa todo en tener por objeto proporcionar es lo que falta, por el orden gradual que facilita todo. Los tejidos ordinarios de algodón, lino y lana, preciso para cubrirse la parte más numeroso de la población, son los que deben fomentarse excitando los capitalistas nacionales o extranjeros al establecimiento de fábrica con las máquinas necesarias, para que los artefactos resulten a un precio moderado, lo que nuca se conseguirá sin este auxilio." Alamán, *Memoria de la Secretaria de Estado y del despacho de Relaciones Interiores y Exteriores*, 1830, 206.

26. "Las minas son la fuente de la verdadera riqueza de esta nación, y todo cuando han dicho conta este principio algunos economistas especulativos, ha sido victoriosamente rebatido por la esperiencia. Asi hemos visto constantemente la agricultura, el comercio y la industria, seguir el progreso de las minas, adelantando con estas y decayendo en la misma proporcion." Alamán, *Memoria presentada a las dos cámaras del Congreso General de la Federacion: por el Secretario de Estado y del Despacho de Relaciones Esteriores é Interiores*, 1825, 37.
27. Tutino, *Mexican Heartland*, 30.
28. "De aquí se sigue la necesidad de emplear muchedumbre de brazos, de máquinas y caballerías, tanto p ra su estracción como para su beneficio, o que dá lugar a inmensos consumos que equivalen a considerabels esportaciones de furtos, y que impulsan a s uvez todas las artes, y en particular la agricultura. Asi es que el fomento que se dá a la minería se dá tambien a estas, y el restablecimiento y prosperiad de todas, y consiguientemente de la nación, es simultáneo." Alamán, *Memoria presentada a las dos cámaras del Congreso General de la Federacion: por el Secretario de Estado y del Despacho de Relaciones Esteriores é Interiores, 1825*, 38.
29. Ávila and Tutino, "Becoming Mexico," 262.
30. Tutino, "El debate sobre el futuro," 1121.
31. "[u]no de los grandes beneficios que produce el progreso de la industria es relacionar todos los ramos [de la economía] entre sí, hacer provechoso para los uno lo que era perdido para los otros, y dar valor aun a las cosas más despreciables." Alamán, *Memoria sobre el Estado de la Agricultura e Industria de la República*, 1843, 30.
32. "La industria fabril fomenta la agricultura por el mismo medio que lo hace la minería, pero de una manera más uniforme y estable que está. No depende de la voluntad del hombre hacer unas terminas en donde se quiere, y así el fomento que ellas puedan promover, está limitado a solo las localidades favorecidas por la naturaleza con este género de riqueza, ya solo el consumo de ciertos artículos indispensables para que el giro, que siendo por sí mismo inestable, tampoco puede producir en fomento permanente. Industria fabril por el contrario, eligiendo las localidades a su arbitrio empleando para sus usos todos los productos naturales, siendo su duración perpetua como lo son las necesidades que probé y los medios que emplea, proporciona la agricultura un fomento permanente, y sus buenos efectos se han de sentir ya en varios ramos cuyos adelantos son palpables merced al progreso de las fábricas, según veremos tratando de cada uno de ellos en particular." Alamán, "Memoria sobre el Estado de la Agricultura y Industria de la República en el Año de 1845," 231–32.
33. Alamán, *Memoria sobre el Estado de la Agricultura e Industria de la República*, 1843, 27.
34. "...pero sí es cierto que hasta los primeros meses del año de diez, del presente siglo, los artistas de Puebla tuvieron una larga época de ocupacion, y toda la felicidad que era compatible con el estado de colonos, mucho en que ocuparse

útilmente, dinero con abundancia . . . ." Antuñano, "Manifiesto del algodón," *Obras*, 9.

35. "lo poco que ha quedado ya, no se puede considerar sino como fragmentos dispersos de un grande edificio, y monumento honorífico del ingenio de los poblanos." Antuñano, "Manifiesto del algodón," *Obras*, 11.
36. ."Parece que el Todopoderoso, sabiendo lo futuro, quiso acabar todo lo viejo de nuestras costumbres y entendimientos, para vestirnos de nuevo, análogamente al gran papel que ibamos a representar desde la época de regeneración, que ya estaba próxima." Antuñano, "Manifiesto del algodón," *Obras*, 11.
37. "Las filas de beligerantes se llenaron de tejedores, que arrojando la lanzadera abrazaban el fusil, inducidos por el entusiasmo fanático que los cegaba." Antuñano, "Manifiesto del algodón," *Obras*, 10.
38. "Como que poco conocíamos, poco apetecíamos, vivíamos contentos, circunscriptos a una esfera de media luz, bien hallados con nuestro fanatismo y nuestros escasos conocimientos, en la generalidad de las ciencias y artes." Antuñano, "Manifiesto del algodón," *Obras*, 9.
39. "y volvieron mendigos á nuestros artesanos, que menos diestros, no pudieron conservar su existencia ya miserable." Antuñano, "Manifiesto del algodón," *Obras*, 12.
40. "Perdieron los artesanos y labradores la esperanza de poderse ocupar útilmente, y salir de la miseria; y los pueblos todos la de prosperar." Antuñano, "Manifiesto del algodón," *Obras*, 12.
41. "el antiguo uso de hilar y tejer, es incompatible con las instituciones liberales de la nación y por lo mismo racionalmente impracticable, y que tambien es disonante con la política que debe guardarse con las Potencias amigas, y el decoro propio." Antuñano, "Manifiesto del algodón," *Obras*, 22.
42. "México es ya independiente y libre, y es poderoso y rico, por la abundancia de su suelo, y por el valor e ingenio de sus hijos: entrado en el rango de nación civilizada, y es preciso que se adorne con los vestidos que le corresponden, so pena de esponerse al desprecio y tal vez a la esclavitud." Antuñano, "Manifiesto del algodón," *Obras*, 23.
43. "el motivo único y verdadero de nuestra miseria, de nuestra escasa ilustración y de nuestras disensiones domésticas: *la falta de la ocupación útil de la mayor parte de los mexicanos, que todo ha de venir de afuera, nada se ha de hacer aquí.* No habiendo ocupación útil, ¿cómo ha de haber utilidades? Sin estas ¿cómo abundancia? ¿Cómo matrimonios? Sin estos ¿cómo población? ¿Cómo virtudes? ¿Cómo paz? ¿Cómo fortaleza nacional? ¿Cómo nada bueno? La necesidad engendra todos los vicios; ella es hija legitima de la ociosidad; luego mientras en México abundan los hombres desocupados, no podrá salir del estado lastímero que presenta ahora." Antuñano, "Manifiesto del algodón," *Obras*, 18.
44. Antuñano fictionalized the opposing position in his *Ampliación*, putting the complaint in the mouth of his fictional weaver: "Sí siñor, lo he leído, y aunque no lo he entendido todo; pero he comprendido muy bien que este siñor que

quiere se pongan aquí esas máquinas, que sin venir acá, ya nos han arruinado, y me es muy sensible que este siñor por estar encalabrinado con las máquinas estrrnajeras, ya se haya hecho odioso para los probes artesanos." See Antuñano, *Ampliación*, 15.

45. Antuñano, "Manifiesto del algodón," *Obras*, 17.
46. Antuñano, *Ampliación*, 24–26.
47. "Reventaría un hombre día y noche y no podría salir de un pobre calzón y camisa de manta. No, siñor, sería una bobería volver a los tiempos de gentilidá." *Ampliación*, 24.
48. "no . . . alcanzaria porque hay muchos objetos nuevos que desear, y que ya forman neesidad en nosotros." Antuñano, *Ampliación*, 25.
49. "la marca del despotismo que aun no se nos borra a los que nacimos bajo su imperio." Antuñano, *Ampliación*, 25.
50. Antuñano, "Manifiesto del algodón," *Obras*, 14.
51. Antuñano, "Manifiesto del algodón," *Obras*, 14, 20. "esta utilidad incitaría a los capitalistas y a los hombres industriosos a formas empresas sobre este ramo, y en el curso de los seis u ocho años, la nación aseguraría este patrimonio pingüe."
52. Antuñano, "Manifiesto del algodón" in *Obras*, 18.
53. "un millón de personas se podría ocupar en cultivarlo, y este número de ciudadanos tendría directamente un modo de pasar más cómodo: adelantarían la educación de sus hijos, y de ello le vendrían a la patria los bienes de que carece: no pararía en esto la ganancia pública; los habitantes de nuestras costas se ocuparían más en el cultivo de este fruto: se enriquecerían muchos directamente por estos ramos: estenderían su brazo ya fuerte a los otros: todas las demás clases participarían indirectamente de este beneficio por el comercio recíproco, y llegaríamos al colmo *del poder, de la riqueza, de la felicidad* . . . Este venturoso dia ha de aparecer, compatriotas: paz, unión, y espíritu público, son los precursores; tras ellos veréis la aurora de este día grande." Antuñano, "Manifiesto del algodón," in *Obras*, 20–21.
54. "A nuevos tiempos, nuevas costumbres." Antuñano, "Manifiesto del algodón" in *Obras*, 22
55. Antuñano, "Manifiesto del algodón" in *Obras*, 18.
56. Antuñano, "Manifiesto del algodón" in *Obras*, 22.
57. "que para la producción usan los mexicanos, torpes y escasos, es preciso que su estado sea pobre." Antuñano, "Pensamientos para la regeneración industrial de México" in *Obras*, 290.
58. For Antuñano, "lo más sano e importante del pueblo [conserva] siempre aquellas costumbres que le dio el sistema colonial, falto de espírito público, yde ninguna manera poderse acomodar, a las liberales leyes democráticas, por el abuso que se hace de ellas." And the current legislatos "dando leyes con profusión pero muy pcoas dirgiidas a mejorar las costumbres para ponerlas al nivel de nuestras amidrables instituciones." Antuñano, *Ampliación*, 9.
59. "civilizar y unir nuestras clases, conforme lo requiere nuestro sistema." Antuñano,"Comercio exterior en México. Segunda parte" in *Obras*, 305.

60. "Las artes han refinado la civilización, como que en ellas obra mucho el entendimiento; y porque sus operaciones, en general, siendo mas suaves que las de la agricultura, moderan el caracter del hombre." Antuñano, *Pensamiento para un plan para animar la industria mejicana*, 34.
61. See Antuñano, *Pensamientos para un plan para animar la industria mexicana*, published originally on 1834.
62. " un lugar a donde nadie puede estar ocioso ni separarse de él, porque las máquinas para andar bien en sus operaciones progresiva, No permiten largas, paradas ni distracciones." Antuñano, "Ventajas políticas, civiles, fabriles y domésticas" in *Obras*, 270.
63. ". . . las máquinas para obrar bien con ellas, no requieren un largo aprendizage, ni comunnmente, grandes fuerzas." . Antuñano, "Ventajas políticas, civiles, fabriles y domésticas" in *Obras*, 267.
64. "Cómo que metidos todos los individuos de una familia en una fábrica, la utilidad quiere de aquella, aunque formada de pequeñas porciones, crece sin aumentar el jornal individual, resultará que la economía jornalera de nuestra fábrica nos pondrá a cubierto de la ruina que la industria extraña por estar puesta bajo economía más estricta, pudiera causar." Antuñano, "Ventajas políticas, civiles, fabriles y domésticas" in *Obras*, 269.
65. "todo lo que se dirija a infundir buena moralidad en los jornaleros, es inmediatamente oportuno para la moral civil y religiosa, para la industria en general, y para los propietarios de los establecimientos." Antuñano, "Ventajas políticas, civiles, fabriles y domésticas" in *Obras*, 268.
66. "Ocupando en ella tambien á las mugeres se saca la ventaja de que los barones estén mas sujetos al lugar y a sus obligaciones cibiles, fabriles y domésticas." Antuñano, "Ventajas políticas, civiles, fabriles y domésticas" in *Obras*, 268.
67. "quizás algunas personas timoratos encontrarán peligros murales en la concurrencia asidua de ambos sexos un mismo lugar, pero reflexionen; que más peligro corre en su casa una mujer joven, ociosa y sola, por la separación de dos o tres veces al día tengan que hacer sus mayores o que ella tenga que salir, que en un lugar bajo la vista de sus deudos, muy concurrido y muy cuidado por los directores y maestros, que comúnmente han de ser personas de juicio." Antuñano, "Ventajas políticas, civiles, fabriles y domésticas" in *Obras*, 270.
68. "Como que los establecimientos de lados comúnmente se han de fijar distantes de las poblaciones, y que en ellos se ocupan gran número de personas, para cuya habitaciones de necesidad levantar edificios, que por sus costos y conservación aunque sean económicos pueden llevar hacer algún día un gravamen ruinoso para estas negociaciones, es sumamente conveniente aumentar las ganancias de cada familia, cobrándoles un moderado arrendamiento por su habitación, lo que se conseguirá fácilmente, admitiendo en en esta casa también las mujeres." Antuñano, "Ventajas políticas, civiles, fabriles y domésticas" in *Obras*, 269.
69. "cuanto mas recursos tengan para subsistir estas personas, están menos espuestas al robo, que ha sido frecuente en nuestros obrajes. SEs mas facil evitar

este vicio, asi como la embriaguez en persona ubicada cerca de la fábrica." Antuñano, "Ventajas políticas, civiles, fabriles y domésticas" in *Obras* 269–70.

70. "beneficios ostensibles que ya está produciendo a la industria y a la moral pública [la industria moderna]." Antuñano, "Breve memoria del estado que guarda la fábrica de hilados" in *Obras*, 245.
71. "concurren gustosos al trabajo, aun los días de media fiesta: la embriaguez y el robo han sido desterrados de aquella mansión; toda la gente es voluntaria, y usa de completa libertad para disponer de su persona después de las horas de trabajo: el aseo en los días de fiesta y un carácter decoroso, se va arraigando en estos operarios." Antuñano, "Breve memoria del estado que guarda la fábrica de hilados" in *Obras*, 246.
72. "[L]os operarios de La Constancia Mexicana están desmintiendo los otros es imputaciones, que se hacía en el carácter mexicano." Antuñano, *Comercio exterior en México. Segunda parte*, 304.
73. "Más de 400 familias se mantienen hoy en Puebla, y en algunos puntos de su departamento, por tejer el hilo de La Constancia," which proved that establishment such as his benefited people of "all qualities and of all opinions." Antuñano, "Breve memoria del estado que guarda la fábrica de hilados" in *Obras*, 246.
74. Antuñano, *Comercio exterior en México. Segunda parte*, 304.
75. "Años hace que tengo el pensamiento de que en la hermosa cañada de más de 9 leguas que a las orillas del río Atoyac ocupan 9 haciendas de mi propiedad (Santo Domingo, La Noria, Cusinaloyan, Apetlachica y la Uranga), se forme el valle de la industria mexicana, componiéndose de 10 o 12 fábricas todas de movimiento hidráulico y de 10 o 12 pueblecitos de labradores arrendatarios de la mayor parte de las tierras de dichas fincas, con el fin de que teniendo a la vez una ubicación y propiedad rural fueran también unos artesanos de la mejor moral que alternativamente atendiesen al campo y a las fábricas de su demarcación para cuyo efecto los pueblos quedarían señalados del modo conveniente." Antuñano, *Obras*, 569.
76. Sánchez, *Las élites empresariales*, 44–45. As had been the norm since viceregal times, no matter how a given elite family's wealth had originated, its leading members made sure to diversify their investsments. In this process, as John E. Kicza has documented, rural holdings were a significant part of a family's portfolio, not only because they had the potential of providing meaningful income, but because landed estates "coinstituted the only form of property or enterprise which was easily divided and transferred acrss generations." *Colonial Entrepreneurs*, 227–28.
77. Bernecker, *De agiostistas y empresarios*, 90–92.
78. Sánchez, *Las élites empresariales*, 45.
79. Potash, *Mexican Government and Industrial Development*, 44.
80. Potash, *Mexican Government and Industrial Development*, 45.
81. "[Estas leyes] no la pueden hacer nacer cuando se halla reducida a la nada."

Alamán, *Memoria de la Secretaria de Estado y del Despacho de Relaciones Interiores y Exteriores*, 1831, 22.

82. "Era menester, pues, pensar en la creación de estos capitales, y aplicarlos al fomento de la industria, dandoles la dirección conveniente." Alamán, *Memoria de la Secretaria de Estado y del Despacho de Relaciones Interiores y Exteriores*, 1831, 22.
83. Potash, *Mexican Government and Industrial Development*, 45.
84. Potash, *Mexican Government and Industrial Development*, 45.
85. Potash, *Mexican Government and Industrial Development*, 49.
86. Potash, *Mexican Government and Industrial Development*, 49.
87. Potash, *Mexican Government and Industrial Development*, 50.
88. "En lugar de someter su gestión al espíritu federal y republicano de la Constitución, lo cual supone una vida pública de instituciones, el gobierno de Bustamante experimenta administrativamente con la combinación de los intereses económicos mediante la formación de fondos y la creación de establecimientos útiles como el Banco." Covarrubias, "Riqueza, Ilustración y población," 133.
89. Potash, *Mexican Government and Industrial Development*, 49.
90. Quoted in Fowler, *Tornel and Santa Anna*, 103.
91. Potash, *Mexican Government and Industrial Development*, 57.
92. Gómez Galvarriato, *The Mexican Cotton Textile Industry*, 5.
93. Potash, *Mexican Government and Industrial Development*, 68.
94. For a recent and clear account about Guerrero's death and the role Alamán might or might not have played in it, see Van Young, *A Life Together*, 465–82.
95. Potash, *Mexican Government and Industrial Development*, 72.
96. Potash, *Mexican Government and Industrial Development*, 84.
97. Potash, *Mexican Government and Industrial Development*, 137.
98. Potash, *Mexican Government and Industrial Development*, 117.
99. Potash, *Mexican Government and Industrial Development*, 134.
100. "estos progresos, aunque maravillosos, hubieran sido insubsistentes, la suerte de la industria mexicana hubiera quedado incierta y vacilante, si los individuos que la ejercen hubiesen permanecido aislados; si sus esfuerzos no fuesen dirigidos a un mismo fin; en una palabra, si no hubiese informado una corporación, que les diese unidad y estabilidad *Memoria sobre el Estado de la Agricultura e Industria de la República, 1843*, 4.
101. Tutino, *Mexican Heartland*, 191.
102. Alamán, "Memoria sobre el Estado de la Agricultura y Industria de la República en el Año de 1845," 233.
103. "introducir hábitos de mayor comodidad, é inspirar el gusto de ciertas necesidades y conveniencias a la masa general de la población." Alamán, "Memoria sobre el Estado de la Agricultura y Industria de la República en el Año de 1845," 232.
104. "el orden social es una cadena en que todos los eslabones se entrelazan, la mejora de costumbres de que de aquí se seguiría, fomentaría de mil maneras las

artes y la labranza, y estas a su vez, proporcionando efectos mas baratos, facilitarían mayor número de goces a esa parte de la sociedad que ahora carece de ellos." Alamán, "Memoria sobre el Estado de la Agricultura y Industria de la República en el Año de 1845," 232.

105. Alamán, "Memoria sobre el Estado de la Agricultura y Industria de la República en el Año de 1845," 235.

106. "[La falta de consumidores] se vencería por medio de una providencia que obligara la clase de que se habla, a presentarse en público siempre vestidos y a proporción de sus facultades, corrigiendolos de algún modo cuando faltaran este precepto." Alamán, "Memoria sobre el Estado de la Agricultura y Industria de la República en el Año de 1845," 233.

107. Fernández de Lizardi sketched these ideas in 1814, when imagining the island of Ricamea in his public paper *El Pensador Mexicano*. He would do so again in *El Periquillo Sarniento*, when he thematized anti-vagrancy in the island of *Saucheofú*. We see this, yet again, in 1824, in the middle of the Second Constituent Congress's recess, in another of his ventures, *Conversaciones del payo y el sacristan* (1824), where these viceregal dispositions echoed. In all of these, we find the insistence on transparency, which sought to actualize the Enlightenment's promise of the progressive extension of the legibility of the world. As Elías J. Palti has written, Fernández de Lizardi put his trust not on the probity of the citizen as individual, but on the system of social controls that, through transparency and public opinion, protected and preserved subjects from the inevitable perversion of their private passions and desires. Like Jean-Jacques Rousseau, in all of his utopian speculations, *El pensador mexicano* described small republics in which "neither the secret machinations of vice, nor the modesty of virtue escaped the notice and judgment of the public." See Palti, *La invención de una legitimidad*, 73. These were republics that sought to make explicit the inner reaches of the citizen's *fuero interno*, to submit it to the "public eye" so as to reveal the appropriateness of the citizen's activity and industriousness to all; and, thus, to make possible, and enforceable, the complete subjection, willingly or not, of the republic to industry.

108. "un consumo de todas clases, que alimentaría por este motivo los rápidos progresos de los artesanos miserables, que aún así es gente muy necesaria y útil, sea cual fuere el estado de situación en que se encuentran." Alamán, "Memoria sobre el Estado de la Agricultura y Industria de la República en el Año de 1845," 233.

109. "[h]ubo un tiempo en que el gobierno español providenció, que la clase media y aún a la ínfima se obligase a andar vestidos." Alamán, "Memoria sobre el Estado de la Agricultura y Industria de la República en el Año de 1845," 233.

110. "hacer un gasto tan superior a sus fuerzas." Alamán, "Memoria sobre el Estado de la Agricultura y Industria de la República en el Año de 1845," 233.

111. "que no todos los de la clase ínfima son tan miserables, pues hay una gran parte que pueden tener ahorros sin ser perjudicados, y estos utilizan algunos reales, de los cuales solo aprovecha su familia una pequeña parte y el resto se

desperdician los vicios, y viéndose obligados los referidos a comprar su vestido, habría por tanto facilidad de disminuir su vida crapulosa, y más ventajas para la moral y la comodidad." Alamán, "Memoria sobre el Estado de la Agricultura y Industria de la República en el Año de 1845," 234.

112. "[a]fortunadamente se cuenta con un pueblo docil, que en muy poco tiempo, acostumbrado a la comodidad y el abrigo, dejaría tener por opresivo este medio, y bendeciría la mano que lo había establecido." Alamán, "Memoria sobre el Estado de la Agricultura y Industria de la República en el Año de 1845," 234.
113. "la de moralizar a los pueblos, o la de proteger por este medio el comercio de efectos extranjeros que monopolizada por su mano." Alamán, "Memoria sobre el Estado de la Agricultura y Industria de la República en el Año de 1845,"235.
114. "cualquiera de estas intenciones que se tuviese, una y otra parecen bien calculadas, y a nosotros nos podrían proporcionar en todas direcciones bellos y útiles resultados." Alamán, "Memoria sobre el Estado de la Agricultura y Industria de la República en el Año de 1845," 235.
115. In any case, Alamán began to push for a monarchy in the late 1840s out of frustration and historical contingency.
116. Van Young, *A Life Together*, 546
117. Gómez Galvarriato, *The Mexican Cotton Textile Industry*, 7.
118. Potash, *Mexican Government and Industrial Development*, 142.
119. Gómez Galvarriato, *The Mexican Cotton Textile Industry*, 8.
120. Baptist, "Towards a Political Economy of Slave Labor," 33–35.
121. Baptist, "Towards a Political Economy of Slave Labor," 33.
122. Baptist, "Towards a Political Economy of Slave Labor," 35
123. Baptist, "Towards a Political Economy of Slave Labor," 35.
124. "los artistas manufactureros de México, que en una dilatada serie de año han visto con color arruinarse y desaparecer la industria nacional de la República, gemían en lo interior de sus desiertos y abandonados talleres, agobiados con el peso inmenso de la miseria." *Semanario artístico*, February 9, 1844, 4.
125. Pérez Toledo, *Los hijos del trabajo*, 189.
126. "La protección de la industria fabril es uno de los ramos más necesarios, como que ella es la fuente de donde puede emanar la felicidad doméstica y pública; sin este ausilio, el género humano estaría siempre presentando cuadros a cual más funestos de miseria y anarquía. Sin esta base, las sociedades no son más que un verdadero caos, y el componerlo y desarrollarlo vendría a ser como sacar de la nada un universo." *Semanario artístico*, February 9, 1844, 3–4.
127. "Se trata nada menos que de la protección de la industria fabril del país, la que influirá poderosamente a sacarla de la abyección en que se ha conservado por tantos años: los artistas con tal medida entrarán en goces de sus derechos, y la nación toda recibirá un positivo bien." *Semanario artístico*, February 9, 1844, 4.
128. "Y vosotros en particular, apreciables y dignos artistas, que vais a ser los fundadores del cngrandecimiento y prosperidad de la más poderosa de las repúblicas; de vosotros pende la buena o mala suerte de ella." *Semanario artístico*, February 9, 1844, 4.

129. "Había resuelto encargarse de la instrucción y propagación de las materias que deben ilustrar a los artesanos, de regularizar sus ideas, organizar sus métodos, familiarizarlos con la lectura, e inspirarles las afición a las letras y el amor a las artes." *Semanario artístico*, January 30, 1844, 1.
130. Pérez Toledo, *Los hijos del trabajo*, 613.
131. Illades, *Estudios sobre el artesanado urbano*, 26.
132. "Una gran parte de nuestra población entregada a la ignorancia y esclava de la preocupación y la rutina ignoa aun los principios de la sana moral, no conoce su importancia ni prevee la influencia que puede tener el arte d ser feliz que es el de conocer y cumplir sus deberes." *Semanario artístico*, February 17, 1844, 1.
133. *Semanario artístico*, February 24, 1844, 1.
134. "Obligado [por los "hábitos de regularidad" que el trabajo hace contraer] a dominarse continuamente, luchando con frecuencia con mil dificutlades, y sufriendo acaso privaciones molestas, se fortalece cada día más; y a medida que los ejercicios son mas duros, su voluntad se robustece y adquiere por la paciencia, el vigor que solo produce una larga perseverancia." *Semanario artístico*, April 20, 1844, 1.
135. *Semanario artístico*, April 20, 1844, 1.
136. *Semanario artístico*, February 24, 1844, 1.
137. Honoré-Antoine Fregier was an administrative police official who, in 1840, wrote *Des Classes dangereuses de la population des grandes villes* (The Dangerous Classes in the Population of Great Cities), a "moral topography" of Paris's "dangerous classes," vagrants, beggars, thieves, prostitutes, etc. According to Richard F. Wetzell, Fregier held that "crime was primarily a product of the vices of the poor: gambling, drinking, sexual excess, and above all, idleness. As a remedy he recommended providing employment and fostering a strong work ethic and healthy morals." See Wetzell, *Inventing the Criminal*, 26.
138. "el que quiera merecer debidamente el titulo de honrado, adviertiendo que la habitud de obrar bien, es en efecto, una cosa natural en los que por su profesion se encuentran tan preparados á ejercer sin esfuerzo las virtudes cristianas y morales" *Semanario artístico*, March 2, 1844, 1.
139. Thompson, *Cultures in Common*, 5.
140. Thompson, *Cultures in Common*, 5.
141. Pérez Toledo, *Los hijos del trabajo*, 325.
142. "El aprendizaje del oficio se iniciaba, como en el pasado colonial, en el momento en que el aprendiz era entregado por sus padres a un maestro, quien se encargaba no sólo de introducirlo y adiestrarlo en el oficio, sino que le proporcionaba alimento y vestido." Pérez Toledo, *Los hijos del trabajo*, 325.
143. "[El maestro] "se constituía *en el custodia moral de aprendices y oficiales*, pues a él se encomendaba el cuidado de la buena conducta y costumbres de sus discípulos así como la dedicación al oficio aprendido." Pérez Toledo, *Los hijos del trabajo*, 60.

144. Marx and Engels, *The German Ideology*, 70.

145. See *Semanario artístico*, March 3 and March 23, 1844.

146. *Semanario Artístico*, April 27, 1844.

147. "La vida del artesano es una verdadera educación moral cuando sabe recoger y aprovechar todas las instrucciones que encierra . . ." *Semanario artístico*, April 20, 1844, 1.

148. "El trabajo es la escuela de la resignación: nos enseña nuestra dependencia, nos recuerda lo que debemos a los demás: corrige y castiga nuestra vanidad, y nos recuerda que la vida humana no es sino un tiempo de prueba y de preparación." *Semanario artístico*, April 20, 1844, 1.

149. "Lo que hace mas falta a los artesanos, y en general a las clases pobres, es el conocimiento verdadero de su situación, y la fuerza bastante para conformarse con ella, es el saber emplear utilmente los recursos que adquieren por medio de su trabajo. No es preciso tirar contra la necesidad, sino saber sufrirla y adaptar a ella la vida. Sin negar que es preciso mucho valor y resignación para soportar la pobreza en sus malos días, el que esto escribe se halla persuadido de que esa misma pobreza laboriosa y económica, puede en tiempos comunes proveer a las necesidades de la vida y aun disfrutar muchas de las comodidades creadas or la civilización. En ninguna clase de sociedad se pueden contentar todos los deseos; lo que falta al operario falta tambien al maestro, y lo que parece deseable a este último, es un objeto de envidia para el director de una fábrica. La medida de lo necesario cambia con la condición del individuo, y por consiguiente la de lo superfluo, y deben cambiar simultáneamente porque nadie está contento con su suerte. Ademas, la pobreza será siempre la espresión más o menos limitada de lo necesario, según la conducta del individuo, el estado de las circunstancias y el número de los miembros de su familia." *Semanario artístico*, June 22, 1844, 1.

150. "Nuestro interés solo sería bastante para aconsejarnos a tener el trabajo diario esa intención que lo abraza como un deber, porque con esta sola sujeción a los designios de la Providencia, haremos su peso más llevadero, mas sufribles sus molestias, mas abundantes sus frutos, y por ultimo, nada habrá difícil ni impracticable a los esfuerzos de la industria artística, el día que se persuadan los artesanos mexicanos de que todo, sin escepción alguna, lo vence el trabajo." *Semanario artístico*, April 20, 1844, 1–2.

151. "En resúmen: pretender las clases colocadas en poco favorables posiciones, salir de ellas con pasos imprudentes educando a sus hijos, casándolos, o colocándolos muy fuera de la esfera en que se hallan, es harto peligroso y la esperiencia lo confirma; peligroso para la familia, amargo para le corazón del elevado, inutil cais siempre para el mundo, para quien, dígase lo que se quiera, no vale tanto la gloria de tener un gran hombre, como la paz general y el bienestar doméstico al as familias." *Semanario artístico*, September 14, 1844, 2.

152. *Semanario artístico*, September 14, 1844, 2.

153. Thompson, *Cultures in Common*, 36.
154. Thompson, *Cultures in Common*, 23.
155. Pérez Toledo, *Los hijos del trabajo*, 189.
156. *Semanario artístico*, February 24, 1844.
157. Pérez Toledo, *Los hijos del trabajo*, 218.
158. *Semanario artístico*, June 6, 1844.
159. Pérez Toledo, *Los hijos del trabajo*, 189.
160. See *Semanario artístico*, February 24 and March 10, 1844.
161. "La seguridad de contar con un ausilio oportuno en las mas frecuentes necesidades de vida, insensiblemente atraerá al operario á depositar en el fondo su pequeña cuota, adquiriendo muy pronto las habitudes de una economía bien entendida y fundada en el amor al trabajo." *Semanario artístico*, June 29, 1844, 1.
162. "La limosna dada a los pobres, hasta cierto punto, los degrada y los humilla, alimenta su pereza y arruina el país, sin dar mayor alivio a los infelices." *Semanario artístico*, September 14, 1844, 1.
163. "Las cajas de ahorros por el contrario, elevan y sostienen la moralidad de los pobres, porque ellos mismos son sus salvadores y sus limosneros: en gratitud se estiende a sí mismo y se exsitan al trabajo con la reocompensa del trabajo mismo que apropian y adjudican" *Semanario artístico*, July 27, 1844, 2.
164. "Los jornaleros y artesanos . . . llegan a persuadirse de que es preciso economizar cuando son jovenes y pueden trabajar e ir juntando algun dinerito para cuando sean viejos y enfermos." *Semanario artístico*, July 27, 1844, 2.
165. "Una caja de ahorros es una institucion anti-revolucionaria por su esencia misma, pues da al prolectario con sus propias obras, y sin despojos ni violencias, parte en los goces de la propiedad territorial." *Semanario artístico*, July 27, 1844, 2.
166. *El Sol*, May 1, 1826, published an article on "Instituciones de beneficiencia" in which they summarized a British pamphlet titled Almanaque de la Caridad, which listed all filantropic institutions in London. Cajas de ahorro, specifically tied to *menestrales*, were mentioned in passing as a tool to guarantee a livelihood in old age.
167. 1839 also saw an extended engagement with cajas de ahorro in the educational *Diario de los niños*, authored by cuban poet Rafael Matamoros y Tellez. *El Cosmopolita*, a liberal weekly, also published a brief note on August 21st, 1839, about the beneficial effects of such institutions in countries across Europe.
168. It is not irrelevant that Cocolapán was, until shortly before the creation of the *cajas*, partly owned by Lucas Alamán, along with the Legrand brothers, French entrepreneurs established in Veracruz. Alamán's foray into industrial manufacturing, guided by his own theoretical knowledge, his experience with the Banco, and inspired by Antuñano's success, ended in near bankruptcy. For a complete account of Alamán's travails, see Van Young's *A Life Together.*
169. "uno de los medios más convenientes para mejorar las costumbres de los artesanos," in that they provided artisans "el huir de las ocasiones de vanas prodigalidades y hacerse de un peculio para sus necesidades y para alivio de su

vejez." Alamán, *Memoria sobre el Estado de la Agricultura e Industria de la República*, 1843, 40.

170. "[Las cajas de ahorro] disminuyen el número de indigentes, y hacen gustar á las personas de poca fortuna de la satisfaccion agradable que nace de la propiedad" Alamán, *Memoria sobre el Estado de la Agricultura e Industria de la República*, 1843, 68.
171. Alamán, *Memoria sobre el Estado de la Agricultura e Industria de la República*, 1843, 68
172. Alamán, *Memoria sobre el Estado de la Agricultura e Industria de la República*, 1843, 68.
173. "entre nosotros deben ser más grande los benéficos efectos de las cajas de ahorros. Nuestros trabajadores adolecen del mismo espíritu de imprevisión, y tienen las mismas tendencias a la disipación de que en todas partes está desgraciadamente notada esta clase de la sociedad. Necesitan por lo mismo que prácticamente los bienes que consiguen los depositantes en las cajas, para ser conducidos por el ejemplo. Tienen necesidad de sus establecimientos para colocar en ellos las sumas pequeñas que les van sobrando, porque son muy propensos a gastar luego que se presenta una tentación de placer o de capricho, y esas tentaciones pasan cuando no se tienen los ahorros a la mano por haberse colocado en las cajas; y puestas las primeras cantidades en depósito, atraen otras, porque solo no guarda y economiza, el que no ha empezado guardar y economizar." Alamán, *Memoria sobre el Estado de la Agricultura e Industria de la República*, 1843, 68.
174. Alamán, *Memoria sobre el Estado de la Agricultura e Industria de la República*, 1843, 69.
175. "por la multiplicación, no por la división de propiedades." Alamán, *Memoria sobre el estado de la agricultura*, 1843, 104–5.
176. See Illades, *Conflict, Domination, and Violence*, 13–27; and Gutiérrez, *El mundo del trabajo y el poder político*.
177. Piccato, *City of Suspects*, 134.
178. Beatty, *Technology and the Search for Progress*, 20.
179. Beatty, *Technology and the Search for Progress*, 13.
180. "[La prensa obrera] funcionó como laboratorio en el que se construyó su representación de la vida social, y donde decantaron los proyectos de modificación y formación de nuevas instituciones laborales." Illades, *Estudios sobre el artesanado urbano*, 68.
181. "es menester unirnos, disciplinarnos, arrojar de entre nosotros las malas costumbres e ideas retrógradas y darnos el abrazo de hermanos para trabajar todos unidos, no por el bien particular de un individuo, sino por el bien de todos." *El socialista*, July 9, 1871, 4.
182. "Si la ley atomizó a los trabajadores al individualizarlos, la prena obrera ayudó a conformar su identidad y a reconstituirlos como colectividad." Illades, *Estudios sobre el artesanado urbano*, 68.

CHAPTER 3

1. Agamben, *The Highest Poverty*, 99.
2. Hale, *Mexican Liberalism*, 275.
3. Schaefer, *Liberalism as Utopia*, 211
4. "si no se ataca el mal en la raíz, aunque se corten las ramas podridas." *El Sol*, November 6, 1824, 578.
5. "Mejor es prevenir ó evitar, que castigar," he noted and insisted that "[l]a ociosidad es el origen de tantos males: multam malitian docui otiositas." *El Sol*, November 6, 1824, 578. The author meant to quote Ecclesiastes 33:29, "multam enim malitiam docuit otiositas," which translates to "For idleness hath taught much evil."
6. "las causas de la desidia, la holgazanería y vicios consiguientes de nuestra plebe; los medios legales, gubernativos y económicos de contenerlos y corregirlos en los ya viciosos, y de preservar de ellos a los que no lo están, [al igual que] los ociosos, vagos y mal entretenidos . . . que si no roban, son materia dispuesta para ello y están en peligro próximo de hacerlo, para satisfacer sus vicios y mantener la decencia exterior que los encubre." *El Sol*, November 6, 1824, 578.
7. "Remitido," *El Sol*, November 23, 1824, 681–82.
8. Hale, *Mexican Liberalism*, 275.
9. Castillo Canché, "El contramodelo de la ciudadanía liberal," 61.
10. Kagan, Marías, and Franco, *Urban Images*, 28.
11. Kagan, Marías, and Franco, *Urban Images*, 28.
12. Kagan, Marías, et al, *Urban Images*, 20–21.
13. Kagan, Marías, et al, *Urban Images*, 20–21.
14. In the past decade, the concept of *policía* has gained currency in the fields of Mexican literature and history, primarily through the works of Gareth Williams and Pablo Piccato. For both critic and historian, the drive behind the slogan *buen gobierno y policía*, commonly attributed to the colonial and early independence period, guides Mexican political and cultural history well into the twentieth century, and, in a certain sense, up to our days. Williams reads police as a name of the practice of power that characterizes Mexican politics, in which, instead of the retreat of sovereign power and the rise of biopower in the form of the distribution and diffusion of power throughout society by means of regularization, administration, and bureaucratization, we have "a total state that strived at all times to suppress the duality of state and society." See Williams, *The Mexican Exception*, 12; and Piccato, *City of Suspects*, 20.
15. Marx, *Economic and Philosophical Manuscripts of 1844*, 86.
16. Maldonado Ojeda, "El derecho de la pereza," 24.
17. The *Decreto XXVIII* circulated in Mexico on April 14, 1821, seven weeks after the the revolutionary proclamation of the Plan de Iguala, in the pages of the *Gaceta del Gobierno de México* on April 14, 1821. The *Decreto XXVIII* of September 11, 1820, abolished, to a certain extent, the *Real Órden* and the *Ordenanza*. The

Decreto brought the question of vagrancy, previously left to the hands of enlightened jurists and the king, up for debate among self-denominated liberals and republicans. For the Spanish legislators of the Cortes, the recruitment of vagrants was a disservice done to the army as an honorable institution. For these Spanish liberals, "[e]nviar a las filas del ejército a personas que se caracterizaban por caracter de las virtudes que constituían los rasgos esenciales del ciudadano era no sólo una afrenta para la institución, sino también un riesgo de que la patria no pudiera ser defendida." Cardona, *La salud pública* 75. They believed that the proper way to battle vagrancy was through rehabilitation. Accordingly, they made "corrección," through hospices and similar institutions of "beneficiencia" the official sentence of the idle. For the whole edifice to work, they would later go on to approve, on December of that year, the *Decreto XL*, which focused on the development of "instituciones de beneficiencia" meant to satisfy the previous charge. Despite the Cortes's break with Hispanic anti-vagrancy traditions, the *Decreto XXVIII* referenced and welcomed the vagrant typology and justifications of both the *Real Orden* of 1745 and the *Ordenanza de Levas* of 1775. Even though the *Decreto*'s abolishment of the *leva* as punitive mechanism fell on deaf ears, its revival of the *Real Orden* and the *Ordenanza de Leva* reactivated, within the political imaginary of independent Mexico, eighteenth-century Spanish anti-vagrancy politics and with it, to a certain degree, the elements of the enlightened Bourbon ideology of governance which spawned it. As Charles F. Walker has said, despite the halting successes of Bourbon urban policy, "their efforts influenced political practice for generations, shaping political responses and alignments even beyond independence" See Walker, "Civilize or Control," 75. It was precisely this legacy that the "ley de vagos" had sought to update. A version of the Cortes's *Decreto* would be circulated, for different reasons, in different regions, and by different publishers, in April 1822, November 1823, October 1824, and October 1825, to mention some instances that precede its definite discussion by the Senate in 1826.

18. "Dejaba atrás la antigua noción enfática en la vagabundería errante, característica de ciertos grupos sociales desde el Medioevo (peregrinos, cruzados, gitanos, etc.), para centrarse en las nuevas formas del trabajo y del ocio social que trajo consigo el desarrollo urbano experimentado por las principales ciudades de la Metrópoli y las de sus colonias americanas durante el siglo XVIII." Maldonado Ojeda, "El derecho de la pereza," 23.
19. Arrom, "Vagos y mendigos," 81–82.
20. Arrom, "Vagos y mendigos," 73–74.
21. Arrom, "Vagos y mendigos," 73–74.
22. Arrom, "Vagos y mendigos," 77.
23. Arrom, "Vagos y mendigos," 77.
24. Maldonado Ojeda, "El derecho de la pereza," 24.
25. Maldonado Ojeda, "El derecho de la pereza," 24.

26. "[S]i el discurso religioso [ya] había criminalizado la supuesta inmoralidad lasciva de los vagabundos, el económico criminalizó la improductividad del desocupado y el itinerante." Hontanilla, "La figura del vago," 516.
27. According to a 1765 addendum to a pair of subsequent "instructions" on the capture of vagrants the actual Real Órden was never published "por superiores motivos," a fact that has widely been ignored in Mexican historiography on the topic. It remained available, however, to jurists and enlightened reformers. With incredible foresight, the author of the addition noted that it was in that 1745 legislation where "con más extension se especificaron las señas de los verdaderos vagamundos." Quoted in Luis Miguel Fernández, *Tecnología, espectáculo y literature*, 122n51.
28. Its full heading read: "*Ordenanza* de Su Majestad en que se previene, y establece el recogimiento de Vagos, y mal-entretenidos por medio de Levas anuales, y se encarga a las Justicias Ordinarias, Salas, y Audiencias criminales el orden judicial, que deben observar; y los cuatro depósitos a donde deben remitirse los que fueren aptos para las armas: Derogando todo Fuero, y *Ordenanzas* contrarias a lo que se dispone en esta, con lo demás que en ella se expresa."
29. "para reducirlas á una regla de policia constante: libre de los inconvenientes, y abusos, que se habian experimentado antes de aora, en su egecucion." *Ordenanza*, 4.
30. "producido los saludables efectos que se deseaban, a causa de no estar simplificado el método del procedimiento, ni dados los medios prácticos . . . ." *Ordenanza*, 22.
31. For Silvia Arrom, the eighteenth-century gendering of vagrancy had to do precisely with the fact that the period's legislation was preoccupied, first and foremost, with incorporating the idle and the vagrant into military service. See Arrom, "Vagos y mendigos," 81–82.
32. Timo H. Schaefer has studied this phenomenon at the municipal level. He argues that army recruitment through banishment had the consequent effect of concentrating "abnormal" behaviors in an institution that progressively became identified by its members' exclusion from the sphere of legality and morality. See Schaefer, *Liberalism as Utopia*, 79.
33. *Ordenanza*, 21.
34. *Ordenanza*, 21.
35. "que no subsista por más tiempo en el Reyno la nota, ni los daños, que trae consigo la ociosidad, en perjuicio de la universal industria del pueblo, de que depende en gran parte la felicidad comun." *Ordenanza*, 22.
36. Maldonado Ojeda. "El derecho de la pereza," 24.
37. Maldonado Ojeda. "El derecho de la pereza," 24.
38. Arrom, *Containing the Poor*, 16.
39. "adoptar con eficacia las providencias que sean más conducentes, no ya a evitar que por su inaplicación se hagan inútiles á la sociedad, sino en procurarles todos los recursos posibles para que, *aunque no quieran*, se enriquezcan y puedan

contribuir suficientemente al socorro de las urgencias del Estado." Quirós, *Ideas Políticas Económicas de Gobierno*, 34–35, my emphasis.

40. The Areopagus, he wrote, once had the power to punish idleness and "preguntar a todo ciudadano sobre el modo con que socorría sus necesidades. La mendicidad y abandono en aquellos que no tienen otro patrimonio que sus brazos deben castigarse por la potestad pública; y esta deberá hacer lo que todo hombre que vegeta en la inaccion, pasa en ella su vergonzosa juventud, y extiende vilmente y con bajeza su mano ácia el rico que podia ser útil al Estado." See Bustamante, *La Abispa*, #2, 10.
41. Stanley and Barbara Stein write, with regards to the usage of the concept of "reform" when refering to the Bourbon dynasty: "The term *reform*, or *reformation*, rarely appears in the discourse of eighteenth-century Spanish analysts, although modern Spanish usage defines *reforma*, *reformismo*, and *reformación* in the very terms (restoration, renovation, and the like) used at that time to describe the Bourbon paradigm. Spanish and other historians have, however, generally adopted *reform* to describe changes sought by Spanish Bourbon governments, particularly under Charles III. At the risk of indulging in Vico's 'scholar's conceit,' attributing to the 'ancients' concepts that emerged at a later time, it seems appropriate to incorporate the term *reform* in Spanish discourse in assaying the achievements of the reign of Charles III. Reform meant calibrated adjustment, methodical incrementalism, never radical change or restructuring." See Stein and Stein, *Apogee of Empire*, 27.
42. Cañizares Esguerra, "Enlightened Reform in the Spanish Empire," 33.
43. Paquette, *Enlightenment, Governance and Reform in Spain*, 71. Paquette insists on the importance of regalism in the face of those who believe it to be a simple euphemism for despotic and absolutist thought. For Paqutte, this sort of position "ignores the crucial, if often-neglected, role played by regalist ideas as catalysts in the crucial, inaugural stages of government reform in the 1750s and 1760s not only in Spain, but equally robust in Pombal's Portugal, Tanucci's Naples, and Du Tillot's Parma." The scholar believes that in the second half of the eighteenth century, regalism moves from a concern with the excesses of the Church's secular power into a "multi-faceted ideology, which justified the extirpation of all obstacles blocking monarchical aggrandizement." An amplification which "coincided with, and was vitalized by, the infusion of European intellectual currents, particularly political economy. See Paquette, "Empire, Enlightenment and Regalism," 115.
44. For an incisive account of the impact of Bourbon ideologies of governance in the Americas and their clash with "derecho indiano," see Albi, "Derecho Indiano vs. the Bourbon Reforms: The Legal Philosophy of Francisco Xavier de Gamboa," 237–39.
45. Paquette, *Enlightenment, Governance and Reform in Spain*, 65.
46. Paquette, "Empire, Enlightenment and Regalism," 115.
47. For Paquette, patriotism provided the discursive authority to avoid accusations

of anti-clericalism or impiousness. See *Enlightenment, Governance and Reform in Spain*, 74.

48. Paquette, *Enlightenment, Governance and Reform in Spain*, 82
49. Paquette traces the notion's popularization in Spain to Ludovico Antonio's *La Pública Felicidad: Un objeto de los Buenos príncipes*, originally published in Venice in 1749. In broad strokes, Muratori argued for the coincidence of the interests of the prince, the state's, and his vassal's. Antonio's *La pública felicidad* was published in Spanish in 1790 by royal decree and circulated widely thereafter. *Enlightenment, Governance and Reform in Spain*, 58.
50. Paquette, *Enlightenment, Governance and Reform in Spain*, 58.
51. Van Young, *A Life Together*, 611.
52. Maldonado Ojeda, *El tribunal de vagos*, 94. Maldonado Ojeda argues that nineteenth-century Mexican anti-vagrancy had little to do, in practice, with the question of social marginalization or subalternity. Breaking with the historiography on the topic, he holds that anti-vagrancy responded to a central aspect of urban society of the time: the need of social subjection and police over wide swaths of popular sectors in a period characterized by los "desajustes originados por la casi permanente crisis económica, no solamente política, en la que el país se sumergiría después de alcanzada su independencia." See Maldonado Ojeda, *El Tribunal de vagos*, 72–73.
53. "La ley que arregla los procedimientos contra vagos, va a mejorar visiblemente la moral pública y a preservarla de los ataques que esa clase de hombres dan continuamente por sus vicios y ociosidad y muy pronto espera el gobierno ver agianzados por esa saludable disposición el crédito y la espiritualidad del sistema republicano" Guadalupe Victoria, *Correo de la Federación*, March 21, 1828, 2.
54. "se le aplicará la pena de 8 años de servicio a las armas o en el ejército permanente o a la marina nacional."*El Sol*, February 28, 1826, 1037.
55. Beattie, *Tribute of Blood*, xxi.
56. Beattie, *Tribute of Blood*, 6.
57. *El Sol*, February 28, 1826, 1037.
58. Sanders, *The Vanguard of the Atlantic*, 6.
59. Like colonization, the question of vagrancy cut through political allegiances. Zavala, one of the law's main supporters, represented the most radical of popular, republican politics of the time.
60. *El Sol*, February 28, 1826, 1038.
61. *El Sol*, March 2, 1826.
62. "Los que fueren declarados vagos por el tribunal serán destinados.—1. al servicio de las armas.—2. a la marina.—3. a la colonización.—4.a casas de corrección" See *El Aguila Mexicana*, May 12, 1826, 3.
63. "librándola de unos hombres inútiles, que están muy próximos a ser criminales; y del perjuicio que sufriría privándola de brazos útiles en otros ramos" *El Sol*, March 15, 1826, 1098.

64. *El Sol*, March 15, 1826, 1098.
65. Here I am paraphrasing Martin Jay, whose work has tackled the question of visibility and modernity, See Jay, *Essays from the Edge*, 78.
66. "de un modo que en el imperio del despotismo no se haría con más escándalo y garbo." *El Sol*, March 21, 1827, 2581.
67. *El Sol*, March 29, 1827, 2671–74.
68. "persecución de hombres de bien, de ciudadanos honrados y de artesanos miserables, que son los que tienen la necesidad de presentarse en la calle," "sin otra calificación que su trage pobre y humilde. *El Sol*, March 29, 1827, 2673.
69. "¿Y a esto se llama una recolección de vagos? ¿Y hay hombre en la república que esto vea y tolere?." *El Sol*, March 21, 1827, 2581.
70. Two Chamber of Deputies' representatives requested a report from the federal government in which it answered whether proper procedures had been followed as stated in the legislation. The Senate, in turn, prohibited *levas* in the Federal District until more information was gathered. Pro-*leva* senators, however, dismissed both positions because they believed their colleagues misunderstood the nature of the raids in question. These had not been regular *levas*, they argued. These had been anti-vagrancy operations. As such, they conformed to existing law—viceregal law—that called for vagrants' persecution and forced recruitment into the army. These senators did not question the fact that the raids might have gotten out of hand. But, if they did, congressmen ought not to fault and prohibit *anti-vagrancy* operations, but the agents that carried it out.
71. For the 1828 Vagrants' Law, see Cámara de Diputados, *Colección de órdenes y decretos*, v.4, 151–53.
72. *Correo de la Federación mexicana*, March 31, 1828, 1–2.
73. *Correo de la Federación mexicana*, March 31, 1828, 1–2.
74. "que no se aprehendiesen a los individuos desconocidos que por su traje y decencia tienen la presunción a su favor." *Correo de la Federación mexicana*, March 31, 1828, 2.
75. "no es extraño que a estos se les hubiese pasado la mano." *Correo de la Federación mexicana*, March 31, 1828, 2.
76. "los que viven sin ganar su subsistencia por medios lícitos y honestos." *El Sol*, March 1, 1826, 2.
77. "Art. 6. Se declaran por vagos y viciosos: Primero. A los que sin oficio ni beneficio, hacienda o renta, viven sin saber de que les venga la subsistencia por medios lícitos y honestos. Segundo. El que teniendo algún patrimonio o emolumento, o siendo hijo de familia, no se le conoce otro empleo que el de las casas de juegos, compañías mal opinadas, frecuencias de parages sospechosos y ninguna demostración de emprender destino en su esfera. Tercero.El que vigoroso, sano, y robusto y aun con lesión que no le impida conocer algún oficio, sólo se mantiene de pedir limosna. Cuarto. El hijo de familia que mal inclinado no sirve en casa y en el pueblo de otra cosa que escandalizar con poca reverencia u obediencia a sus padres, y con el ejercicio de malas costumbres,

sin propensión o aplicación a la carrera que le ponen." *El Sol*, March 8, 1828, 1.

78. Quoted in Warren, *Vagrants and Citizens*, 87; and in Pérez Toledo, *Los hijos del trabajo*, 243.
79. Warren, *Vagrants and Citizens*, 87.
80. Schaefer, *Liberalism as Utopia*, 76
81. Schaefer, *Liberalism as Utopia*, 76
82. Schaefer, *Liberalism as Utopia*, 76
83. Warren, *Vagrants and Citizens*, 87.
84. Warren, *Vagrants and Citizens*, 99.
85. Warren, *Vagrants and Citizens*, 99.
86. The memorandum was titled: "Circular de la secretaría de relaciones. Padrón para elección de diputados y prevenciones en cuanto a cargos, casas de prostitución, de juego o escándalo y acerca de educación a juventud." While dated August 8, the circular was published and circulated as a broadsheet on August 11.
87. Three years before, in 1831, Carlos María Bustamante had excerpted, in *La Voz de la Patria*, Spanish lawyer Hipólito Villaroel's *Enfermedades políticas que padece la capital de esta Nueva España*, which had remained unpublished despite being written in 1785 and 1787. As Ana Sabau has recently shown, like the supporters of the 1834 memorandum, Villaroel proposed, between 1785 and 1787, a census as part of a series of policies to tackle Mexico City's surplus population, which he believed endangered and harmed the body politic. Bustamante's recuperation of Villaroel speaks to the viceregal returns of the 1830s, and in Sabau's words, the "continuities of colonial strategies into the postindependence period." Sabau, *Riot and Rebellion in Mexico*, 69, 79. In 1790, three years after Villaroel finished his work, viceroy Juan de Güemes Padilla, Count of Revillagigedo commissioned the first viceroyalty-wide general census, with the purpose of recruiting for militia duty, but also because he believed that such data could improve the enlightened governance of the territory. See Dominic Keith Peachey, "The Revillagigedo Census," 66. For a more thorough account of the emergence of the Revillagigedo census and the debates it sparked, see Saborit, *El virrey y el capellán: Revilla Gigedo, Alzate y el censo de 1790*.
88. "Circular de la secretaría de relaciones," 296.
89. "Circular de la secretaría de relaciones," 298–99.
90. "Circular de la secretaría de relaciones," 296.
91. "Circular de la secretaría de relaciones," 298.
92. "Circular de la secretaría de relaciones," 297.
93. "Providencia de la secretaría de relaciones. Excitación para que se persiga y ocupe a los vagos," 460–61.
94. "Circular de la secretaría de relaciones," 300.
95. "Circular de la secretaría de relaciones," 299.
96. Arrom, "Vagos y mendigos," 73–74.
97. "Circular de la secretaría de relaciones," 298.

98. "[La] real órden del 16 de noviembrre de 1767, repetida en 785 y 786, y comunicada a todos los tribunales en cédula de 11 de septiembre de 1788." "Circular de la secretaría de relaciones," 298.
99. The piece was published, in installments, on January 29, February 5, 9, 16, and 23, 1836.
100. "el público, que en su mayoría no es compuesto de literatos, ni los libros andan en manos de todos." *El Mosquito Mexicano*, January 29, 1836, 2.
101. *El Mosquito Mexicano*, January 29, 1836, 2.
102. *El Mosquito Mexicano*, February 9, 1836, 2.
103. "que todos son libres para trabajar o no," but they were mistaken, for "la libertad legal es de otro orden y no puede haberla para perjudicar a la sociedad, como efectivamente la perjudican los ociosos, vagos y mal entretenidos, de cuyo gremio salen todos los criminales y malhechores." *El Mosquito Mexicano*, February 16, 1836, 2.
104. *Diario del Gobierno de la República Mexicana*, April 25, 1842, 458.
105. "es cosa muy grata no hacer nada, y eligen la vida ociosa." *Diario del Gobierno de la República Mexicana*, April 25, 1842, 458.
106. "porque pasando la niñez y juventud en la ociosidad, será sumamente dificultoso lograr de ellos una conveniente aplicación; y ni la vigilancia del gobierno ni el celo de los magistrados, pueden después cortar la raíz del mal." *Diario del Gobierno de la República Mexicana*, April 25, 1842, 458.
107. "es mejor dejar morir a los holgazanes, que mantenerlos en la holgazanería" *Diario del Gobierno de la República Mexicana*, April 25, 1842, 458.
108. "Elhombre, repetimos, jamás es vil ni despreciable por su oficio. Toda la vez que tenga una ocupación útil al estado, sea cual fuere, debe ser acogido entre sus buenos hijos. El querer subsistir sin trabajar, esto es lo que lo degrada, y lo constituye un ser vil." *El Siglo Diez y Nueve*, July 15, 1842, 4.
109. "con quienes ningunas consideraciones deben tenerse, si no es para corregir su excesos." *El Siglo Diez y Nueve*, July 15, 1842, 4.
110. "Los vicios y la holgazanería hacen decaer las fortunas privadas, y esta decadencia produce más adelante la de la nación." *El Siglo Diez y Nueve*, July 15, 1842, 3.
111. The law was approved on January 28, 1845. The broadsheet was published on February 7, signed by Mucio Barquera, president of the Departmental Assembly. *El Monitor Constitucional*, February 7, 1845, 1.
112. *El Siglo Diez y Nueve*, February 18, 1845, 4.
113. "Desde luego se conoce que todos estos serán todo lo que se quiera, pero no vagos: un hombre muy industrioso puede no respetar a sus padres o maltratar a su muger y sin embargo, dista infinito de ser vago. Pero ¿quién no ve que solo la Inquisición podía autorizar ciertas investigaciones? Entre los dominios de la legislación y los de la moral hay un límite que no se puede traspasar: la moral desciende hasta los más íntimos senos de la conciencia; pero a las leyes les es vedado entrar más allá de los umbrales de una casa. El que no respeta ni obedece a sus padres es un perverso que falta a uno de los más santos preceptos de

la moral y de la religión; pero nadie tiene el derecho de inquirir si comete esta falta . . . Lo repetimos: el legislador que traspasa el quicio de la puerta, restablece la Inquisición, ataca directamente la libertad individual: perturba el orden social: trastorna los fundamentos de la moral pública . . . No hay un lado por donde no aparezca esta ley atentatoria a los sagrados derechos de la independencia, la seguridad y la libertad personal. Creemos que la asamblea departamental de México, no tuvo facultades para darla: que si las tuvo, las ha usado de un modo inconsiderado y peligroso; y finalmente, que esa misma asamblea, o la autoridad a quien corresponda, procederá desde luego a impedir que surta sus funestísimos efectos . . ." *El Siglo Diez y Nueve*, February 18, 1845, 4.

114. *El Siglo Diez y Nueve*, October 28, 1845, 4.

115. "pues los vagos no solo viven del sudor de otros, sino que con su mal ejemplo, muchos se vuelven lo mismo que ellos." *El Monitor Constitucional*, February 27, 1845, 2.

116. In this, I disagree with Silvia Arrom's precision that, after an experiment of two decades (1828–48), the conflict between the needs of the state and the civil rights of the vagrant was settled in favor of the former. For Arrom, the republic that came out of the US-Mexico war fully adopted viceregal anti-vagrancy and jettisoned its republican iteration. Arrom, "Documentos para el estudio del Tribunal de Vagos," 221. In my estimation, while it is true that the July 1848 law reaffirmed the videregal disposition of the 1845 law's definitions, between 1849 and 1852, we see a renewed attempt at the normalization of a "modern" conception of vagrancy.

117. The July 1848 decree proposed, according to Arrom, a simpler system in which "alcaldes could qualify and sentence vagrants directly (within 48 hours), and the Tribunal would intervene only when the accused appealed the sentence." The decree, published in the press of the time, came accompanied by a reprinting of the 1845 law's text. Arrom, "Documentos para el estudio del Tribunal de Vagos," 221.

118. The proyecto de ley itself was embedded in a longer report by the Ministry that proposed a new code for "procedimientos en el juicio criminal," published in *El Siglo Diez y Nueve* between June 2 and June 6, 1849. the sections relating to vagrancy are found on June 3 and June 6 in particular.

119. "teniendo oficio honesto no lo ejerce habitualmente, sino que vaga la mayor o considerable parte de los días." *El Siglo Diez y Nueve*, June 6, 1849, 1.

120. See *El Siglo Diez y Nueve*, July 30, 1849, 115–116. Note that *El Siglo Diez y Nueve*'s editors began to use continuous pagination starting on January 1, 1849.

121. "La naturaleza misma del delito está marcando la pena, de modo que no es posible equivocarse en su elección." *El Siglo Diez y Nueve*, July 30, 1849, 116.

122. "obligados a ejecutar las mas asquerosas faenas públicamente, a la luz del día y las más veces casi desnudos, [los acusados] pierden hasta los últimos restos de pudor y de moralidad, y se entregan al más asqueroso cinismo. ¿Y se creerá todavía que por tales medios se puede conseguir la corrección de los condenados

a esta pena?" *El Siglo Diez y Nueve*, July 30, 1849, 116.

123. "miseria, el abandono y la falta de educación de los padres," which "hace que la infancia y la juventud de los hijos se pasen en la ociosidad, o bien en el desempeño de quehaceres domésticos" *El Siglo Diez y Nueve*, July 30, 1849, 116.

124. "¿Diremos por eso que aquellos infelices no son culpables? De ninguna manera; diremos sí que la mitad de la culpa del delito porque se les persigue no las tienen ellos."*El Siglo Diez y Nueve*, July 30, 1849, 116.

125. "Todo esto a primera vista parece difícil, y se cree que coarta la voluntad de los ciudadanos; pero no es así." *El Siglo Diez y Nueve*, August 26, 1849, 227.

126. "se sabría, como debe saberse, cuál es la profesión de cada uno, los medios que tiene para vivir y aun las horas que emplea en su trabajo. Esto, dígase lo que se quiera, es una positiva garantía, pues cuando un hombre sabe que la autoridad vigila sobre sus acciones, procura que estas sean buenas, y si no tiene en qué emplearse, por el temor del castigo busca una ocupación, a la que necesariamente se aficiona después, cuando reconoce las ventajas que de ella saca. El hombre que trabaja, el que saca una subsistencia regular sin esponer su vida, no se lanza a la vía detestable y peligrosa del crimen; pero cuando las administraciones descuidan sus deberes sobre este punto, los vagos se multiplican, y he aquí el gérmen de todos los males." *El Siglo Diez y Nueve*, August 26, 1849, 227.

127. The proto-sociological conception of vagrancy foreshadowed the language of the "social question." Yet, the "social question" was slow to permeate in Mexico's political discourse, despite its availability in the sources read by the figures studied here. Historian Holly Case has written that "many of the issues that informed discussion of "the social question" [after the 1820s] had been in circulation prior to their crystallization under that heading," but the emergence of the phrase itself in Europe was important because it emphasized the "effort to raise the profile of particular issues into the realm of significant concerns, or problems of both domestic and international importance, and to usurp the role of the scholastic question." Case, "The 'Social Question,' 1820–1920," 753. In nineteenth-century Mexico, Mariano Otero was the first to address the "social question" explicitly, adopting the phrase directly from Víctor Considerant, in his 1842, "Ensayo sobre el verdadero estado de la cuestión social y política que se agita en la República Mexicana" [Essay on the real state of the social and political questions that stirs the Mexican Republic]. There, Otero argued that one of the intellectual roadblocks in Mexico was the tendency, by politicians, to disregard "las cuestiones sociales por las políticas" (the social questions for the political), and, as a result, to discard the former because they are seen as irrelevant for the larger transformation of society. Otero, "Ensayo," 64. Otero was unique in his emphasis on the social question and, along with the circumscription of vagrancy and its new sociological conception and the 1848 Dirección de Colonización, seen in the first chapter, represented a series of idiosyncratic loose strands that would fail to coalesce into a form of "social liberalism" until late in the nineteenth-century. For Charles Hale, Otero's social

analysis "represented a significant departure in Mexican social thought." Hale believes that, perhaps, "because of Otero's early death in 1850 at the age of thirty-three, and because of his involvement in politics after 1842, he did not develop his ideas further." Hale, *Mexican Liberalism*, 185. Whatever the reason, Hale concludes, Otero's sociological approach "departed from the mainstream of liberalism—the tradition of 1833 and 1857." Hale, *Mexican Liberalism*, 187.

128. Maldonado Ojeda, "El derecho de la pereza," 19.

129. "[La verdadera riqueza] consiste en que a nadie falte ocupación provecosa y acomodada a sus fuerzas, con que poder mantenerse y criar sus hijos aplicados . . . [y esto] ecsige de la autoridad pública, no solo que procure por cuantos medios estén a su alcance el trabajo indispensable a todas las clases, sino que se vigile y castigue a aquellos hombres que, sin tener ocupación honesta son . . . nocivos y corruptos." *El Siglo Diez y Nueve*, January 9, 1851, 35.

130. Manuel Comeiro y Penido's *Derecho administrativo español* was published just the previous year, in 1850. Colmeiro y Penido was a moderate liberal jurist, political economist, and, eventually, politician, part of a generation, caught between liberal "radicalism" and monarchical conservatism, dedicated to the development of a scientific, yet Catholic, approach to Spanish Administrative Law. His *Derecho Administrativo Español*, was groundbreaking in its attempt to modernize the precepts of Spanish governance.

131. "La ociosidad puede ser voluntaria o forzosa en los individuos; accidental o habitual; simple o calificada. La voluntaria supone un vicio, un verdadero desarrollo de costumbres, que la administración está obligada a corregir por el bien del vicioso, por la seguridad de todos y para evitar el mal ejemplo. La forzosa es una desgracia particular hija de la ignorancia, ya de la improvisación, o resultado de ciertas causas generales imposibles de contrarrestar por un hombre solo. Éste género de ociosidad inocente, o esta falta de trabajo, debe ser remediada por el influjo de la caridad pública, si no bastasen los auxilios de la privada.- La ociosidad accidental, aunque voluntaria, no es el vicio mismo, sino sus anuncios; es la semilla, no el fruto. Como son desórdenes leves todavía y por lo común privados; faltas, en fin, de conducta doméstica, más bien entran en la esfera de la moral, que caen bajo el imperio de la administración. Las autoridades políticas pueden sin embargo combatirlos indirectamente, inspirando a los pueblos, por medio de la educación, el amor al trabajo, y alentando la perseverancia con el estímulo de la recompensa. La habitual envuelve un estado de guerra con la sociedad, el hombre vive en oposición con el interés general, y es su constante enemigo.- En la ociosidad simple, hay peligro de turbar el orden público; en la ociosidad calificada, o acompañada de circunstancias agravantes, el orden público está de hecho perturbado. La primera se combate con medios preventivos, dentro de los límites del poder administrativo; la segunda es un delito común, que debe ser reprimido y castigado por la autoridad judicial competente.' Dedúcese, pues, de todo lo espuesto, que siempre la autoridad es la que directa o indirectamente tiene que prevenir la vagancia, y

evitar a la sociedad los males que ella le origina; póngase en práctica todos los medios represivos, procúrese la educación del pueblo, por la cual no nos cansaremos de clamar; desarróllese la industria; protéjase de preferencia la agricultura; empréndase obras públicas de utilidad pública; vigílese que la caridad no sea ciega ni indirecta, y entonces la vagancia quedará reducida, que con pocos esfuerzos logrará la administración contenerla y destruirla." *El Siglo Diez y Nueve*, January 9, 1851, 35.

132. "La primera [political rights] le señala sus fuentes, la segunda [civil jurisprudence] le traza sus límites, le comunica sus principios la tercera [public economy] y la última [statistics] le sugiere datos y noticias." Colmeiro, *Derecho administrativo español*, vol.1, v.
133. Administrative governance was understood to have two elements. On the one hand, there was a technical element, which dictated its principles and its invariable laws; and, on the other, a political element, which is variable and depends on the particular society and responds always to present circumstance.
134. Maldonado Ojeda, "El derecho de la pereza," 18–19
135. Maldonado Ojeda, "El derecho de la pereza," 19–20.
136. Williams, *The Mexican Exception*, 12.
137. See, for example, Guillermo Prieto's "On Freedom to Work."
138. Maldonado Ojeda, *El Tribunal de Vagos*, 209.
139. If until the 1870s, policing had been at the hand of the neighbors themselves and civilian agents hired for this purpose, by 1879 a police force was created and institutionalized under the Gendarmería Municipal. From then on, Piccato writes, "[t]he police force was to be composed of full-time members, clearly distinguished from the civilian population by their uniforms and accountable to their superiors rather than to their neighbors—whose relations with the force were to be kept within strict limits." Piccato, *City of Suspects*, 5.
140. "Es vago: el que careciendo de bienes y rentas, no ejerce alguna industria, arte u oficio honestos para subsistir, sin tener para ello impedimento legítimo." Medina y Ormaechea, *Código Penal Mexicano*, v.1, 560.
141. The sentences of yore—colonization, forced impressment into the army—were long gone, and the constellation of deviant acts that had once been folded into the category—drunkenness, theft, etc.— had been separated and treated as autonomous phenomena. See Article 855 in Medina y Ormaechea, *Código Penal Mexicano*, v.1, 563.

CONCLUSION

1. Calderón de la Barca, *Life in Mexico*, 53.
2. This vignette paraphrases and expands on Calderón de la Barca, *Life in Mexico*, 53.
3. This vignette of retail in the city builds on Kicza, *Colonial Entrepreneurs*, 127–28.
4. "En el mundo moral como en el mundo físico, todo está enlazado, todo tiene

su causa y fin." Otero, Ensayo sobre el verdadero estado de la cuestión social y política, 23.

5. "[La propiedad es] el principio generador, [el] hecho que modifi[ca] y comprend[e] a todos los otros y del que sal[en] como de un origen común todos los fenómenos sociales que parecen aislados. Otero, Ensayo sobre el verdadero estado de la cuestión social y política, 27.
6. "Tenía una fisonomía propia, y que en nada se parecía a las sociedades europeas, con las que siempre nos estamos comparando, tan sólo porque hemos tomado prestados los nombres de su organización social, sin tener en manera alguna sus partes constitutivas." Otero, *Ensayo sobre el verdadero estado de la cuestión social y política*, 29.
7. "[Un] examen árido de la constitución de la sociedad considerada bajo sus relaciones puramente materiales; y suplico que se atienda todavía, porque sin comprender este conjunto es imposible formar una idea exacta de nuestras cuestiones sociales" (37). Otero, Ensayo sobre el verdadero estado de la cuestión social y política, 37.
8. Otero, *Ensayo sobre el verdadero estado de la cuestión social y política*, 37.
9. Schaefer, *Liberalism as Utopia*, 215.

Bibliography

NEWSPAPERS

Correo de la Federación
Diario del Gobierno de la República Mexicana
El Águila Mexicana
El Cosmopolita
El Despertador Americano
El Fénix de La libertad
El Monitor Constitucional
El Monitor Republicano
El Mosquito Mexicano
El Oriente
El Siglo Diez y Nueve
El Sol
El Universal
Gaceta Imperial de México
La voz de la religión
Semanario artístico
Semanario de la industria mexicana

PAMPHLETS AND COLLECTED SOURCES

Actas del Congreso Constituyente Mexicano. Vol. 3. Edited by José Barragán Barragán. Mexico: UNAM, 1980.

"Circular de la Secretaría de Relaciones. Padrón para elección de diputados y prevenciones en cuanto a cargos, casas de prostitución, de juego o escándalo y ccerca de educación a juventud." In *Recopilación de leyes, decretos, bandos, reglamentos, circulares y providencias de los supremos poderes de los Estados Unidos Mexicanos*, edited by Basilio José Arrillaga, 296–319. Mexico: Imprenta de J.M Fernández de Lara, 1835.

Alamán, Lucas. "Memoria de la Secretaria de Estado y del Despacho de Relaciones Interiores y Exteriores Del Año 1832." In *Obras de D. Lucas Alamán. Documentos diversos (inéditos y muy raros). Tomo Primero*, 339–433. Vol. 9. Mexico: Editorial Jus, 1945.

Alamán, Lucas. *Memoria sobre el Estado de la Agricultura e Industria de la República.* México: Imprenta de Lara, 1843.

Alamán, Lucas. "Memoria sobre el Estado de la Agricultura y Industria de La República en el Año de 1844." In *Obras de D. Lucas Alamán. Documentos Diversos (inéditos y muy raros). Tomo Segundo*, 131–220. Vol. 10. Mexico: Editorial Jus, 1945.

Alamán, Lucas. "Memoria sobre el Estado de la Agricultura y Industria de la República en el Año de 1845." In *Obras de D. Lucas Alamán. Documentos Diversos (inéditos y muy raros). Tomo Segundo*, 221–319. Vol. 10. Mexico: Editorial Jus, 1945.

Alamán, Lucas. *Memoria de la Secretaria de Estado y del despacho de Relaciones Interiores y Exteriores*. Mexico: Imprenta del Águila, 1830.

Alamán, Lucas. *Memoria de la Secretaria de Estado y del Despacho de Relaciones Interiores y Exteriores*. Mexico: Imprenta del Águila, 1831.

Alamán, Lucas. *Memoria presentada a las dos cámaras del Congreso General de la Federacion: por el Secretario de Estado y del Despacho de Relaciones Esteriores é Interiores.* Mexico: Imprenta del Supremo Gobierno de los Estados Unidos Mexicanos, 1825.

Antuñano, Estevan de. "Breve memoria del estado que guarda la fábrica de hilados de algodón Constancia Mexicana y la Industria de este Ramo." In *Obras. Documentos Para la Historia de la Industrialización en México, 1833–1846*, 241–62. Vol. 1. Mexico: Secretaria de Hacienda y Crédito Público, 1979.

Antuñano, Estevan de. "Comercio Exterior en México. Segunda Parte." In *Obras. Documentos Para la Historia de la Industrialización en México, 1833–1846*, 303–6. Vol. 1. Mexico: Secretaria de Hacienda y Crédito Público, 1979.

Antuñano, Estevan de. "Manifiesto del algodón." In *Obras. Documentos Para la Historia de la Industrialización en México, 1833–1846*, 4–29. Vol. 1. Mexico: Secretaria de Hacienda y Crédito Público, 1979.

Antuñano, Estevan de. "Memoria breve de la industria manufacturera de México." In *Obras. Documentos Para la Historia de la Industrialización en México, 1833–1846*, 223–36. Vol.1. Mexico: Secretaria de Hacienda y Crédito Público, 1979.

Antuñano, Estevan de. "Pensamientos Para La Regeneración Industrial de México." In *Obras. Documentos Para la Historia de la Industrialización en México, 1833–1846*, 275–98. Vol. 1. Mexico: Secretaria de Hacienda y Crédito Público, 1979.

Antuñano, Estevan de. "Ventajas políticas, civiles, fabriles y domésticas que por rara ocupación tambien a las mugeres en las fabricas de maquinaria moderna que se estan levantando en Mexico, deben recibirse." In *Obras Obras.*

Documentos Para la Historia de la Industrialización en México, 1833–1846, 265–72. Vol.1. Mexico: Secretaria de Hacienda y Crédito Público, 1979.

Antuñano, Estevan de. *Pensamientos para un plan para animar la industria mejicana*. Puebla: Imprenta de Campos, 1834.

Azcárate y Lezama, Juan F. *Un programa de política internacional*. Mexico: Editorial Porrúa, 1970.

Barragán Barragán, José, ed. *Actas del Congreso Constituyente Mexicano*. Vol. 3. Mexico: UNAM, 1980.

Bustamante, Carlos María. *El Gabinete Mexicano*. Vol. 2. Mexico: Imprenta de Lara, 1842.

Bustamante, Carlos María. *La Abispa de Chilpancingo*. Mexico: Imprenta de D. Mariano Ontíveros, 1821.

Calderón de la Barca, Frances. *Life in Mexico, during a Residence of Two Years in That Country*. London: Chapman and Hall, 1843.

Cámara de Diputados. *Colección de ordenes y decretos de la Soberana Junta Provisional Gubernativa y Soberanos Congresos Generales de la Nación Mexicana*. Vol. 4. Mexico: Imprenta de Galván, 1829.

Carlos III, Rey de España. *Ordenanza de S.M En Que Se Previene, y Establece El Recogimiendo de Vagos, y Mal-Entretenidosp or Medio de Levas Anuales, y Se Encarga a Las Justicias Ordinarias, Salas, y Audiencias Criminales El Orden Joduicial, Que Deben Observar; y Los Quatro Depósitos à Donde Deben Remitirse Los Que Fueren Aptos Para Las Armas: Derogando Todo Fuero, y Ordenanzas Contrarias à Lo Que Se Dispone En Èsta, Con Lo Demàs Que En Ell Se Expresa*. Oficina de Francisco Díaz Pedregal, Impresor del Principado de Asturias, 1775.

Colmeiro y Penido, Manuel. *Derecho administrativo español*. Vol. 1. Madrid: Librería de Angel Calleja, 1850.

Guerrero, Vicente. *Manifiesto del ciudadano Vicente Guerrero, Segundo Presidente de Los Estados Unidos Mexicanos, a sus compatriotas*. Mexico: Imprenta del Águila, Dirigida por Jose Ximeno, 1829.

JMR. *Lo que interesa a La Patria. Por El Artesano y su Amigo*. Mexico: Imprenta Americana de José María Betancourt, 1821.

Maza, Francisco de la. *Código de colonización y terrenos baldíos de la República Mexicana*. Oficina tip. de la Secretaría de fomento, 1893.

Medina y Ormaechea, Antonio. *Código penal mexicano*. Vol. 1. Mexico: Imprenta del Gobierno en Palacio, 1880.

Ortiz de Ayala, Tadeo, José Antonio de Echávarri, and Mariano Barbabosa. *Bases sobre las que se ha formado un plan de colonización en el Ysmo de Hoazacoalco ó Tehuantepec: para los beneméritos ciudadanos militares y particulares que busquen un asilo de paz y quieran dedicarse con utilidad propia y del estado, en unión de los capitalistas é industriosos extrangeros de todo el mundo á la agricultura*. Imprenta Nacional del Supremo Gobierno, 1823.

Ortiz de Ayala, Tadeo. *México considerado como nacion independiente y libre, ó sean algunas indicaciones sobre los deberes mas esenciales de los mexicanos.* C. Lawalle Sobrino, 1832.

Ortiz de Ayala, Tadeo. *Resumen de la estadística del Imperio Mexicano.* Mexico: Imprenta de Doña Herculana del Villar y socios., 1822.

Otero, Mariano, "Ensayo sobre el verdadero estado de la cuestión social y política que se agita en la república mexicana." In *Obras Completas I*, edited by Jesús Reyes Heroles, 1–94. Mexico City: Editorial Porrua, 1967

Pesado, José Joaquín. "[Carta a Lucas Alamán Remitiéndole Un Artículo Sobre Colonización]," November 1849. 298. Lucas Alamán Papers, 1598–1853, Benson Latin American Collection, General Libraries, University of Texas at Austin.

Prieto, Guillermo. *Obras Completas.* Edited by Boris Rosen Jélomer. Vol. 21. Mexico: Consejo Nacional para la Cultura y las Artes, 1997.

Prieto, Guillermo. "On Freedom to Work. Report on the Speech before Congress on November 5, 1874." In *Liberty in Mexico. Writings on Liberalism from the Early Republican Period to the Second Half of the Twentieth Century*, edited by José Antonio Aguilar Rivera, translated by Janet M. Burke and Ted Humphrey, 344–52. Indianapolis: Liberty Fund.

Proyecto de ley sobre colonización, presentado a la deliberación del Honorable Congreso Del Estado de Veracruz, por su comisión respectiva de la Cámara Del Senado. Veracruz: Imprenta del Gobierno, 1826.

Proyectos de colonización presentados por la junta directiva del ramo, al Ministro de Relaciones de la República Mexicana En 5 Julio de 1848. Mexico: Imprenta de Vicente García Torres, 1848.

"Providencia de La Secretaría de Relaciones. Excitación Para Que Se Persiga y Ocupe a Los Vagos." In *Recopilación de leyes, decretos, bandos, reglamentos, circulares y providencias de los Supremos Poderes de Los Estados Unidos Mexicanos*, edited by Basilio José Arrillaga, 460–61. Mexico: Imprenta de J.M Fernández de Lara, 1835.

Quirós, José María. *Ideas políticas económicas de gobierno.* Veracruz: Imprenta del Gobierno Imerial Mexicano, 1821.

SECONDARY SOURCES

Agamben, Giorgio. *The Highest Poverty: Monastic Rules and Form-of-Life.* Stanford, CA: Stanford University Press, 2013.

Albi, Christopher Peter. "Derecho indiano vs. the Bourbon Reforms: The Legal Philosophy of Francisco Xavier de Gamboa" In *Enlightened Reform in Southern Europe and Its Atlantic Colonies, c. 1750–1830*, edited by Gabriel Paquette, 229–59. London: Routledge, 2009.

Alcázar Molina, Cayetano. *Las colonias alemanas de Sierra Morena.* Madrid: Universidad de Murcia, 1950.

Aljovin de Losada, Cristóbal. "Ciudadano y vecino en Iberoamérica, 1750–1850: Monarquía o República." In *Diccionario político y social del mundo iberoamericano. La era de las revoluciones, 1750–1850.* Edited by Cristóbal Aljovin de Losada, Joao Feres Junior, and Javier Fernández Sebastián, 179–305. Madrid: Fundación Carolina, 2009.

Almonte, Juan. *Noticia estadística sobre Tejas*. Mexico: Ignacio Cumplido Impresores, 1834.

Altable, Francisco. "Ilustración y utopismo en el noroeste de Nueva España. El pensamiento económico español del siglo xviii en las proyecciones de José Rafael Rodríguez Gallardo y José de Gálvez." In *El mito de una riqueza proverbial: Ideas, utopías y proyectos económicos en torno a México en los siglos XVIII y XIX*. Edited by Francisco Altable, José Enrique Covarrubias, Richard Weiner, and Edward Beatty, 19–78. Mexico: UNAM, 2015.

Anna, Timothy A. *The Mexican Empire of Iturbide*. Lincoln: University of Nebraska Press, 1990.

Araya Espinoza, Alejandra. "Guerra, Intolerancia a la ociosidad y resistencia: Los discursos ocultos tras la vagancia. Ciudad de México 1821–1860." *Boletín Americanista*, no. 52 (2002): 22–55.

Aravamudan, Srinivas. *Enlightenment Orientalism: Resisting the Rise of the Novel*. Chicago: University of Chicago Press, 2012.

Arrom, Silvia M. *Containing the Poor: The Mexico City Poor House, 1774–1871*. Durham, NC: Duke University Press, 2000.

Arrom, Silvia M. "Documentos para el estudio del Tribunal de Vagos, 1828–1848: Respuesta a una problemática sin solución." *Anuario Mexicano de Hisotria Del Derecho* 1 (1989): 215–35.

Arrom, Silvia M. "Vagos y mendigos en la legislación mexicana, 1745–1845." In *Memoria del IV Congreso de Hisotria del derecho mexicano*, edited by Beatriz Bernal, Vol.1:71–87. Mexico: UNAM, 1988.

Ávila, Alfredo. *Camino de Padilla. México y Manuel Mier y Terán en 1832*. Ciudad Victoria: Instituto Tamaulipeco para la Cultura y las Artes, 2016.

Ávila, Alfredo. *Para La Libertad. Los republicanos en tiempos del Imperio, 1821–1823*. Mexico: UNAM, 2004.

Ávila, Alfredo, Virginia Guedea, and Ana Carolina Ibarra. *Diccionario de la Independencia de México*. Mexico: Universidad Nacional Autónoma de México, 2010.

Ávila, Alfredo, and John Tutino. "Becoming Mexico. The Conflictive Search for a North American Nation." In *New Countries: Capitalism, Revolutions, and Nations in the Americas, 1750–1870*, edited by John Tutino, 233–77. Durham, NC: Duke University Press, 2017.

Badiou, Alain. "The Courage of Obscurantism." *The Symptom*, 11, 2010. http://www.lacan.com/symptom11/?p=163.

Baptist, Edward. "Towards a Political Economy of Slave Labor: Hands, Whipping-Machines, and Modern Power." In *Slavery's Capitalism. A New History of*

American Economic Development. Edited by Sven Beckert and Seth Rockman, 31–61. Philadelphia: University of Pennsylvania Press, 2016.

Bartra, Roger. *Agrarian Structure and Political Power in Mexico*. Translated by Stephen K. Ault. Baltimore, MD: Johns Hopkins University Press, 1994.

Beattie, Peter M. *The Tribute of Blood: Army, Honor, Race, and Nation in Brazil, 1864–1945*. Latin America Otherwise. Durham, NC: Duke University Press, 2001.

Beatty, Edward. "Riqueza, polémica y política: pensamiento y políticas económicas en México (1765–1911)." In *El mito de una riqueza proverbial: Ideas, utopías y proyectos económicos en torno a México en los siglos XVIII y XIX*. Edited by Francisco Altable, José Enrique Covarrubias, Richard Weiner, and Edward Beatty, 243–294. Mexico: UNAM, 2015.

———. *Technology and the Search for Progress in Modern Mexico*. Oakland, CA: University of California Press, 2015.

Benson, Nettie Lee. "Territorial Integrity in Mexican Politics, 1821–1833." In *The Independence of Mexico and the Creation of the New Nation*, 275-307. Irvine, CA: UCLA Latin American Center Publications, 1989.

Bernecker, Walther L. *De agiotistas y empresarios: En torno de la temprana industrialización mexicana (Siglo XIX)*. Mexico: Universidad Iberoamericana, 1992.

Burden, David K. "Reform Before La Reforma: Liberals, Conservatives and the Debate over Immigration, 1846–1855." *Mexican Studies/Estudios Mexicanos* 23, no. 2 (Summer 2007): 283–316.

Cañizares Esguerra, Jorge. "'Enlightened Reform' in the Spanish Empire: An Overview." In *Enlightened Reform in Southern Europe and Its Atlantic Colonies, c. 1750–1830*, edited by Gabriel Paquette, 33-36. London: Routledge, 2009.

Cardona, Álvaro. *La salud pública en España durante el Trienio Liberal, 1820–1923*. Madrid: Consejo Superior de Investigaciones Científicas, 2005.

Caro Baroja, Las 'nuevas poblaciones' de Sierra Morena y Andalucía: un experiment sociológico en tiempos de Carlos III." *Clavileño: Revista de la Asociación Internacional del Hispanismo*. 18 (1952): 52–64.

Case, Holly. "The 'Social Question,' 1820–1920." *Modern Intellectual History* 13, no. 3 (2016): 747–75.

Castillo Canché, Jorge I. "El contramodelo de la ciudadanía liberal. La vagancia en Yucatán, 1812–1842." In *Encrucijadas de La Ciudadanía y La Democracia. Yucatán, 1812–2004*. Edited by Sergio Quezada, 61–82. Mérida: Universidad Autónoma de Yucatán, 2005.

Chang, Jason Oliver. *Chino: Anti-Chinese Racism in Mexico, 1880–1940*. Champaign: University of Ilinois Press, 2017.

Charbit, Yves. "The Political Failure of an Economic Theory: Physiocracy." Translated by Arundhati Virmani. *Population (English Edition)*. 57:6 (Nov-Dec 2002): 855–83.

Congost, Rosa, and Pablo F. Luna. *Agrarian Change and Imperfect Property*. Turnhout: Brepols Publishers, 2018

Corcoran, Steve. "Thermidorian." *The Badiou Dictionary*. Edited by Steven Corcoran. Edinburgh: Edinburgh University Press, 2015: 352–58.

Corredera, Edward Jones. "Labouring Horizons: Passions and Interests in Jovellanos's Ley Agraria." *Dieciocho* 38:2 (Fall 2015): 267–90.

Covarrubias, José Enrique. *En busca del hombre útil: un estudio comparativo del utilitarismo neomercantilista en México y Europa, 1748–1833*. Mexico: Universidad Nacional Autónoma de México, 2005.

Covarrubias, José Enrique. "Riqueza, Ilustración y población en el pensamiento mexicano, 1821–1847." In *El mito de una riqueza proverbial: Ideas, utopías y proyectos económicos en torno a México en los siglos XVIII y XIX*. Edited by Francisco Altable, José Enrique Covarrubias, Richard Weiner, and Edward Beatty, 79–118. Mexico: UNAM, 2015.

Covarrubias, José Enrique, and Matilde Souto Mantecón. *Economía, ciencia y política estudios sobre Alexander von Humboldt a 200 años del Ensayo político sobre el reino de la Nueva España*. Mexico: Instituto Mora, 2012.

Covarrubias, José Enrique, and Richard Weiner. Introduction to *El mito de una riqueza proverbial: Ideas, utopías y proyectos económicos en torno a México en los siglos XVIII y XIX*. Edited by Francisco Altable, José Enrique Covarrubias, Richard Weiner, and Edward Beatty, 7–18. Mexico: UNAM, 2015.

Enrigue, Alvaro. *Ahora me rindo y eso es todo*. Mexico: Editorial Anagrama, 2018.

Fernández, Luis Miguel. *Tecnología, espectáculo, literatura: Dispositivos ópticos en las letras españolas de los siglos XVIII y XIX*. Santiago de Compostela: Universidad Santiago de Compostela, 2006.

Foucault, Michel. *Security, Territory, Population: Lectures at the Collège de France 1977–1978*. Edited by Michel Senellart. Translated by Graham Burchel. New York: Picador, 2009.

Foucault, Michel. *The Birth of Biopolitics: Lectures at the Collège de France, 1978--1979*. Edited by Michel Senellart. Translated by Graham Burchel. New York: Picador, 2010.

Fowler, Will, ed. *Forceful Negotiations: The Origins of the Pronunciamiento in Nineteenth-Century Mexico*. Lincoln: University of Nebraska, 2010.

Fowler, Will. *Mexico in the Age of Proposals, 1821–1853*. London: Greenwood Press, 1998.

Fowler, Will. *Tornel and Santa Anna: The Writer and the Caudillo, Mexico, 1795–1853*. London: Greenwood Press, 2000.

Gaillardet, Frederic, and James L. Shepherd. *Sketches of Early Texas and Louisiana*. Austin: University of Texas Press, 2013.

Gómez Galvarriato, Aurora. *The Mexican Cotton Textile Industry: An Overview*. Documentos de Trabajo Del Centro de Investigación y Docencia Económicas 438. Mexico: CIDE, 2008.

González Navarro, Moisés. *La colonización en México, 1877–1910*. Mexico: Estampillas y Valores, 1960.

Gutiérrez, Florencia. *El mundo del trabajo y el poder político. Integración, consenso y resistencia en la Ciudad de México a fines del Siglo XIX*. Mexico: El Colegio de Mexico, 2011.

Gutiérrez Negrón, Sergio. "Instituent Fictions: The Exceptional Present, The Junta Nacional Instituyente and Mexico's First Post-Independence Fiscal Plan (1822)." *Journal of Latin American Studies*, 2021, 1–26. https://doi.org/10.1080/13569325.2021.1978957.

Hale, Charles A. *Mexican Liberalism in the Age of Mora, 1821–1853*. New Haven, CT: Yale University Press, 1968.

Hale, Charles A. "The Liberal Impulse: Daniel Cosío Villegas and the Historia Moderna de México." *The Hispanic American Historical Review* 54, no. 3 (1974): 479–98.

Hämäläinen, Pekka. *The Comanche Empire*. New Haven, CT: Yale University Press, 2008.

Harcourt, Bernard E. *The Illusion of Free Markets: Punishment and the Myth of Natural Order*. Cambridge, MA: Harvard University Press, 2011.

Hernández, José Ángel. *Mexican American Colonization during the Nineteenth Century: A History of the U.S.-Mexico Borderlands*. Cambridge: Cambridge University Press, 2012.

Herrejón Peredo, Carlos. "Grito de Dolores." In *Diccionario de La Independencia de México*. Edited by Alfredo Ávila, Virginia Guedea, and Ana Carolina Ibarra, 194–97. Mexico: UNAM, 2010.

Hontanilla, Ana. "La figura del vago en la España Ilustrada." *Revista de Estudios Hispánicos* 50, no. 2 (June 2016): 509–31.

Howren, Alleine. "Causes and Origin of the Decree of April 6, 1830." *The Southwestern Historical Quarterly* 16, no. 4 (1913): 378–422.

Illades, Carlos. *Conflict, Domination, and Violence: Episodes in Mexican Social History*. New York: Berghahn Books, 2017.

Illades, Carlos. *Estudios sobre el artesanado urbano del siglo XIX*. 2nd ed. Mexico: Universidad Autónoma Metropolitana, 2001.

Illades, Carlos, and Adriana Sandoval. *Espacio social y representación literaria en el Siglo XIX*. Mexico: Universidad Autónoma Metropolitana, 2000.

Jaeggi, Rahel. *Critique of Forms of Life*. Translated by Ciaran Cronin. Cambridge, MA: Harvard University Press, 2018.

Jameson, Frederic. *The Political Unconscious: Narrative as a Socially Symbolic Act*. Ithaca, NY: Cornell University Press, 2014.

Jay, Martin. *Downcast Eyes: The Denigration of Vision in Twentieth-Century French Thought*. Berkeley: University of California Press, 1993.

Jay, Martin. *Essays from the Edge: Parerga and Paralipomena*. Charlottesville: University of Virginia Press, 2011.

Jessop, Bob, and Stijn Oosterlynck. "Cultural Political Economy: On Making the Cultural Turn Without Falling into Soft Economic Sociology." *Geoforum*, no. 39 (2008): 1155–69.

Jovellanos, Gaspar. *"Report on the Agrarian Law" (1795) and Other Writings*. Edited by Gabriel Paquette. New York: Anthem Press, 2016.

Kagan, Richard L., Francisco Marías, and Fernando M. Franco. *Urban Images of the Hispanic World, 1493–1793*. New Haven, CT: Yale University Press, 2000.

Kazanjian, David. *The Brink of Freedom: Improvising Life in the Nineteenth-Century Atlantic World*. Durham, NC: Duke University Press, 2016.

Kelly, Edith Louise, and Mattie Austin Hatcher. "Tadeo Ortiz de Ayala and the Colonization of Texas, 1822–1833, I." *The Southwestern Historical Quarterly* 32, no. 1 (1928): 74–86.

Kicza, John E. *Colonial Entrepreneurs: Family and Business in Bourbon Mexico City*. Albuquerque: University of New Mexico Press, 1983.

Knight, Alan. "Mexican Peonage; What Was It and Why Was It?" *Journal of Latin American Studies* 18, no. 1 (May 1986): 41–74.

Kow, Simon. *China in Early Enlightenment Political Thought*. New York: Routledge, 2017.

Legrás, Horacio. *Culture and Revolution: Violence, Memory, and the Making of Modern Mexico*. Austin: University of Texas Press, 2017.

López, Laura Angélica Moya, and Margarita Olvera Serrano. "La sociología mexicana de Daniel Cosío Villegas: recuento de un legado." *Sociológica* 21, no. 62 (Fall 2006): 109–38.

Luna, Pablo F. "Property, Dominium, and the Hispanic Enlightenment on Both Sides of the Atlantic in the Second Half of the Eighteenth-century." In *Agrarian Change and Imperfect Property*, 87–104. Turnhout: Brepols Publishers, 2018.

Lund, J. *The Mestizo State: Reading Race in Modern Mexico*. Minneapolis: University of Minnesota Press, 2012.

Maison, Hippolytte and Charles Dubouchet. *La colonización francesa en Coatzacoalco*. Veracruz: Universidad Veracruzana, 1986.

Maldonado Ojeda, Lucio Ernesto. *El Tribunal de Vagos de la Ciudad de México (1828–1867) o La Buena Conciencia de la Gente Decente*. Mexico: Suprema Corte de Justicia de la Nación, 2018.

Maldondo Ojeda, Lucio Ernesto. "El derecho de la pereza en el México del siglo XIX." In *Pereza, revolución y desarrollo empresarial en México: Siglos XIX y XX*, edited by Óscar Flores, 12–48. México: Centro de Estudios Históricos UDEM, 2011.

Marx, Karl. *Capital: A Critique of Political Economy. Volume One*. Translated by Ben Fowkes. New York: Penguin Books, 1982.

Marx, Karl, and Friedrich Engels. *The Economic and Philosophic Manuscripts of 1844 and the Communist Manifesto*. New York: Prometheus Books, 2009.

Marx, Karl, Friedrich Engels, and C. J. Arthur. *The German Ideology*. New York: International Publishers, 1970.

McCaa, Robert. "The Peopling of Nineteenth-Century Mexico: Critical Scrutiny of a Censured Century." *Statistical Abstract of Latin America* 30 (1993): 603–33.

Nancy, Jean Luc. *Noli Me Tangere: On the Raising of the Body*. New York: Fordham University Press, 2009.

Nemser, Daniel. "Biopolitics in Latin America." In *The Encyclopedia of Postcolonial Studies*, 1–7. Malden, MA: Wiley Blackwell, 2016.

Olveda Legaspi, Jaime. "La abolición de la esclavitud en México, 1810–1917." *Signos Históricos* 29 (January-June, 2013): 8–34.

Ortega y Medina, Juan. *Humboldt y Mexico*. Mexico: UNAM, 1995.

Palti, Elías José. *La invención de una legitimidad: Razón y retórica en el pensamiento mexicano del siglo XIX*. Mexico: Fondo De Cultura Economica, 2005.

Pani, Erika. *Para mexicanizar el Segundo Imperio: El imaginario político de los imperialistas*. Mexico: El Colegio de México, 2001.

Paquette, Gabriel. *Enlightenment, Governance, and Reform in Spain and Its Empire 1759–1808*. London: Palgrave Macmillan UK, 2008.

Paquette, Gabriel. "Empire, Enlightenment and Regalism: New Directions in Eighteenth-Century Spanish History." *European History Quarterly* 35, no. 1 (2005): 107–17.

Paquette, Gabriel, ed. *Enlightened Reform in Southern Europe and Its Atlantic Colonies, c. 1750–1830*. New York: Taylor & Francis, 2016.

Peachey, Dominic Keith. "The Revillagigedo Census of Mexico, 1790–1794: A Background Study." *Bulletin of the Society for Latin American Studies*, no. 25 (1976): 63–80.

Pérez Toledo, Sonia. *Los hijos del trabajo: los artesanos de la Ciudad de México, 1780–1853*. Mexico: El Colegio de México, Universidad Autónoma Metropolitana Iztapalapa, 1996.

Piccato, Pablo. *City of Suspects: Crime in Mexico City, 1900–1931*. Durham, NC: Duke University Press, 2001.

Poovey, Mary. "Between Political Arithmetic and Political Economy." In *Regimes of Description: In the Archive of the Eighteenth-century*, edited by J. B. Bender and M. Marrinan, 61–76. Stanford, CA: Stanford University Press, 2005.

Postone, Moishe. *Time, Labor, and Social Domination. A Reinterpretation of Marx's Critical Theory*. Cambridge, MA: Cambridge University Press, 1993.

Potash, Robert. *Mexican Government and Industrial Development in the Early Republic: The Banco de Avio*. Amherst: University of Massachusetts Press, 1983.

Pratt, Mary Louise. *Imperial Eyes: Travel Writing and Transculturation*. New York: Routledge, 1994.

Read, Jason. *The Micro-Politics of Capital: Marx and the Prehistory of the Present*. Albany: State University of New York Press, 2003.

Reinert, Sophus A. *Translating Empire: Emulation and the Origins of Political Economy*. Cambridge, MA: Harvard University Press, 2011.

Rojas, Rafael. "El México de Iturbide. Indicios de Un Imaginario Imperial." *Política y Gobierno* VI, no. 2 (1999): 479–97.

Rojas, Rafael. *Los derechos del alma: Ensayos sobre la querella liberal-conservadora en Hispanoamérica (1830–1870)*. Mexico: Taurus, 2014.

Sabau, Ana. *Riot and Rebellion in Mexico: The Making of a Race War Paradigm*. Austin: University of Texas Press, 2022.

Saborit, Antonio. *El virrey y el capellán: Revilla Gigedo, Alzate y el censo de 1790*. Mexico: Nexos, 2018.

Salmerón Sanginés, Pedro. "El mito de la riqueza de México, variaciones sobre un tema de Cosío Villegas." *Estudios de Historia Moderna y Contemporánea de México*, no. 26 (2003): 127–52.

Sanchez, Evelyne. *Las élites empresariales y la independencia económica de México: Estevan de Antuñano, o Las vicisitudes del fundador de la industria textil moderna (1792–1847)*. Puebla: Benémerita Universidad Autónoma de Puebla, 2013.

Sanchez, Evelyne. "Una ciudadanía experimental.: La creación de colonias rurales desde el Porfiriato hasta los años 1940." *Naveg@mérica. Revista electrónica editada por la Asociación Española de Americanistas*, no. 3 (2009).

Sánchez, Karla. "Entrevista a Yásnaya Elena A. Gil. 'La Lengua Tiene Una Carga Política.'" *Letras Libres*, March 2021. https://letraslibres.com/revista/entrevista-a-yasnaya-elena-a-gil-la-lengua-tiene-una-carga-politica.

Sanders, James E. *The Vanguard of the Atlantic World: Creating Modernity, Nation, and Democracy in Nineteenth-Century Latin America*. Durham, NC: Duke University Press, 2014.

Schaefer, Timo H. *Liberalism as Utopia: The Rise and Fall of Legal Rule in Post-Colonial Mexico, 1820–1900*. Cambridge, MA: Cambridge University Press, 2017.

Sierra, Carlos J. *Tadeo Ortiz de Ayala; viajero y colonizador*. Mexico: Secretaría de Hacienda, 1965.

Simon, Joshua. *The Ideology of Creole Revolution: Imperialism and Independence in American and Latin American Political Thought*. Cambridge, MA: Cambridge University Press, 2017.

Spear, Jennifer M. "Beyond the Native/Settler Divide in Early California." *The William and Mary Quarterly*, Vol. 76, No. 3 (July 2019): 427–34.

Stein, Barbara H., and Stanley J. Stein. *Crisis in an Atlantic Empire: Spain and New Spain*, 1808–1810. Baltimore, MD: Johns Hopkins University Press, 2014.

Stein, Barbara H., and Stanley J. Stein. *Edge of Crisis: War and Trade in the Spanish Atlantic, 1789–1808*. Baltimore, MD: Johns Hopkins University Press, 2009.

Stein, Stanley J., and Barbara H. Stein. *Apogee of Empire: Spain and New Spain in the Age of Charles III, 1759–1789*. Baltimore, MD: Johns Hopkins University Press, 2004.

Stein, Stanley J., and Barbara H. Stein. *Silver, Trade, and War: Spain and America in the Making of Early Modern Europe*. Baltimore, MD: Johns Hopkins University Press, 2000.

Taylor, Charles. *A Secular Age*. Cambridge, MA: Harvard University Press, 2009.

Thompson, E.P. *Customs in Common*. New York: Penguin Books, 1993.

———. *The Making of the English Working Class*. New York: Vintage Books, 1966.

Torget, A. J. *Seeds of Empire: Cotton, Slavery, and the Transformation of the Texas Borderlands, 1800–1850*. Chapel Hill: University of North Carolina Press, 2015.

Trotsky, Leon. *The Revolution Betrayed: What Is the Soviet Union and Where Is It Going?* New York: Pathfinder Press, 1983

Tutino, John. "El debate sobre el futuro de México: En busca de una nueva economía, 1830–1845." *HMex* 65, no. 3 (2016): 1119–92.

Tutino, John. "The Americas in the Rise of Industrial Capitalism." In *New Countries: Capitalism, Revolutions, and Nations in the Americas, 1750–1870*. Edited by John Tutino, 25–70. Durham, NC: Duke University Press, 2016.

Tutino, John. *The Mexican Heartland: How Communities Shaped Capitalism, a Nation, and World History, 1500–2000*. Princeton, NJ: Princeton University Press, 2017.

Van Young, Eric. *A Life Together: Lucas Alamán and Mexico, 1792–1853*. New Haven, CT: Yale University Press, 2021.

Vázquez Semadeni, María Eugenia. "Azcárate y Lezama, Juan Francisco." In *Diccionario de La Independencia de México*. Edited by Alfredo Ávila, Virginia Guedea, and Ana Carolina Ibarra, 24–27. Mexico: Universidad Nacional Autónoma de México, 2010.

Walker, Charles F. "Civilize or Control? The Lingering Impact of the Bourbon Urban Reforms." In *Political Cultures in the Andes, 1750–1950*. Edited by Nils Jacobsen and Cristóbal Aljovín de Losada, 74–95. Durham, NC: Duke University Press, 2005.

Warren, Richard. *Vagrants and Citizens: Politics and the Masses in Mexico City from Colony to Republic*. New York: Rowman & Littlefield Publishers, 2007.

Weiner, Richard. "Antecedents to Daniel Cosío Villegas's Post-Revolutionary Ideology: Justo Sierra's Critique of Mexico's Legendary Wealth and Trinidad Sanchez Santos's Assault on Porfirian Progress." *Mexican Studies/Estudios Mexicanos* 30, no. 1 (Winter 2014): 71–103.

Weiner, Richard. "El declive económico de México en el siglo XIX: Una perspectiva cultural." *Signos Históricos*, no. 12 (December 2004): 68–93.

Weiner, Richard. "La riqueza legendaria de México: Lectura selectiva del legado del Ensayo político de Humbolt." In *Economía, ciencia y política estudios sobre Alexander von Humboldt a 200 años del Ensayo político sobre el reino de la Nueva España*. Edited by José Enrique Covarrubias and Matilde Souto Mantecón, 261–91. Mexico: UNAM, 2012.

Wetzell, Richard F. *Inventing the Criminal: A History of German Criminology, 1880–1945*. Chapel Hill: University of North Carolina Press, 2003.

Williams, G. *The Mexican Exception: Sovereignty, Police, and Democracy*. New York: Palgrave Macmillan, 2011.

Index

www.ingramcontent.com/pod-product-compliance
Lightning Source LLC
LaVergne TN
LVHW091528200926
848483LV00002B/331
9780826505545